SCRIPTURE AND TRANSLATION

Indiana Studies in Biblical Literature

Herbert Marks and Robert Polzin,
general editors

SCRIPTURE AND TRANSLATION

MARTIN BUBER

AND

FRANZ ROSENZWEIG

Translated by Lawrence Rosenwald with Everett Fox

INDIANA UNIVERSITY PRESS
BLOOMINGTON & INDIANAPOLIS

Published in German as *Die Schrift und ihre Verdeutschung*

Buber selections copyright 1936 by Martin Buber

"Warum und wie wir die Schrift übersetzten" copyright 1993 by The Estate of Martin Buber

"Die Schrift und das Wort" by Franz Rosenzweig is translated by permission of Kluwer Academic Publishers from *Franz Rosenzweig: Der Mensch und Sein Werk,* Band 3, *Zweistromland* (The Hague: Martinus Nijhoff, 1984), pp. 777–83. Copyright 1984.

Remaining Rosenzweig selections © Athenäum Verlag GmbH, Frankfurt a.M.

Translation © 1994 by Indiana University Press

The paper used in this publication meets the minimum requirements of American National Standard for Information Sciences—Permanence of Paper for Printed Library Materials, ANSI Z39.48-1984.
Manufactured in the United States of America

Library of Congress Cataloging-in-Publication Data

Buber, Martin, 1878–1965.
  [Schrift und ihre Verdeutschung. English]
  Scripture and translation / Martin Buber and Franz Rosenzweig ; translated by Lawrence Rosenwald with Everett Fox.
    p. cm. — (Indiana studies in biblical literature)
  Translation of: Die Schrift und ihre Verdeutschung.
  Includes bibliographical references and index.
  ISBN 0-253-31272-8 (cloth : alk. paper)
  1. Bible. O.T.—Translating. 2. Bible. O.T. German—Versions— Buber-Rosenzweig. I. Rosenzweig, Franz, 1886–1929. II. Title. III. Series.
  BS449.B8313   1994
  221.5—dc20   93-32629
  1 2 3 4 5 99 98 97 96 95 94

For Alan Kenneth Rosenwald,
1916–1991

CONTENTS

PREFACE

Lawrence Rosenwald

This book is the product of two collaborations: first, of course, the great collaboration between Martin Buber and Franz Rosenzweig, and second the lesser but equally cordial and respectful collaboration between Everett Fox and myself. It was Fox who first saw the importance of having the book translated and set the process in motion; I brought to his passionate admiration for the book an equally passionate inclination to translate it. The actual drafting of the translation has been largely my work. But the product, the finished book, is ours together, and has been shaped by both of us. I did a first draft; Fox read this knowledgeably and carefully, made valuable suggestions, and annotated points concerning Bible and biblical studies. I then gratefully incorporated his annotations and most of his suggestions into the text, though in some cases I sought to find other solutions than those he had proposed to the problems he had rightly identified. Then he read this second draft, and set the process of revision in motion again—a process that stops now not from lack of interest or from a delusory sense that the translation is perfect, but on the ground of *ars longa, vita brevis*.

The constraints on translating the expository prose of scholars are pretty clear, and for the most part this translation is done in accord with those constraints. There are some exceptions, though, because Buber and Rosenzweig are more interesting writers than most scholars are; in their writing there is, as both Buber and Rosenzweig like to say of biblical narrative, no What separable from a How. In particular, their essays are often organized either locally or generally around small groups of crucial and crucially linked words, groups rather like the *Leitwörter* they identify in the Bible. I have attempted to retain these patterns, though by diverse means. Where possible I have devised an equivalent pattern. In other places I have retained the German terms and annotated them. In this respect the translation seeks, in Rosenzweig's adaptation of Schleiermacher's phrase, to move not only the text toward the reader but also the reader toward the text.

Some particular problems have arisen because translating this book has meant, after all, translating into English a German text that is partly

ix

about translating a Hebrew text into German. Often, therefore, a central point has to do with the distinction between one German rendering of a Hebrew phrase and another, and the trick has been to make these points clear to a reader of English. To do that I have done whatever seemed necessary. For rendering Buber and Rosenzweig's own translations of biblical passages I have most often simply quoted Fox's own Bible translations, which more than any other versions in English are in accord with (though they are not a servile imitation of) Buber and Rosenzweig's own work.[1] (For passages in books of the Bible that Fox has not yet translated he made translations as needed.) In certain cases, where using Fox's translation would have obscured Buber's or Rosenzweig's point, I have silently modified the translation to make the point clear. In rendering other German translations of the Hebrew Bible, usually quoted to illustrate some putative error of fact or principle, I have had to be more opportunistic, doing whatever seemed necessary to produce an English rendering exhibiting Buber's sense or Rosenzweig's of the particular inadequacy of the German rendering. (Luther's translation in particular I have often rendered by quoting older English translations, most often those of the Geneva Bible, or sometimes by making a pastiche of them.) Where I despaired of finding an equivalent rendering I have quoted and glossed the German. The technical difficulties of this process have been considerable, and have sometimes seemed crippling. It has at such times been comforting for me to remember that Buber liked to refer to the problems of making a German translation of the Bible as a subset of the general problems inherent in finding equivalents in a western language for patterns in a semitic language; in that framework the differences between German and English largely disappear, and the task of this translation seems more legitimate. In this context and generally I have tried in translating to imagine not what Buber and Rosenzweig would have written had they *written in* English, but rather what they would have written had they *translated into* English.

The title of the book presented a particular problem. *Die Schrift und ihre Verdeutschung* might arguably be translated "Scripture and its Germanization" rather than "Scripture and Translation." Buber and Rosenzweig are in fact uncomfortable with *Übersetzung*, the German word normally rendered "translation." Both often prefer *Übertragung*; in general the translation retains this distinction, usually translating *Übertragung* by "rendering," though component by component the two German words are more similar than "translation" and "rendering" are, the former mean-

---

1. *In the Beginning* (New York: Schocken, 1983) and *Now These Are the Names* (New York: Schocken, 1986), now reprinted as *Genesis and Exodus* (New York: Schocken, 1991).

ing "to set something over," the latter "to carry something over." But on occasion Buber and Rosenzweig also prefer *Verdeutschung*, "Germanization." This distinction the translation ordinarily does not try to reproduce, on the ground that the reader encountering "Germanization" would be misled by it to think that the point being made pertains only to translation from Hebrew into German and not to translation generally. And if this is true of individual sentences in the text it is all the more true for the title itself—it is hard to imagine an anglophone reader drawn to a book called *Scripture and Its Germanization*.

This book appears as part of a series dedicated to literary studies of the Bible. Its annotations, therefore—aside from those already discussed, intended to illuminate Buber and Rosenzweig's verbal schemes—are chiefly intended for students and scholars in biblical and Jewish studies, i.e., are intended to make things clear that such readers might find bewildering: the numerous manifestations of Buber and Rosenzweig's deep, learned rootedness in classical, European, and of course above all German, secular culture. But we hope the translation will be read also by translators, by Bible scholars of all sorts, and by intellectuals generally; so we have also identified biblical quotations, glossed some liturgical and Talmudic and rabbinic references and phrases, and identified a good number of the scholars Buber and Rosenzweig refer to by last name alone. The one thing the annotations do not include is any citation of the scholarly literature subsequent to Buber and Rosenzweig's work.

Buber and Rosenzweig's original notes are not marked; editorial notes end with the phrase "[eds.]." In some cases an editorial note directly follows an original note; in these cases the phrase "[eds.]" refers only to the paragraph it concludes. Editorial interpolations into original notes are enclosed in []'s. Buber's cross-references to *pages* have in part been changed to cross-references to *essays*, and in part incorporated into the index; Buber's occasional errors of citation have been silently corrected.

Finally comes the pleasant task of acknowledging gratitude: to Ed Greenstein, Norman Janis, Joseph Reimer, Cynthia Schwan, and Werner Weinberg, who gave sympathetic and rigorous readings to some or all of these translations in draft; to David Aaron, Marc Brettler, Thomas Hansen, and Jens Kruse, who gave generously of their expertise to solve particular problems I'd encountered; and especially to Herbert Marks, who with the grace of a diplomat mixed sympathy and exhortation to help move the project along. My greatest debt, and greatest regret, are expressed in the dedication.

THE BOOK IN
ITS CONTEXTS

Everett Fox

Die Schrift und ihre Verdeutschung was first published as a collection by Schocken Verlag (Berlin) in 1936. It brings together a range of pieces, originally either articles or lectures, by Martin Buber and Franz Rosenzweig dealing with their view of the nature (*Wesen*) of the Hebrew Bible and the problems of its translation. The reader will find here, initially, ruminations on the unity of the Bible, its focus on message (*Botschaft*), and its grounding in oral recitation. In addition, the essays set forth a methodology for reading biblical texts, based on the perception of sound patterns such as the repetition of key words; they discuss the reading and translating of Scripture by major figures in German culture (Luther, Moses Mendelssohn, Goethe); and they are supplemented with detailed replies to early critics of the unique German translation of the Bible which Buber and Rosenzweig "undertook" beginning in 1925.

This bare-bones description of the book does not do justice to the programmatic fervor underlying its contents. *Die Schrift und ihre Verdeutschung* is not merely about biblical poetics, close reading, translation theory, or cultural history—although it deals with all these issues in depth and in an entirely original manner. Neither does it reply to critics of the Bible translation solely in the interests of splitting philological hairs. It is above all a passionate, even utopian plea for the revival of the Bible's ability to speak in living words, to renew what Buber called "the dialogue between heaven and earth." In these essays, Buber and Rosenzweig seek to demonstrate how the Bible presses art into the service of a Teaching, and how a translation designed to lead the attentive listener-reader back to the syntactic and stylistic workings of the Hebrew text may serve that end.

The date of publication is of some moment. In the essay "The How and Why of Our Bible Translation" (Appendix II), Buber observes that the translation work was chronologically bracketed by a German assault on the

xiii

Hebrew Bible. The desire to separate the "Old Testament" from the New
had its roots in the ancient Marcionite heresy; it became an issue in
German culture before World War I and was eventually revived in the wake
of the Nazi attempt to purge "Jewish influences" from German society and
culture. Against this background, and given what the book has to say about
the Hebrew Bible's claims upon the spirit, it is all the more remarkable that
it could have been published in 1936.[1]

From the biographical side, it could well be that having completed the
translation of Psalms, Buber could finally allow himself to be prevailed
upon to gather "explanatory" material on the translation as a kind of stock-
taking.[2] Certainly by 1936 his own focus had shifted from secluded scholarship to the daunting task of bolstering the deeply wounded morale of the
German Jewish community, for which he had become centrally responsible, not only as a symbolic leader but also as one engaged in the day-to-day
education of Jewish adults. In this period he did translate the book of
Proverbs and begin to wrestle with Job, but he was not to return to translating the Bible with full attention until the 1950s.

The essays themselves date from several years earlier. Except for four of
them written in the 1930s ("On Translating the Praisings," "*Leitwort* and
Discourse Type," "A Suggestion for Bible Courses," and "The How and Why
of Our Bible Translation") and two from 1930 in memory of Rosenzweig,
who had died the previous December ("On Word Choice in Translating the
Bible" and "From the Beginnings of Our Bible Translation"), the bulk of
the material presented here stems from 1925-1929, the period during
which Buber and Rosenzweig did their collaborative translation work. They
are, in a sense, working papers on the principles and practice of translating
the Hebrew Bible, born, not from theorizing alone, but from the experience of wrestling with the Hebrew text itself. Consequently this volume is a
rare phenomenon in the annals of Bible translation: it contains a gold mine
of information about the history, underlying philosophy, and word selection employed by the translators. It functions as the companion piece to the
drafts and extensive notes and correspondence on the translation that are
found in the Martin Buber Archives in Jerusalem,[3] which perhaps give the
best insight into the translators' thinking and methods.[4]

---

1. On Nazi practices toward Jewish publishing in Germany, cf. Jacob Boas, "The Shrinking
World of German Jewry 1933-1938," *Leo Baeck Institute Year Book* 31 (1986), pp. 241-244.

2. Cf. Buber's opening remarks in the Foreword. Two other events produced parallel results:
Rosenzweig's death led to the writing of "From the Beginnings of our Bible Translation," and
probably Buber's emigration to Palestine eventually produced "The How and Why of Our
Bible Translation."

3. A portion of the translation papers, for many years in the possession of Nahum Glatzer,
exists also at the Leo Baeck Institute in New York.

4. Cf. my dissertation, "Technical Aspects of the Translation of Genesis of Martin Buber and
Franz Rosenzweig" (Brandeis University, 1975); Rachel Bat-Adam, *Arbeitspapiere zur*

Despite the assured tone and sometimes complex explication of the translators' ideas, examination of archival material reveals that their actual method of translation in fact evolved over time, albeit a short one. Early drafts of Genesis, for instance, show that the striking choice settled upon by the translators for rendering the biblical name of God (YHWH)—upper case personal pronouns—was only the last in a series of experiments. Then, too, the central exegetical technique employed in the Buber-Rosenzweig text—the repeating of word-stems in German where roots repeat in Hebrew (*Leitwörter*)—was not applied with thorough consistency until the second, revised edition of the Pentateuch (published 1930). Indeed, that second edition represents a fundamental move toward greater clarity, less obfuscation, and greater constancy to the principles set forth in the essays in this book.[5]

It is the completion of the translation of Exodus (spring of 1926) that appears to lie behind the changes from the first to the second edition. Since the differences between the two versions are relatively minor from Leviticus on, we are entitled to surmise that having completed nearly half of the Pentateuch, Buber and Rosenzweig felt compelled to revise extensively and to make peace, as it were, with their method.[6] The results are evident in the present volume: a number of the articles here date from precisely the period of revision (most notably, "*Leitwort* Style in Pentateuch Narrative"[7]). What is remarkable in all this is that the solidifying of the translation methodology took place so quickly; this is perhaps attributable to the urgency brought on by Rosenzweig's fatal illness, as well as by both men's gifts of concentration and hard work.

Nevertheless, an evolution in practical method should not be confused with an evolution in the translators' general perception of the Bible. From the first drafts in mid-1925, to the version of the second edition currently available (for the Pentateuch, 1976[8]), the Buber-Rosenzweig translation is distinguished by a consistent goal: the evocation of a spoken sacred text, a text that is to be brought to life by the reader and hearer. This is in line with

Verdeutschung der Schrift (Band IV/2 of Rosenzweig, *Gesammelte Schriften*) (Dordrecht: Martinus Nijhoff, 1984); and the forthcoming publication of the Genesis material by Dafna Mach.

It should be mentioned that the explanatory volume on the Jewish Publication Society's Torah translation (Harry M. Orlinsky, *Notes on the New Translation of the Torah* [Philadelphia: Jewish Publication Society, 1970]) while illuminating and extremely valuable, fails to reflect the vigorous committee debates that were part of the translation process.

5. Cf. my "Technical Aspects," pp. 161-185, for details about the changes; and also my "Franz Rosenzweig as Translator," *Leo Baeck Institute Year Book* 34 (1989), pp. 377.

6. Cf. Bat-Adam, *op. cit.*, p. 24.

7. The biblical quotations that appear in the article stem from the revision work (and appear in later editions), although the first editions of Genesis and Exodus had only recently appeared in print.

8. This edition, originally appearing in 1968, contains final changes made by Buber shortly before his death.

the ancient Jewish tradition of recitation/chanting of Scripture in public, but it goes beyond formal practice. Buber and Rosenzweig aimed at liberating the biblical text, and its German equivalent, from the "fetters" of written language, and while they paid close attention to the traditional Jewish accent system (*ta'amei ha-miqra'*) printed in Hebrew Bibles, they did not feel duty bound to accept them where they believed that their own line divisions would further the spokenness of the text. The result is refreshing and at the same time startling. One is confronted with the oldest, most familiar of texts and stories, and literally forced to see—and thus to hear—them in a different manner. While the system of "breathing units" into which Buber divided the German text is open to dispute in the details, its value and effect are not. It is a system that above all slows the reader down, giving him or her the time and space to look for unusual modes of expression, emphases, and connections within the text. Buber called this kind of reading "absolute attentiveness" (*vollkommene Aufmerksamkeit*).

All this is well illustrated in the present volume, which presents a classic statement of the Bible's spokenness. What does not always appear in these essays, however, is the explicit connection between Buber and Rosenzweig's biblical translating and exegesis and the more general religio-philosophical underpinnings which they brought to their work. Readers familiar with *The Star of Redemption, I and Thou,* and numerous other works of the two thinkers will not fail to make the connection. However disparate might have been their views on Jewish law and Zionism, Buber and Rosenzweig were of one mind in their approach to the centrality of language and dialogical speech. They often expressed their views on these concepts through the medium of interpreting the biblical text.

It would take a separate essay to trace the relationship of the Bible to Buber's "way of dialogue" and to the development of Rosenzweig's "speech-thinking." Fortunately, these journeys have been the subject of recent penetrating analysis by Michael Fishbane, and need not be discussed here at length. Fishbane's article "The Biblical Dialogue of Martin Buber"[9] beautifully explicates Buber's goal of sensitizing the reader to the voice embedded in the text in order to hear the voice potentially present in his/her own life. Similarly, Fishbane's "Speech and Scripture: The Grammatical Thinking and Theology of Franz Rosenzweig"[10] sets forth the profound (and sometimes opaque) reading to which Rosenzweig subjected selected passages from the Bible in the *Star.* Here the connection is forged between the spoken word, biblical exegesis, and the process of "making-oneself-ready" to respond to life in dialogical terms.

---

9. In *The Garments of Torah* (Bloomington: Indiana University Press, 1989), pp. 81-90.
10. Ibid., pp. 99-111.

But despite the obvious connections between the translators' philosophy and their philology, as it were, it should not be assumed that their work is merely an attempt to lift a philosophical system wholesale onto the biblical text. As I have suggested above, it was the experience of working with the text itself, and wrestling with the challenge of translation, that produced the results. The Rosenzweig that appears in the Bible translation goes beyond the Bible exegete of the *Star of Redemption* and the translator of portions of Jewish liturgy,[11] while the Buber encountered in the translation is a man whose poetic inclinations are necessarily held in check by the exigencies of biblical grammar. He could not do with the Bible what he had done with Hasidic texts decades earlier, if only because his attitude toward the biblical text (and that of Rosenzweig as well) was fundamentally different. The presuppositions of the translation are not only nineteenth century notions about language and languages, but also a reflection of a position long held in Jewish tradition: that the precise wording and style of the Bible are the primary vehicle through which Voice and Teaching (*Torah*) are fully conveyed. In this view, a translation designed to echo the Hebrew helps to point the way to the biblical message, whereas an "idiomatic" one (which defines most other current translations) will of necessity distort the text beyond recognition.[12]

In a series devoted to studies in biblical literature, a major context in which *Scripture and Translation* must be viewed is that of contemporary Bible scholarship. Here too there have been other evaluations in recent years;[13] I shall add only some background and general observations.

Neither Buber nor Rosenzweig was trained as a biblical scholar. They were, however, conversant with the Bible scholarship of their day, Rosenzweig through material brought to him during the translation work, and Buber much more fully through his own research. The Buber Archives contain lists of books related to biblical studies that Buber kept close at hand, and these are what one might expect: a host of lexica, modern commentaries and exegetical notes and articles (mostly in German[14] and English), many earlier German translations (Jewish and Christian), and

---

11. Cf. my "Franz Rosenzweig as Translator," pp. 372-375.

12. Cf. the path-breaking essay of Edward L. Greenstein, "Theories of Modern Bible Translation" (in *Essays on Biblical Method and Translation* [Atlanta: Scholars Press, 1989], pp. 85-118), which places B-R in the context of contemporary translations.

13. Cf. Glatzer, "Buber as an Interpreter of the Bible," in Paul Arther Schilpp and Maurice Friedman, eds., *The Philosophy of Martin Buber* (LaSalle, IL: Open Court Press, 1967), pp. 361-380; James Muilenberg, "Buber as an Interpreter of the Bible" (ibid.), pp. 381–402; Meir Weiss, *"Be-sod siaḥ ha-miqra',"* in Buber, *Darko shel Miqra'* (Jerusalem: Mosad Bialik, 1964), pp. 9-33; Michael Fishbane, "Martin Buber's *Moses,"* in *The Garments of Torah*, pp. 91-98.

14. E.g., the commentaries of Rudolf Kittel, Bernhard Duhm, Franz Delitzsch, and Eduard König.

rabbinic texts. In reference to their contemporaries, Rosenzweig had a particular fondness and respect for Benno Jacob, the commentator on Genesis and Exodus; Buber carried on a wide-ranging correspondence with a number of biblical scholars such as N. H. Tur-Sinai (then Torczyner); and the valuable work of Arnold Ehrlich (d. 1919) is often cited in the discussions. It is apparent that the translators (especially Buber, who held the major responsibility for accurate understanding of the Hebrew) spared no effort to be familiar with current trends in the field, including in Semitics. It should, however, be borne in mind that they completed a good portion of their work prior to some of the major developments in biblical scholarship of this century, such as the many archaeological discoveries (e.g., at Ras Shamra, Qumran, Deir Alla) that have led to advances in understanding both the cultural and linguistic backdrop to the emergence of the Hebrew Bible. Buber attempted to incorporate some of these into his later books (*The Kingship of God, Moses,* and *The Prophetic Faith*), but it is not clear that they figured to any great extent in his revisions of the second edition of the translation in the 1950s and 1960s.

The other area of background to the translation that should be noted is pre-modern material. A glance at the translators' written discussions on the opening chapters of Genesis alone[15] demonstrates that they frequently utilized the major ancient versions of the Bible—the Septuagint, Samaritan version, Vulgate, Symmachus, and Targums—although they rarely, if ever, emended the text. In the area of grammatical exegesis, Buber and Rosenzweig also made extensive use of the medieval Jewish commentators, who are represented in early archival material by Rashi, Ibn Ezra, Kimhi, Gersonides, Nahmanides, Samuel ben Meir, and Isaac Abravanel.[16] The translation papers in which these works are cited make for surprisingly lively reading, as they weave the commentators' suggestions in with Buber's and Rosenzweig's, thereby creating, rather in the manner of the commentaries themselves, a living conversation on the text.

Equally or more important than the tools used in the translation, of course, is the approach itself. There are four areas in which the translators set out their principles, and which have been the subject of some controversy: the unity of the Bible, its oral origins, the translators' use of the "leading-word" technique, and their philological method.

Buber and Rosenzweig treated the Bible as an organic whole.[17] While nei-

---

15. Cf. my "Technical Aspects," which covers the early Genesis material.

16. Ironically, it was not yet appreciated in the 1920s to what extent the medievals anticipated many solutions to textual problems that have since been solved by work in comparative Semitics.

17. Cf. especially the essays "The Unity of the Bible," "On Translating the Praisings," and "A Suggestion for Bible Courses."

ther completely disavowed the possibility of textual layers or historical change, Rosenzweig remained distrustful of then-regnant Source (or "Higher") Criticism, and Buber opted for a model of biblical composition that stressed cumulative addition rather than the pasting together of discrete sources. Here they reveal themselves to be part of a general trend especially among Jewish biblical scholars of their time, some of whom (such as Benno Jacob and Umberto Cassuto) in fact devoted strenuous efforts to discrediting the Wellhausen model.[18] Buber and Rosenzweig's approach did not stem from a desire to defend the doctrine of the Torah's divine origin as such, but rather from the perception that, beyond possible earlier stages of composition, the Hebrew Bible is an anthology that frequently cross-references itself, an anthology in which terms and concepts are explained by their complementary use in differing contexts. Along the same lines, the translators felt that the traditional Masoretic text-form was all that could be relied upon with certainty; Rosenzweig even wrote in a note to Buber that by translating "R" (the "Redactor" or final editor of the Torah), they could at least ensure that their work would not look foolish to posterity, since R would in any event outlive biblical criticism![19] The translation, then, like a number of recent "literary" readings of the Bible, seems to operate from a largely ahistorical viewpoint. The redactorial approach might today fall under the recognized rubrics of "rhetorical criticism" or "canonical criticism," but might well be attacked for ignoring a theoretically more complex evolution for the biblical text and the institutions represented therein. Buber did devote a good deal of energy in later books to setting forth his theories about the development of biblical religion—but his method was unorthodox and was vigorously criticized (he felt it necessary to write two new introductions to *The Kingship of God*, dealing with his critics).

Recent scholarship suggests that the evolutionary and "final product" approaches to the Bible need not live in mutual antagonism, and may even come to function as complementary views of the text.[20] The practitioners of so-called synchronic analysis of the Bible seem to be admitting the validity of historical factors, and the diachronic-minded critics appear to be more

---

18. Cf. Joel Rosenberg, *King and Kin* (Bloomington: Indiana University Press, 1986), p. 8.

19. Note on Gen. 2:7; cf. Fox, "Technical Aspects," p. 113.

20. A particularly suggestive and insightful study on the growth of biblical literature that combines various approaches is David Damrosch, *The Narrative Covenant* (San Francisco: Harper & Row, 1987). A more sweeping approach, utilizing the insights of many disciplines, is explicated by James W. Flanagan, *David's Social Drama* (Sheffield: Almond Press, 1988), and "New Constructs in Social World Studies," in David Jobling, Peggy L. Day, and Gerald T. Sheppard, eds., *The Bible and the Politics of Exegesis* (Cleveland: Pilgrim Press, 1991), pp. 209-223.

21. Cf. Richard Eliot Friedman, "The Hiding of the Face: An Essay on the Literary Unity of Biblical Narrative," in Jacob Neusner, Baruch A. Levine, and Ernest S. Freirichs, eds., *Judaic Perspectives on Ancient Israel* (Philadelphia: Fortress Press, 1987), pp. 207-222; and David Noel Freedman, *The Unity of the Hebrew Bible* (Ann Arbor: University of Michigan Press, 1991).

interested in a holistic view than previously.[21] Given these developments, the
essays dealing with biblical unity in this book will provide but one approach
to the topic, albeit an eloquent one. Yet the B-R translation will survive as a
text through which, because of its careful attention to style and syntax, one
can essay both literary and historical criticism of the Bible in translation.

A second area for consideration—the Bible's spokenness—is also problematic in its precise formulation by Buber and Rosenzweig. As previously
noted, the translators viewed the Bible as essentially a spoken document,
similar to much of ancient literature. Buber lays out his presuppositions in
this regard in the Foreword to *Moses* (1944):

> That this early saga [referring to the Exodus traditions], close as it is to
> the time of the event, tends to assume rhythmical form, can well be
> understood. It is not due solely to the fact that enthusiasm naturally
> expresses itself in rhythm. Of greater importance is the basic idea charac-
> terizing this stage of human existence that historical wonder can be
> grasped by no other form of speech save that which is rhythmically artic-
> ulated, of course in oral expression (a basic concept which is closely asso-
> ciated with the time-old relation between religion and magic). This is
> sustained by the wish to retain unchanged for all time the memory of the
> awe-inspiring things that had come about; to which end a transmission in
> rhythmical form is the most favorable condition.[22]

The problem, of course, is that we simply do not possess enough evidence
to support the idea that the Bible is an oral document in the same sense as
the epic poems of Homer (or those of other cultures). Earlier attempts to
fit the Bible into an epic or even rhythmic scheme have largely failed or
remained unproven; research on the nature of oral literature[23] has shown
that it is difficult to conclusively prove on purely formal grounds how much
of the Hebrew text originated in oral recitation. The Bible itself is of little
help in answering the question, since it portrays instances of writing alongside the recitation of poetry and song in various periods. In addition, the
notion of the Bible's original spokenness smacks heavily of nineteenth-cen-
tury Romanticism, and Buber's statement (in "The How and Why of Our
Bible Translation") that he came to this view in conjunction with the study
of other ancient religious literatures[24] is telling.

A shift in focus may preserve the contribution of the Buber-Rosenzweig

---

22. Buber, *Moses* (Atlantic Highlands, NJ: Humanities Press International, 1988), p. 14.

23. Cf. Jan Vansina, *Oral Tradition: A Study in Historical Methodology* (Chicago: Aldine
Publishing Co., 1965); and Robert Culley, "Oral Tradition and Old Testament Studies,"
Semeia, vol. 5 (1976).

24. Greenstein, *op. cit.*, pp. 105-106, sees such a unifying approach to traditional literatures
as related to ideas of Herder and Nietzsche (among others).

translation. While we may never be able to identify the precise medium in which biblical texts originated, we may be able to make use of the fact that the Bible was read aloud in antiquity, and that the kinds of exegesis found throughout this book would indeed have made sense to a culture that read virtually all of its literature that way.[25] A declaimed Bible—in the sacrificial prescriptions of Leviticus no less than in the artfully constructed narratives of Genesis—does reveal something significant that a printed Bible does not, by way of aurally highlighting emphases and connections within the text. A translation that is meant to be read aloud consequently may well foster a deeper understanding of the text, provided that the translator/reader does not stretch the text's suggestiveness beyond reasonable limits by seeing connections and allusions everywhere. At the same time, taking this approach will assuredly not answer questions about the prehistory of the biblical text; those questions will continue to bedevil biblical scholars for years to come.

Arising from the Bible's oral character is the third aspect of the Buber-Rosenzweig methodology, and indeed one of Buber's enduring contributions: the "leading-word" (*Leitwort*) technique. Here Buber tries to show how "attentiveness" to the repetitions of Hebrew roots can provide a key to understanding the thematics at work in numerous biblical narratives. His "*Leitwort* Style in Pentateuch Narrative," dealing with the Tower of Babel, Korach's rebellion, Jacob's encounters with Esau, and the Abraham cycle,[26] is a classic example of literary exegesis of the Bible, and has often been cited by later studies.[27] Similarly thought-provoking readings may be found elsewhere in the present volume, as well as throughout Buber's later writings on the Bible. I might add that I have found the *Leitwort* technique extraordinarily useful in the classroom and in literary analysis.[28] It is indeed striking how frequently the Bible makes use of paranomastic repetition of this kind, and how frequently a satisfying reading may be derived from it.

A recent article by Yairah Amit[29] has taken Buber to task on the *Leitwort*, citing vagueness in his definition of the technique and subjectivity in his choices of leading-words within specific stories. She also finds him unclear

---

25. I have made this point in my *Genesis and Exodus* (New York: Schocken Books, 1991), pp. xiv.

26. The Abraham material is likewise treated in "Abraham the Seer" (in *On the Bible* [New York: Schocken Books, 1968], pp. 22-43).

27. E.g., Robert Alter, *The Art of Biblical Narrative* (New York: Basic Books, 1981), pp. 92ff.; Shimon Bar-Efrat, *Narrative Art in the Bible* (Sheffield: Almond Press, 1984), pp. 136, 212; Michael Fishbane, *Text and Texture* (New York: Schocken Books, 1979), pp. 12, 35; Meir Weiss, *The Bible from Within* (Jerusalem: Magnes Press/Hebrew University, 1984), pp. 56-57.

28. Cf. my *Genesis and Exodus*, and "The Samson Cycle in an Oral Setting," *Alcheringa: Ethnopoetics* 4:1 (1978), pp. 51-68.

29. Yairah Amit, "The Multi-Purpose 'Leading Word' and the Problems of Its Usage," *Prooftexts* 9 (1989), pp. 99-114.

on the important question of whether the technique was embedded at an early stage of biblical literary development or is primarily the work of a later editor. Here Buber appears to be guilty of a practice that has been raised regarding some of his other writings as well: he seems to combine certainty of interpretation with a blurring of the overall concept, or to put it another way, the line between subjectivity and objectivity is itself blurred. Thus, for instance, Buber's ethics have been criticized because they do not clearly establish moral absolutes, while calling for an ill-defined "response of the whole person."[30] Buber's assertion that, instead of proposing a system, he merely "points the way" becomes, in the eyes of some, a form of waffling.

In answer to the first two objections, Buber would undoubtedly send the critic back to his—and the biblical—text. Certainly one cannot *prove* exegetical claims; one can only demonstrate plausibility, and Buber has tried to make it clear that the *Leitwort* approach is suggestive rather than definitive. The Bible, he avers, does not provide spelled-out morals at the end of stories, but rather, by leaving aural clues, alerts its audience to central themes and concerns. In the light of this fact, Buber's own interpretation of a specific passage or book—stunning as many of them are—may not even be the issue. What is perhaps more important is that some form of leading-word reading, judiciously applied, remains valuable as one of the tools for cracking the biblical code. It remains the one aspect of Buber and Rosenzweig's work that is referred to more than any other by modern literary critics of the Bible. And its usefulness extends beyond the genre of narrative, to legal and poetic texts of the Bible as well (an example of the latter may be found in Buber's "On Translating the Praisings").

Amit's historical objection is not so easily parried. Buber viewed the biblical text as having arisen from a "proto-biblical" core of traditions and stylistics, which grew into a full-fledged text through an evolving but unified community of spirit. If this was not the case—and the majority of biblicists today would concur that it was not—then the role of *Leitwörter* is more difficult to assess in the historical development of the text. The technique simply may not be a tool that answers historical questions.

A final approach to the Bible and its translation that is explicated in this book concerns the philological practices of Buber and Rosenzweig. In a number of cases, the translation of important terms is based on the belief that biblical words retain their "primal," root meanings, and that only by bringing them out in translation can the reader confront the depths of biblical thinking. Two examples might be the word usually rendered "altar" and the four-letter name of God (YHWH). Deriving Hebrew *mizbeaḥ* from

---

30. Cf. Marvin Fox, "Some Problems in Buber's Moral Philosophy," in Schilpp and Friedman, eds., *op. cit.*, pp. 151-170.

the root that normally means "to slaughter [for sacrifice]," Buber and Rosenzweig depart from the conventional "altar" (which for them has too post-sacrificial a ring) and render it by the primitive-sounding *Schlachtstatt* (slaughter-site). But one could make the case that the translators have failed to take into account that sacrificial slaughtering usually took place beside the biblical altar, not on it, and that grain as well as animal life was offered up. Some of the same difficulties arise in connection with other terms, especially those used in the book of Leviticus. What would Buber have done had he had access to the work of Jacob Milgrom[31] and Baruch Levine[32] on the cult? It is difficult to speculate on the answer.

A more serious case occurs with the name of God (YHWH), where Buber on several occasions[33] pushed vigorously for an understanding of the name as indicating God's unwavering presence among the Israelites. YHWH in this reading means "He Who Is There," and the translators subsequently utilized HE / HIM / YOU etc. in every place that the Tetragrammaton occurs as a way of highlighting that particular meaning. As compelling and powerful a reading as this is, it is hard to imagine it being accepted by most biblical scholars at the present time, based on the derivation Buber proposes.[34] And it raises the more general questions of whether it is possible to recover primal meanings of biblical words, and whether those meanings, if uncovered, truly remain embedded in the text, to be consciously felt by the audience.[35]

One last time, I shall defend the translation, in general if not in particular. The interpretation of the name of God (which is also discussed below in Rosenzweig's essay "'The Eternal,'"), however philologically questionable it may be, is useful in approaching the force of the Hebrew text *as it came to be read*. And the same might be said for a number of B-R's etymologies. Some of these are based on the philology available to Buber at the time of translation and revision; some reflect Midrashic sources insofar as they illuminate the biblical text rather than solely teaching a Rabbinic moral; and some are simply based on B-R's own deeply felt sense of what

31. Jacob Milgrom, *Studies in Cultic Theology and Terminology* (Leiden: E. J. Brill, 1983); *Leviticus 1-16* (Anchor Bible vol. 3) (New York: Doubleday, 1991; and *The JPS Torah Commentary: Numbers* (Philadelphia: Jewish Publication Society, 1990).

32. Baruch A. Levine, *In the Presence of the Lord* (Leiden: E. J. Brill, 1974); *The JPS Torah Commentary: Leviticus* (Philadelphia: Jewish Publication Society, 1989).

33. Cf. *Moses*, pp. 48-55; *The Prophetic Faith* (New York: Macmillan, 1977), pp. 27-29.

34. Buber understands Heb. *hyh* as carrying the connotation "to be present"; many contemporary scholars find the meaning "to cause to be" more convincing.

35. Theodor Gaster once verbally made the same criticism of B-R, using the English word *trivia* as his example: how many English speakers are aware that the word derives from the Latin *trivium*, "three roads/crossroads," indicating a place where common folk gather? For a general critique of this kind of translating, cf. James Barr, *The Semantics of Biblical Language* (Oxford: Oxford University Press, 1967).

the text is trying to teach—including the sense that "popular etymology" sometimes takes precedence over scholarly etymology within the Bible. If contemporary scholars feel that such an approach betrays an exclusively canonical or post-canonical bias, it is up to them to supply the correction where they deem it necessary.[36] But it must also be said that the Buber-Rosenzweig translation, through its etymologies, has the merit of forcing a reconsideration of the meaning of numerous concepts in the Bible—in itself a valuable exercise.

An example of the validity of the translation's rendering of terminology might be the case of the Hebrew root *tm'*, whose nominal form is still commonly rendered "uncleanness." Such a translation is of little help in furthering an understanding of the biblical Weltanschauung; Buber-Rosenzweig adopts the positive term (avoiding "un-" for like concepts) *makel* ("stain"; I would suggest the alternative "pollution," for reasons of accuracy and clarity). This rendition clarifies *tum'ah*, not as a lack of something but rather as a miasmic force that must be ritually dealt with. As another example, one might mention the issue of the translation of biblical names, which the Buber-Rosenzweig version uses within the text itself where the translators felt that the connotation of a name is an important feature of the text. Whether one agrees with the interpretation of the name Yaakov/Jacob given by B-R (*Fersenschleicher*, "Heel-Sneak"), or questions why Buber did nothing about the pun inherent in Job's name, is beside the point; what is important is that the issue of names thus leaves the realm of the footnote and returns to where it is often a factor: in the sounding out of the biblical text.

The approach to the text espoused in *Die Schrift und ihre Verdeutschung* has been compared to the kind of "close reading" advocated in current literary criticism of the Bible, and the book has been cited in many works taking that point of view.[37] One might even have expected the book (and the translation) to have become the launching point for the literary movement that has arisen in biblical studies since the 1970s. But as Shemaryahu Talmon notes,[38] this has not been the case. For one thing, the book appeared at a historically unfortunate moment, and the Jewry for which it was at least partially intended was destroyed. Additionally, Buber and Rosenzweig's antipathy for main-line Bible criticism distanced them from others in the field. But a more far-reaching reason why *Die Schrift und ihre Verdeutschung* never became the spearhead of the biblical literary movement lies in its thrust

36. This is what I have been seeking to do in my English renditions of Pentateuchal books, which are based on the insights of B-R. Cf. my *Genesis and Exodus*.
37. Cf. note 27.
38. Talmon, "Zur Bibelinterpretation von Franz Rosenzweig und Martin Buber," in Wolfdietrich Scmied-Kowarzik, *Der Philosoph Franz Rosenzweig (1886-1929). Bd. II: Die Heranforderung jüdischen Lernens* (Freiburg: K. Alber, 1988), pp. 284-285.

and its tone. As I noted at the beginning of this introduction, the essays, without exception, bespeak a commitment to recovering the Word embedded in the biblical text, so that it may address "people today" (cf. Buber's opening essay). That is, the book is the product of an essentially religious mentality, if unconventionally so. In contrast, virtually all of the major books on literary Bible studies demonstrate a more modest program. Works by Meir Sternberg,[39] Shimon Bar Efrat,[40] and others[41] clearly approach the Bible as an object of description, in order to illustrate its narrative workings. This can lead either within—to a better understanding of the text itself—or without—to the Bible as a paradigmatic narrative for the student of literature. The enraptured tone of *Die Schrift und ihre Verdeutschung*, on the other hand, signals a great divide between it and much of what is currently being written about biblical literature. From the opening essay, Buber's "People Today and the Jewish Bible," the book dares to keep its gaze trained on what the Bible itself purports to be—a record of the encounter between the human and the divine. Few contemporary literary scholars would write that way, and indeed many of the early critics of the translation did not fully understand what was at stake.[42]

But it must be remembered that Buber and Rosenzweig belonged to an

---

39. Sternberg, *The Poetics of Biblical Narrative* (Bloomington: Indiana University Press, 1985). On the opening page of his introduction, he writes:

> What goals does the biblical narrator set himself? What is it that he wants to communicate in this or that story, cycle, book? What kind of text is the Bible, and what role does it perform in context? These are all variations on a fundamental question . . . : the question of narrative as a functional structure, a means to a communicative end, a transaction between the narrator and the audience on whom he wishes to produce a certain effect by way of certain strategies. (p. 1)

40. Bar Efrat, *Narrative Art in the Bible* (Sheffield: Almond Press, 1989). He introduces his study in the following terms:

> The purpose of this book is to provide a guide to the biblical narrative as a literary work of art. It aims at presenting a way of reading which is based on the employment of tools and principles current in the study of literature, and it combines summary and methodical survey with the observation of new aspects. . . . It is my hope that the approach presented here, focusing on the artistic shape of biblical narrative, will contribute to a more profound and exact understanding of these narratives as well as to a fuller appreciation of their beauty. (pp. 7-8)

41. Cf. also Adele Berlin, *Poetics and Interpretation of Biblical Narrative* (Sheffield: Almond Press, 1983), and Robert Alter and Frank Kermode, *The Literary Guide to the Bible* (Cambridge: Harvard University Press, 1987).

42. Lawrence Rosenwald's forthcoming *Prooftexts* article, "Translation as Vocation: On the Reception of Buber and Rosenzweig's Bible." Also to be noted is Fernanda Eberstadt's fine review essay of four books on Exodus (including my own translation), "The Uses of Exodus," (*Commentary* [June 1987], pp. 25-33), in which she laments the loss of the sense of the sacred in much of contemporary work on the Bible.

age that was in the process of rejecting a world full of contradictions: the triumph of European civilization alongside a brutal colonialism; a fascination with the religions of the East alongside the growing secularization of society; and talk of universalism alongside a blind, rampant nationalism—all of which came to a head in the catastrophe of one world war and led to a second. In this context, Rosenzweig's major struggle with Hegelian philosophy and Buber's turning from academic life to cultural Zionism and Hasidic teaching (at least his version of it) made it almost inevitable that they would see in the sources of Judaism, particularly the Bible, more than merely objects of intellectual engagement or even reverence. *Scripture and Translation*, then, and the Buber-Rosenzweig Bible translation along with it, does not properly belong to the narrowly conceived category of literary criticism, but, like so much of the thinking of these two men, is meant to break out into the world of the living, pressing for "realization" (*Bewährung*) in real life. Fishbane has summarized it well:

> In all this, Buber's goal was neither an esthetic nor an historical appreciation of the "literary structures" of the Bible for their own sake. Rather, the purpose of such critical alertness to biblical language was to properly penetrate the life of faith of ancient Israel, for the sake of an historical understanding that is inseparable from a reader's self-renewal. Buber thus had no use for programs of a so-called objective, historical-philological scholarship, which eclipsed the enduring meaning of the text; nor was he interested in a private subjectivization of the text, which obscured or ignored its concrete, historical otherness. For him, the two approaches were one and inseparable—when properly pursued; and he profoundly believed that his own hermeneutical presuppositions and strategies of reading were conducive to that end.[43]

In the final analysis, a musical analogy may be of help in assessing the enterprise represented in this book. The celebrated conductor Arturo Toscanini was, like Buber and Rosenzweig, a man of the nineteenth century, for whom art had an almost religious significance. His most successful performances have a revelatory character about them; for many listeners they were and still are capable of provoking a fresh attitude toward familiar music. Toscanini was known as a "literalist," but in actuality he took a variety of liberties with scores[44] that if publicized would have shocked some of

---

43. Fishbane, "On Buber's *Moses*," *op. cit.*, p. 95. Cf. Glatzer, *op. cit.*, p. 366, for essentially the same view.

44. The most blatant case is Toscanini's recorded performance of Tschaikovsky's *Manfred Symphony*, where he cut fully fifteen pages from the score of the fourth movement in the interests of tightening the piece. But he made changes in other works as well, adding a few timpani parts to the storm movement of the Beethoven Sixth Symphony and the first movement of the Eighth Symphony.

his more worshipful adherents. He saw himself as the dutiful servant of the composer and the score, yet in the very act of trying to keep his own personality out of his interpretations, he injected an element that was immediately identifiable and highly individualistic.

Buber and Rosenzweig, too, sought to present the biblical text in its purity, *come è scritto*, attempting to faithfully lay bare its inner structure and rhetorical force. But in truth there is no such thing as a neutral reading of the Bible, any more than there is a "correct" performance of a Beethoven symphony. The Buber-Rosenzweig translation and the essays in this book are nothing so much as they are the record of an extraordinary reading—a monumental peformance, in the positive sense of the term. To the extent that they are able to illuminate and deepen our understanding of the Bible, they will survive.

But the truly enduring value of Buber and Rosenzweig's biblical work will be its ability to re-engage its readers in the process of learning to hear the biblical text anew, with all that implies. Whether, seventy years[45] after the translation first burst on the scene, this is possible in the English-speaking world, remains to be seen. But "in any case the end is not our business, but the commencement and the commencing."[46]

---

45. Cf. Rosenzweig's letter to Eugen Mayer of 30 December 1925, where he hopes for, seventy years hence, a return from the "Babylonian Exile" of the Bible from Germany to which he feared the translation would lead. Quoted by Buber in "The How and Why of Our Bible Translation," in Appendix II, below.

46. Ibid.

BUBER AND ROSENZWEIG'S CHALLENGE TO TRANSLATION THEORY[1]

Lawrence Rosenwald

> When you have done justice to the meaning, stop.
> —Marianne Moore

I: Prologue

My aim in this introduction is to make a case for the translational program of Martin Buber and Franz Rosenzweig. I have taken my audience to be anglophone translators in the widest possible sense of that phrase: all those who in speaking and writing and reading English have assimilated the anglophone tradition of translational thought. I have shaped my case accordingly. It begins with an account of the anglophone tradition of translation theory intended to reveal the translational ideas that most speakers of English share but few reflect on. It then presents the Buber-Rosenzweig program as a challenge to those ideas. It asks whether those ideas are sound, what their roots and uses and consequences are, what their strengths and weaknesses are. Then, point by point, it proposes ideas from the Buber-Rosenzweig program as deliverances from the limitations that the ideas of our own tradition imply.

I intend, as noted, to make a case. But I am not trying to replace old orthodoxies with new, nor do I believe that good theory guarantees good

1. My thanks to David Aaron, Eva Brann, Everett Fox, Edward Greenstein, Norman Janis, Jonathan Knudsen, Mary Lefkowitz, Herbert Marks, Christoph Schmidt, and Cynthia Schwan for their careful reading or hearing of earlier drafts of this essay; my special thanks to Professor Stéphane Moses, who as director of the Franz Rosenzweig Research Center for German-Jewish Literature and Cultural History made it possible for me to pursue my studies of these matters in the Buber Archive in Jerusalem.

practice or bad theory bad practice. I do believe that theory *constricts* practice, and that Buber and Rosenzweig's ideas can give anglophone translators more room to maneuver in.

II: The Anglophone Tradition

A: Dryden

The anglophone tradition of translation theory begins with John Dryden,
whose beguilingly plainspoken and commonsensical ideas still affect our
thinking. Dryden distinguishes among three types of translation:
metaphrase, paraphrase, and imitation.[2] Metaphrase is a rendering of the
original "word by word, and line by line" (237); Dryden's example is Ben
Jonson's translation of Horace's *Ars Poetica*. Paraphrase, or "translation with
latitude," is a rendering of the original not word for word but sense, more
or less, for sense: "the author is kept in view by the translator, so as never to
be lost, but his words are not so strictly followed as his sense; and that too is
admitted to be amplified but not altered" (237). Dryden's example here is
Edmund Waller's translation of *Aeneid* IV; we might in its place put
Dryden's own classic translations of Ovid and Vergil, or Pope's of Homer.
Imitation, Dryden says, is

> an endeavour of a later poet to write like one who has written before him,
> on the same subject; that is, not to translate his words, or to be confined
> to his sense, but only to set him as a pattern, and to write, as he supposes
> that author would have done, had he lived in our age, and in our country.
> (239)

Dryden's example here is Abraham Cowley's Pindar. Imitation renders not
sense but style, in the sense of style we use when we say, *le style, c'est l'homme*;
we praise an imitation not by saying that it renders this or that line or
thought of Vergil, but that it is in general Vergilian.

Dryden's terms themselves imply tendentious notions regarding language and translation: that we can keep an author "in view" while following
his sense and not his words; that sense can be "amplified" without being
"altered"; and, most importantly, that we can distinguish clearly among
words, sense, and manner in the first place. But to those implied notions he

---

2. Dryden, "Preface to Ovid's Epistles," in W. P. Ker, ed., *Essays of John Dryden* (Oxford:
Clarendon Press, 1900), 1:237. All subsequent quotations from Dryden are drawn from Ker's
edition of this essay, and their location indicated by page numbers in the text.

adds a more explicit argument as well, in favor of paraphrase and against metaphrase and imitation. Against metaphrase he writes, "too faithfully is, indeed, pedantically: 'tis a faith like that which proceeds from superstition, blind and zealous" (237). Later, warming to his task, he writes,

> [Verbal translation is] much like dancing on ropes with fettered legs: a man may shun a fall by using caution; but the gracefulness of motion is not to be expected: and when we have said the best of it, 'tis but a foolish task; for no sober man would put himself into a danger for the applause of escaping without breaking his neck. (238)

Metaphrase Dryden dismisses absolutely. Imitation he accepts in certain cases: where the original author is as "wild and ungovernable" (240) as Pindar (not a "regular intelligible author" [240] like Vergil or Ovid), and the imitator as gifted as Cowley. In other cases, however—and clearly most cases are other cases—he rejects it, noting that most of the arguments in its favor bear only against metaphrase and not against paraphrase. He settles, then, on paraphrase, as the happy medium that remains: "imitation and verbal version are, in my opinion, the two extremes which ought to be avoided; and therefore . . . I have proposed the mean betwixt them" (241).

B: Since Dryden

The most important figure in the history of anglophone translation since Dryden is Ezra Pound, and Pound has had two strong and strongly opposed effects on our habitual thought. First, he gave new prestige to the range of translational possibilities extending from paraphrase to imitation. The *Homage to Sextus Propertius, Cathay,* and the "Sea-Farer" were simply better poems than were any extant translations of these texts. They brought into English poetry important excellences largely missing from it; often, moreover, they brought precisely the excellences that scholars had attributed to the poems Pound translated. No one who cared for poetry and the translation of poetry could after Pound dismiss imitation as Dryden had.

But Pound's work also fostered the now common rupture between those students of translation who cared for poetry and those who cared for scholarship. Some scholars criticized Pound's translations savagely, as if lexical and grammatical accuracy were sufficient criteria for judging translation. Pound and his allies responded as if lexical and grammatical accuracy were irrelevant criteria for judging translation. The quarrels make entertaining reading, but the habits of thought they encouraged were disastrous: an automatic association between philological precision and poetic impotence on the one hand, and between translational freedom and poetic power on the other.[3] Since Pound, it has been a common presumption that the scholar-translator is a graceless pedant and the poet-translator an ignoramus. These presumptions entail distorted ideas of both philology and poetry. But they are no less persuasive for that.

Of the major literary translators active in English since Pound's time, few *in their translations* have "altered the sense" of the poems as Pound did, or even as Dryden did. True, they often elect not to reproduce the source-language patterns of rhyme and meter; but at least they know what these patterns are. Most have worked either from their own expert understanding of the source language or in close collaboration with a respected philologist or native informant, and in fact such collaboration has become almost a normative practice. Many have produced translations that unlike Pound's or Dryden's can almost be used as trots; many who translate poems have chosen to have their translations appear facing the originals, as if to invite readers to use them for just that purpose. Some have produced translations similar to the Ben Jonson version of Horace that Dryden singled out for censure. Some have produced texts for humanities courses, versions of classic texts that philologists feel comfortable teachng from. Moreover, right-wing paraphrases of this sort have won most of the big translation prizes.[4] The extraordinary Homeric imitations of Christopher Logue, on the other hand, the most remarkable achievement in imitation since Pound's *Homage*, have won none of them.

In their comments and essays, however, these same translators take sharply different positions. They locate the thing a translator is to aim at rendering either, like Dryden, not in the words of a poem but in its sense or, like Pound, not in its sense but in some aspect of its manner. Robert Lowell writes, "I have been reckless with literal meaning, and labored hard to get the tone." He, unlike many of these translators, has in fact been reckless with literal meaning. Richard Howard has not been; but he writes in the preface to his scrupulous Baudelaire translations that he has worked to approximate what Baudelaire called his "secret architecture," not his outward form. Robert Bly puts the investigation of a poem's sense second in his *Eight Stages of Translation*, leaving it to be superseded by the claims of tone and sound. John Hollander says that, to give someone a sense of the Roman poet Martial, he would send that person not to J. V. Cunningham's translations of Martial but to Cunningham's own original epigrams. Edwin Honig

---

3. For a richly documented account of the quarrels see Humphrey Carpenter, *A Serious Character* (Boston: Houghton Mifflin, 1988), especially pp. 145-146, 156-157, 265-274, 323-344.

4. See the various editions of *Literary and Library Prizes* (New York: R. R. Bowker) for the winners of such awards as the Bollingen Poetry Translation Prize, the P.E.N. Translation Prize, the National Book Award for translation, the Translators Association prizes, and the American Book Award for translation.

notes that ten of the eleven translators interviewed for *The Poet's Other Voice* agree that a translation should not sound like a translation, as if by espousing that ideal they could guard against any falsely conservative reading of their practice.[5]

I quote as exemplifying these characteristics two passages from Honig's interviews, one with Richard Wilbur and one with Robert Fitzgerald.

> *Wilbur:* I like something that Jackson Mathews once said, when he was speaking well of my translation of *Tartuffe*. Instead of describing it as word-for-word faithful, he said that it was thought-for-thought faithful. Now if you propose to be thought-for-thought faithful, which means not leaving out any of the thoughts of the original, you can chuck particular words that don't have handsome equivalents in your own language.

> *Honig:* It's clear that translation can never be word-for-word.[6]

Wilbur here simply restates the crucial point of Dryden's program, the invidious distinction between word and thought. But he states it as something fresh and novel, and clearly it retains for him (and for Honig) a productive vitality. Then he goes beyond it, casually asserting the right to "chuck" words lacking "handsome equivalents." Wilbur's own brilliant translations "chuck" many fewer words than Dryden's do; but nowhere in the essays do we find Dryden asserting the license to "chuck" so off-handedly.

In the other passage, Fitzgerald singles out for praise a line of Wilbur's translation of Villon. Villon wrote,

> Dites-moi où, n'en quel pays,
> Est Flora, la belle Romaine,
> Archipiades ni Thäis,
> Qui fut sa cousine germaine . . .

Wilbur translated this as

> Tell me where, on lands or seas,
> Flora the Roman belle has strayed,

---

5. Lowell, *Imitations* (New York: Farrar, Straus & Giroux, 1961), p. xi; Howard, *Les Fleurs du mal* (Boston: David R. Godine, 1988), p. xx; Bly, *The Eight Stages of Translation* (Boston: Rowan Tree Press, 1983); Hollander, interview in Edwin Honig, *The Poet's Other Voice: Conversations on Literary Translation* (Amherst: University of Massachusetts Press, 1985), pp. 39-49; Honig, ibid., p. 201.

6. Honig, p. 92.

Archipiades or Thäis,
Who put each other in the shade.

Fitzgerald comments,

> Now, the French says of the second of these dead lovelies—two courte-
> sans, as he understood them—that she was the *cousine germaine* of the first.
> In what respect was she a first cousin? She was first cousin in respect to
> her beauty. Now Wilbur found in English idiom a lovely phrase for what
> one beauty does to another beauty. She puts her in the shade, if she can,
> and he translates that line, "who put each other in the shade"—literally
> utterly remote from the French. But, my point is that had Villon been
> using our language, and had he found that idiom, that same phrase, he
> would have been delighted to use it in that place.[7]

Wilbur's solution substitutes an image of rivalry for Villon's image of kinship, so we might not want to say so confidently that Villon would have been
"delighted to use it." The really interesting point, though, is that
Fitzgerald's own fluent translations seldom "alter the sense" of the original
so greatly. His practice, we might say, is Dryden's practice as modified by his
own philological rigor; but his theory is Dryden's as modified by Pound.

So is the theory of most of the major anglophone translators now working. The movement leftward from Dryden in theory balances the movement rightward from Dryden in practice; on the whole we are where
Dryden started, the heirs of a remarkably consistent, productive, and narrow tradition of literary translation.[8]

C: An Excursus on English Bible Translation

Readers trained in biblical studies will object that the collective work of the
early English Bible stands strongly against the tradition so far described.
Such readers know that that Bible does indeed render its original "word for
word," indeed word *by* word. The English biblical "and," for example,

---

7. Honig, pp. 104-105.
8. While writing this introduction I saw in a remainder catalogue this remark of Stephen
Mitchell's, in the foreword to his version of the *Tao Te Ching*: "with great poetry, the freest
translation is sometimes the most faithful. 'We must try its effect as an English poem,' Dr.
Johnson said: 'that is the way to judge of the merit of a translation.' I have often been fairly literal—or as literal as one *can* be with such a subtle, kaleidoscopic book as the *Tao Te Ching*. But
I have also paraphrased, expanded, contracted, interpreted, worked with the text, played with
it, until it became embodied in a language that felt genuine to me. If I haven't always translated Lao-tzu's words, my intention has always been to translate his mind." Clearly Dryden's
ideas are still with us.

results from the early translators' decision to render consistently the Hebrew Bible's *vav*-connective. The same translators consistently render construct-nouns by construct-nouns devised to correspond to them: "son of man" for *ben-adam,* "bread of affliction" for *leḥem laḥatz.* They render a single recurring Hebrew word by a single recurring English word. The King James version in particular goes so far as to indicate by italics all words in the translation not corresponding to words in the original.[9]

But these same translators make no case for their practice; indeed, they make a case against it.[10] William Tyndale writes in a wonderful polemical passage,

> They will say [the Bible] cannot be translated into our tongue, it is so rude. It is not so rude as they are false liars. For the Greek tongue agreeth more with the English than with the Latin. And the properties of the Hebrew tongue agreeth a thousand times more with the English than with the Latin. The manner of speaking is both one, so that in a thousand places thou needest not but to translate it in to the English word for word. . . .[11]

This is no case for metaphrase, for retention of this or that aspect of the original text even at the cost of straining English idiom. Rather Tyndale is arguing that, given the similarity he finds between English and Hebrew, no choice between metaphrase and paraphrase is necessary; rendering word for word will of itself magically yield sense for sense and manner for manner. The King James translators go further:

> . . . we have not tied ourselves to an uniformity of phrasing, or to an identity of words . . . that we should express the same notion in the same particular word; as for example, if we translate the Hebrew or Greek word once by *Purpose,* never to call it *Intent;* if one where *Journeying,* never *Traveling;* if one where *Think,* never *Suppose;* if one where *Pain,* never *Ache;* if one where *Joy,* never *Gladness,* etc. Thus to mince the matter, we

---

9. See further on these matters Gerald Hammond's excellent *The Making of the English Bible* (New York: Philosophical Library, 1983).

10. The exception is the Catholic Rheims-Douay Bible, translated from St. Jerome's Vulgate but also modeled on St. Jerome's notion "that in other writings it is enough to give in translation sense for sense, but that in Scriptures, lest we miss the sense, we must keep the very words" (in Brooke Foss Westcott, *A General View of the History of the English Bible* (London: Macmillan, 1872), p. 259).

This notion of a two-value system is a powerful one, which nourishes Luther's thought about translation also. But the Rheims-Douay Bible was a translation of a translation; it was a Catholic translation in a Protestant country; it was, above all, a translation full of incomprehensible Latinisms and at odds with the populist aim of Bible translation generally. It had little influence on anglophone translational thought.

11. As quoted in David Daniell, ed., *Tyndale's New Testament* (New Haven: Yale University Press, 1989), p. xxii.

thought to savor more of curiosity than wisdom, and that rather it would breed scorn in the Atheist, than bring profit to the godly reader. For is the kingdom of God become words or syllables?[12]

To this rhetorical question the writers' own translational practices answer, "yes." But the answer the question demands is of course "No!" The only authoritative practitioners of metaphrase thus articulate an authoritative denunciation of it, and the practice of metaphrase gives rise to a theory of paraphrase.

The established Bible translators today only perpetuate that theory. Eugene Nida, arguing for "dynamic equivalence" and against "formal equivalence," simply refurbishes Dryden's distinction between sense and word. Harry Orlinsky, rightly understanding the early English Bible as metaphrase, disparages it as "mechanical" and states forthrightly that "it is precisely this philosophy of literal, mechanical translation which the New Jewish Version has set out to discard." He gives an explicit answer to the King James translators' question, stating categorically that "a Hebrew term may have several nuances, depending on the context . . . it is incorrect, if not misleading, to reproduce that term by a single English term throughout."[13]

In sacred and secular translation alike, then, the program of paraphrase has become centrist, central, and dominant; and that program, with all its presuppositions, is to some extent our program, whether we arrive at it by theoretical reflection or simply by learning the language we speak.

III: Buber-Rosenzweig in Context

A: *Word-for-Word, Word, and* Leitwort

Dryden characterizes metaphrase as translating "word for word."[14] He treats this phrase as if its meaning as a translational program were self-evident; he does not explain it, only argues against it. In fact, though, it is anything but self-evident:

---

12. Edgar J. Goodspeed, ed., *The Translators to the Reader: Preface to the King James Version 1611* (Chicago: University of Chicago Press, 1935), p. 36.

13. Nida, *Toward a Science of Translating* (Leiden: Brill, 1964) and, with Charles Taber, *The Theory and Practice of Translation* (Leiden: Brill, 1969), both *passim*; Orlinsky ed., *Notes on the New Translation of the Torah* (Philadelphia: Jewish Publication Society, 1970), pp. 13, 19, 25.

14. Actually, "word for word *and line by line.*" This second point, i.e., the relation between the order of the original and the order of the translation, is implicitly dealt with later, in the section on the *cola.* See below, "A Translation of the Bible."

Faust: I feel impelled to open the master text
And this once, with true dedication,
Take the sacred original
And make in my mother tongue my own translation.
  (He opens a Bible)
It is written: In the beginning was the Word.
Here I am stuck at once. Who will help me out?
I am unable to grant the Word such merit,
I must translate it differently
If I am truly illumined by the spirit.
It is written: In the beginning was the Mind.
But why should my pen scour
So quickly ahead? Consider that first line well.
Is it the Mind that effects and creates all things?
It *should* read: In the beginning was the Power.
Yet, even as I am changing what I have writ,
Something warns me not to abide by it.
The spirit prompts me, I see in a flash what I need,
And write: In the beginning was the Deed![15]

Each of Faust's choices renders the Greek sentence word for word. In all of them, that is, he is a "literal" or "verbal" translator, a metaphraser. He is, moreover, writing prose, and thus not subject to the constraints Dryden says hamper a metaphraser in rendering verse. But none of this seems to make his task very easy, or even to define it very clearly. It seems, in fact, that in rejecting metaphrase the anglophone tradition disparages as mechanical and constrained a choice of great artistry and dizzying freedom: *which* word for word, and why?

The anglophone tradition has characteristically addressed that subordinated question much as Faust does. He opens the Bible, and then opens either the lexicon on his desk or the lexicon of his memory. The rendering of *logos* as "word" is the first rendering a memory or a lexicon would provide: a default-option rendering, automatic and unthinking. No very interesting mental operation is necessary for Faust to produce it. The operations get more interesting when Faust asks the important translational question of whether this rendering of *logos* makes sense of the local context, the sentence and paragraph, in which it occurs. For that is in fact Faust's question; he is "unable to grant the Word such merit" because his rendering of the word here has to bear the weight of what is predicated of it later in the chapter: "the *logos* was with God, and God was the *logos* . . . all things were made

---

15. Louis MacNeice, *Goethe's Faust* (New York: Oxford, 1960), p. 44, and see also below, "From the Beginnings of Our Bible Translation."

by the same [*logos*], and without that same [*logos*] nothing is made that has been made." When, moreover, Faust replaces "mind" with "power," the argument he hints at is the same: that the rendering must make true and reasonable the statement, "the *logos* effects and creates all things."

The anglophone tradition has often posed the question of translating the word in terms of the oppositions Faust enacts. Lexicon renderings like "word" have been associated with pedantry, with servility, and with philology. Reflective renderings like "mind" and "power" have been associated with deliberation, with interpretation, and with the admirable translational quest to have the original make sense. Faust's brooding over the specific and idiomatic meaning of a word in its local context has in the anglophone tradition become one of the translator's central tasks. And through the performance of that task, translation in the anglophone tradition has been consistently vigorous and occasionally dazzling.

Sometimes, though, even eminent anglophone translators are inexplicably blind to evident patterns in their texts, blind with the sort of blindness that comes not from inattention to detail but from constricting presumptions, and at those moments it seems that these Faustian oppositions need to be reconsidered. One example may stand for many. Every reader of the *Aeneid* in Latin has felt how central the word *pius* is to the character of Aeneas and to the meaning of the book is a whole. Most readers, therefore, recognize when they read of Aeneas' encounter with Mezentius' son Lausus that something extraordinary is happening. Aeneas has just wounded Mezentius, and is about to kill him, but Lausus comes to his father's aid. Aeneas taunts Lausus: *fallit te incautum pietas tua* ("your *pietas* deceives you who are reckless"). Then he wounds him mortally. Then, seeing Lausus dying, he is touched—*et mentem patriae subiit pietatis imago* ("and the image of his own fatherly *pietas* [i.e., Aeneas' *pietas* toward his father] touched his mind") —and he says to the dying youth, *quid pius Aeneas tanta dabit indole dignum* ("what shall *pius* Aeneas give [you] that is worthy of such a nature?").[16] That *pius* Aeneas should reproach Lausus for *pietas*, as if that virtue now stood lower in his scale than prudence; that he should then see in Lausus not *pietas* as folly but *pietas* as the central trait of his own character; that he should in the end reassert his identity as *pius* Aeneas, blind to the tension between these two experiences—all this dramatizes plainly and brilliantly the pressure put on Aeneas' identity by the stress of war and the constraints of his mission. But neither of the two principal contemporary translations of the epic retains the drama of the three utterances. Robert Fitzgerald retains the first two: "Filial piety makes you

---

16. R. A. B. Mynors, ed., *P. Vergili Maronis Opera* (Oxford: Oxford University Press, 1983), X: 812-826.

lose your head," "filial piety... wrung his own heart"—but simply omits the
third: "how will Aeneas reward your splendid fight?"[17] Allen Mandelbaum
retains the third: "what can the pious/ Aeneas give to match so bright a
nature?" But this is of little use, because the resemblance between the
third utterance and the first two has been completely effaced: "your loy-
alty/ has tricked you into recklessness," and "the image of/ his love for his
own father touched his mind."[18] Surely something is wrong when a theory
of translating blurs, as it seems to here, even so evident and central a literary effect as this.

Buber's notion of *Leitwort* poses the question of translating the word in
terms that help us get past such impasses. A *Leitwort* is to a text what a
Leitmotif is to a Wagner opera:[19] a thematic word or word-complex. Buber
and Rosenzweig use the word inconsistently, applying it sometimes to patterns they attribute to the original maker of a passage, sometimes to patterns they attribute to an intermediate or final redactor. The unity of the
notion lies not in its meaning for criticism, however, but in its meaning for
translation; as Rosenzweig wrote, "Buber discovered this secret of biblical
style *in translating*" (my italics).[20] In translation, a *Leitwort* is simply a word
or word-complex that the translator must translate consistently in all its
recurrences, i.e., must translate in such a way that wherever the *Leitwort*
recurs in the original, its equivalent recurs in the translation.[21]

For the idea of *Leitwort* to have meaning, however, we have to know not
only what *Leitwörter* are but also what they are not. On this Buber and
Rosenzweig have less to say. But one passage in Buber's essay on the Psalms
at least defines the issue:

> where necessary and appropriate [the translator] will reproduce a single
> Hebrew word-family by a single German one, not one by many or many by
> one. "Where necessary," since with words given little or no mental empha-
> sis, this principle may be eased or annulled. . . . And "where appropriate,"
> since often the special conditions of a passage will impose the obligation
> to treat it as an exception. . . . Translators of the Bible are subject [both

---

17. Robert Fitzgerald, tr., *The Aeneid* (New York: Vintage, 1984), X: 1137–55.

18. Allen Mandelbaum, tr., *The Aeneid of Virgil* (New York: Bantam Classic, 1981), X: 1114-33.

19. On the relation between the Wagnerian *Leitmotif* and the Buberian *Leitwort*, see Yairah
Amit, "The Multi-Purpose 'Leading Word' and the Problems of Its Usage" (*Prooftexts* 9 [1989],
pp. 99-114). Amit has a lot of interesting things to say about Buber's idea but misses its relation
to translational practice.

20. In "The Secret of Biblical Narrative Form."

21. Often, especially when Buber and Rosenzweig seek to treat a word-root as a *Leitwort*, they
draw their rendering of it from its etymology; but sometimes they do not, and there is no necessary connection between an etymological rendering and a *Leitwort*-rendering. On etymological translation see George Steiner, *After Babel* (New York: Oxford University Press, 1977), pp.
322-333, and Henri Meschonnic, *Pour la poétique V: Poésie sans réponse* (Paris: Gallimard, 1978),
pp. 203-207.

to] the law speaking from the peculiar claim of the individual passage and
the law speaking from the biblical totality. . . . In every case we ask about
what will produce the higher value for the intention of the rendering,
and make our decision accordingly.[22]

Buber defines three categories: *Leitwörter*, unemphasized words, and words
bearing a special meaning in their immediate context. In practice, however, the second category pretty much disappears into the third, since
words felt as unimportant inevitably get translated according to their meaning in context. The translator's choice lies between the two categories
remaining; the translator's task, therefore, is to weigh the claims of local
context against the claims of global context.

Buber gives no useful advice about how that weighing should be done; he
refers the translator only to the criteria of "necessary" and "appropriate,"
and demands that the translator decide in accord with "the higher value for
the intention of the rendering"—as if any translator would consciously
decide otherwise! But we can see how intelligently Buber and Rosenzweig
work with the two categories in detail. In "*Leitwort* and Discourse Type," his
brilliant close reading of Exodus 32-34, Buber identifies the thematic resonances of, for example, ʿ*am* and ʿ*alah*; and the translation lets those resonances be heard. In a wonderful passage of "Scripture and Luther,"
Rosenzweig descends to "the lower layers" of language to trace deeper verbal linkages:

> . . . the text begins again and again by saying that in the tent of the *moʿed*
> God will *hivaʿed* himself to man above the ark of the ʿ*edut*. . . . this is not
> exactly made clear when Kautzsch writes that God reveals himself in the
> tent of revelation above the chest of the law, nor when Luther writes that
> God bears witness to himself in the tent of meeting above the chest of wit-
> ness, nor yet, though more nearly, when Luther in earlier editions writes
> that God bears witness to himself in the tent of attestation above the chest
> of witness. The text speaks of none of these things. The lexically related
> meanings are here of no help to the translator, if at any rate he believes in
> the significance of the connection that Scripture makes so emphatic. Here
> he must descend to the depths, where in the components ʿ*ad*, "until," and
> ʿ*od*, "still," the concrete sense of the verbal group is revealed: spatial and
> temporal *presence*. God makes himself *present* in the tent of the *presence*
> above the ark of the recalling-to-*presence* of the covenant made at Sinai.[23]

By putting extraordinary stress on the language, the translation lets these
resonances be heard also. Names, too, are sometimes identified as carriers

---

22. "On Translating the Praisings."
23. Section VII, "Scripture and Luther."

of thematic meaning and treated almost as *Leitwörter:* "Adam," "Eve," "Cain," "Jacob," "Noah" are all accompanied in the text by glosses of that thematic meaning.[24]

Rejections of *Leitwort* renderings are not for the most part articulated so explicitly.[25] There are some exceptions, happily; we find in the working papers fascinating suggestions from Rosenzweig for modulating from occurrence to occurrence the translation of the Hebrew words *ruaḥ* and *tehom.*[26] We also find a letter of Rosenzweig's trying to work out a *Leitwort* rendering for *baʿal,* one that would encompass the three senses of "owner," "husband," and "god." As the editor of the papers notes, however,

> Buber not only made no use of Rosenzweig's proposal to find a single German root for the three senses of *baʿal;* he did not even render the "husband" sense consistently, giving [in Gen. 20:3] *Gemahl* but in Exod. 21:3 *Gatte.* . . . Even the sense of "owner" is rendered inconsistently; Exod. 21:29 *Eigner,* but Judges 9 *Bürger.*[27]

But probably Buber's "inconsistency" is in fact his reasonable rejection of the proposal to take the word as a *Leitwort* in the first place. In many other cases, *Leitwort* renderings are rejected silently. The French Bible translator André Chouraqui translates the *bereshit* of Gen. 1:1 as *entête* ("at the head"), drawing on the word's rootedness in *rosh,* "head."[28] Buber and Rosenzweig translate the word "im Anfang" ("in the beginning"), thus obscuring the connection between it and *rosh* in all its various occurrences, presumably because they do not regard the word or word-root as thematic in the text. In general, in fact, we find in their text strikingly few of Chouraqui's radical etymological renderings, and in each instance can discern the rejection of a possible *Leitwort.* And to set against the thematically translated names, we

---

24. They usually give the transliterated name, then a comma, then the meaning: "Chava, Leben." This does not in the end work all that well, partly because it is at odds with their principle of providing translation without commentary. But their investigation of the problem at least shows by contrast how little the anglophone tradition has contributed here; outside of some translations of comedy, few translators deal at all *in the text* with the meaningfulness of names, whatever they may do in the commentary. No English translation of the *Odyssey* translates the thematically meaningful name of Odysseus, no English translation of the *Oedipus Rex* the thematically meaningful name of Oedipus.

25. There are two reasons for this. For one thing, devising *Leitwort* renderings was clearly more gratifying than rejecting them, so it led to ampler discussion. Also, Rosenzweig's paralysis meant that all of his comments had to be written down, so the working papers contain far more of his comments than they do of Buber's, and Buber, who had devised the notion of *Leitwort* in the first place, was nonetheless far more likely than Rosenzweig was to reject a *Leitwort* rendering.

26. Rosenzweig, *Arbeitspapiere zur Verdeutschung der Schrift* (Dordrecht: Martinus Nijhoff, 1984), Rachel Bat-Adam, ed., pp. 4 and 32–33, bearing on Genesis 1 and 6.

27. Ibid., pp. 63–65.

28. *La Bible: Entête* (Paris: Desclée de Brouwer, 1974), tr. André Chouraqui, p. 15.

note the numerous names possessing semantic meaning but not treated as having thematic meaning, e.g., Jonah, "dove" (perhaps); the translation ignores the meaning and simply transliterates the name.

We can now clarify Faust's translational situation. "Word" is not just a lexicon rendering; it is also the most plausible rendering if *logos* is taken to be a *Leitwort*. Faust must choose it if, when *logos* next occurs, in John 2:2, he wants to be able to translate, "[his disciples] believed... the word which Jesus had said," so as to link Jesus as word to the words Jesus speaks. (*Logos* could also be taken to be part of a *Leitwort* family, a family including not only *logos* but also *legô*, "to speak." In that case it would have to be rendered by "speech" or "speaking.") If Faust chooses "mind" or "power" or "deed" he does so because he finds the claims of context stronger than the claims of linkage. None of this determines his choice between the thematic and the occasional rendering, or among the three occasional renderings he considers; but it does specify the consequences his choice and our choices of this sort will have, the kind of analysis they must be based upon, and the translational possibilities a free deliberation over such choices might open up.

B: Cola, *Sense, and the Form-Content Distinction*

The most important aspect of the B-R translation program for theory is the making of the *cola*, the lines of the translation, because this helps us past the impasse we get to by thinking in terms of "sense," and "sense" is certainly the central term in anglophone translation theory. But to make the connection will take an extended argument.

"Sense" is a hard term to puzzle out. As Dryden uses it, it must mean something distinct from "word" yet also distinct from "style" or "manner." It must, moreover, be something unitary; none of the uses of the "sense" of a word that refer to one sense of many can matter here. When we turn to the *Oxford English Dictionary*, we find first that often "sense" is quoted precisely in connection with the activity of translation. Thus the King James Bible translators write, "there bee some wordes that bee not of the same sense every where"—i.e., in a paraphrase they must be translated differently according to context. "Sense" thus used means, circularly, simply what an original passage and its translation by paraphrase have in common. This makes for a problem, of course, namely that the translator cannot learn the practice of translation from the idea of "sense" because "sense" is already the product, or the goal, of that practice, and cannot be understood apart from it.

But we also find in the OED a number of citations referring to "sense" in connection with activities like summarizing a message, interpreting a prophecy, or deciphering an allegory. "Sense" as used in these examples is a reduction, a gist. Hence the phrase "sense verses": "a passage, context, or set of sentences, expressed in bare prose, used as material for the composition of Latin or Greek verses." This is clear, at any rate, and not circular. Moreover, it is precisely this reductive quality in "sense" that makes it attractive, because it is this quality that makes "sense" ordinary and egalitarian. William Empson gets brilliantly at the appeal of "sense" by describing the opposition between it and "sensibility":

> *Sensibility* names a special power of sensing, and . . . *sense* is radically opposed to it. . . . *sensibility* will come to praise a special type of person, whereas *sense* will carry a sturdy agreement with the common man. . . . The suasive power of [*sense* in the Augustan period] seems to come from treating all reactions or good judgements as of one sort, though, in fact, they presumably range from the highest peaks of imaginative insight, or the greatest heart-searchings of "enthusiasm," to fundamental but humble processes like recognising a patch of colour as a table. *Sense* tells you to concentrate on the middle of the range, the man-size parts where we feel most at home; and it can do this because the simple use of the trope (which is now taken as a pattern) is an appeal to you to show a normal amount of good judgement, "like everybody else."[29]

Empson is of course studying the word as it denotes a personal quality, but he illuminates it also as it denotes a textual quality. The sense of the text, the gist of it, as opposed to the finicky details of the words, will "carry a sturdy agreement with the common man"; "sense" is what is produced when we "concentrate on the middle of the [textual] range," attending principally neither to the verbal details nor to the intangible personal tone; "sense" appeals to us "to show a normal amount of good [literary] judgement," to resemble neither the Puritanical pedants of verbal translation nor the irresponsible libertines of imitation. The sense of a text would then be what is produced by a translator having sense rather than sensibility.

Thus defined, "sense" is clear enough, and its power is intelligible enough. The problem, though, is that its power gives authority to a conception of translation as reduction. The distinctions between summary and whole, message and prophecy, moral and allegory, prose and poetry all inevitably support the distinction between content and form; and that distinction, which few will argue for but many use, is in thinking about translation and translation theory a severely corrupting error.

---

29. Empson, *The Structure of Complex Words* (Ann Arbor: University of Michigan Press, 1967), pp. 256-262.

Accordingly, Henri Meschonnic[30] founds his devastating critique of most biblical translation on a critique precisely of that distinction, arguing that maintaining the distinction leads us inevitably to make one of two wrong choices:

> on the one side substance, sense, assigned to the domain of pragmatism, functionalism, instrumentalism; on the other, form. Excess in either direction remains *within the limits of the polarity, which it does not affect because it is still inside it.* The predominance of sense in society is not in the least disturbed by an esthetic of form, whose excesses themselves harm the functionality of [its] discourse and are excluded from instrumentalism even as they reinforce it. . . . We must reject, therefore, both together and separately, these two poles of translation, these two partialities that exist only in and by the idea of sign, with a dispensable *signifiant* and an all-encompassing *signifié.*[31]

This trenchant argument is not new, of course. What is new is Meschonnic's idea for getting outside the polarity: to attend neither to sense nor to form but to *rhythm.* He has devoted numerous essays to this notion, and then, as if not satisfied with them, has also written a 700-page *Critique of Rhythm.* But the notion itself is simple enough. Meschonnic means by rhythm a characteristic of every text, not one only of oral or poetic or literary texts; he means by the rhythm of a text its organization of meaning in time. As a translator, he seeks to render that organization in time at least partly by shaping a corresponding organization in space. Typography then is crucial for him; he remarks, "there is a strict correspondence between translational technique and typography. Not only for the Bible. For Kafka too, for example."[32] This may seem obscure, but there is a commonsensical core to it. Whenever as translators we have to choose how to paragraph or punctuate or lineate a text, we find experientially that this typographical decision is in fact a decision about textual rhythm in Meschonnic's charged sense of that term. We find that these apparently peripheral decisions, affecting what bibliographers significantly call the "accidentals" of a text, require of us a full understanding of every aspect of the text: sound and diction, rhythm and prosody, grammar and syntax, argument and rhetoric, tone and register, and the meaning that arises out of the unhierarchized relations among all these. Textual critics have known this for a long time, of course; but

---

30. *Les Cinq Rouleaux* (Paris: Gallimard, 1970); *Pour la poétique II* (Paris: Gallimard, 1973), pp. 305-454; *Pour la poétique V,* pp. 187-268; *Jona et le signifiant errant* (Paris: Gallimard, 1981). Meschonnic's work seems to me the most important work on biblical translation and translation generally since Buber and Rosenzweig's own.

31. Meschonnic, *Jona,* pp. 33-34.

32. Ibid., p. 56.

translators have often ignored it. They have ignored the complex typographical meanings of the original: the fonts Kafka stipulated, the illuminated capitals of medieval manuscripts, the idiosyncratic expressive punctuation of Shakespeare's sonnets. They have also ignored the typographical possibilities available for translation in cases where the original text leaves them open, not only in the Bible but in, say, the one-paragraph essays of Montaigne or the punctuationless texts of Greek and Latin.

It is in this context that the *cola* become of theoretical consequence. Not, however, the *cola* as Buber and Rosenzweig describe them, or at least not in all the ways in which they describe them.

Making the lines is presented in the essays and the working papers as part of an attempt to reveal the Bible's essential spokenness; the lines themselves are supposed to represent phrases of spoken utterance, the breaks between them the breathings of the speaker. But "spokenness" can mean several things. It can mean, and to Buber sometimes does mean, orality—i.e., the characteristics that distinguish oral poetry from written. In the anglophone tradition, it usually means conversationality: the distinctive quality of what particular people actually say, in ordinary conversation with other particular people at a particular place and time. Anglophone literary translators and poets have worked hard to attain spokenness in this sense. Robert Frost is a master of it: "and that has made all the difference." Robert Bly, who quotes this line of Frost as exemplifying "sentence sound," devotes three of his eight stages of translation to making sure that the translation will have this quality.[33]

In neither of these senses, however, would the idea of spokenness and the *cola* manifesting it mean much for translation theory generally; few would deny that an essentially oral text should be translated in such a way as to reflect its orality, or that an essentially conversational text should be translated in such a way as to reflect its conversationality, and the only critical disputes would concern the facts of the case: whether the text in question was in fact an essentially oral or conversational text. As it turns out, however, neither the discussions of the *cola* in the working papers nor the actual *cola* themselves reflect spokenness in either of these senses. Whether the Hebrew Bible is oral poetry or not, the German text of the Buber-Rosenzweig translation simply does not exhibit the oral traits of the Greek text of Homer. Nor, unlike Luther's translation, does it have "sentence sound."[34] "Sentence sound" is precisely what it does *not* have, because that

33. Bly, *Eight Stages*, p. 26.

34. I base this assessment on my own sense of the text but also, gratefully, on that of my colleague Jens Kruse of the Wellesley College German Department, who said that the passages he had read seemed to him to have "almost no tone at all."

On Siegfried Kracauer's interesting and hostile assessment of the translation's tone, see below, "The Bible in German."

is something we hear chiefly in our own time and place, secondarily in times and places we know at second-hand, and not at all in a language as placeless and timeless as is that of Buber and Rosenzweig's Bible.[35] The chief characteristic of their text is rather a typographically articulated analytical clarity.[36] Rosenzweig in "Scripture and Word" suggestively compares the making of *cola* with a great scholar's explicatory reading aloud: "The apparent singsong of Talmud study, i.e., the musical "setting" of the sentence as read, sets up the logical understanding of it; Hermann Cohen similarly "set" difficult sentences of Plato and Kant even in reading them aloud."[37] Such passages, along with the working discussions of how to lineate the text, rightly suggest that the *cola* manifest not orality or tonality but Meschonnic's idea of *rhythmicality:* the quality not of a spoken text but of an intelligibly recitable one. Tonality reflects the rootedness of a text in a particular social situation; rhythmicality reflects its relation to an intelligible meaning articulated in and through time.

This needs some elaboration. In arguing to retain "the first 'and' in the world," i.e., "*and* the earth was without form and void," Rosenzweig wrote, "if it were not affected, I would give it its own line. But it cannot be omitted."[38] The imagined proposal makes clear the actual nature of the *cola:* not the reader's necessary breathings, not the formulae of oral poetry or the phrases of quotidian conversation, but the articulation of textual rhythm, the speedings and slowings and stoppages of its motion as these constitute its meaning. Rosenzweig articulates these ideas more generally in a wonderful passage from "Scripture and Word":

> We must free from beneath the logical punctuation that is sometimes its ally and sometimes its foe the fundamental principle of natural, oral punctuation: the act of breathing.
> Breath is the stuff of speech; the drawing of breath is accordingly the natural segmenting of speech. It is subject to its own law: that we cannot speak more than twenty, at most thirty words without taking a deep breath (and not just a catch-breath)—often indeed we can say only five to ten words. But within this boundary the distribution of breath-renewing silences follows the inner order of speech, which is only occasionally determined by its logical structure, and which for the most part mirrors

---

35. Albrecht Schaeffer praises in the translation its "Germanness in a higher sense . . . the supratemporality of its poetical language" ("Bibel-Übersetzung: Aus Anlass der neuen von Martin Buber und Franz Rosenzweig," *Preussische Jahrbücher* 225:1 [July 1926]), p. 73.)

36. Josef Wohlgemuth notes rightly that in reading the translation "monitoring *with the eyes* is absolutely necessary" (*Jeschurun* 13:1/2 [January-February 1926], p. 12; my italics).

37. Q.v.

38. *Arbeitspapiere*, pp. 3-4. See also below, Appendix I, "A Reply," on the effect of relineating certain passages in 1 Samuel; for a more extended example, see the discussion of how to lineate Gen. 2:4 in *Arbeitspapiere*, pp. 12-14.

directly the movements and arousals of the soul itself in its gradations of energy and above all in its gradations of time.

Thus the movement of speech is segmented into units of equal value, temporally equal breaths, so to speak (but *only* so to speak)—from the isolated "Yes" of God's confirmation of human disobedience to the elaborate naming of the five kings against whom the four went out (Gen. 14:2). Sentences that in unambiguous logic are distinct and so separated by periods—say, Cain's appalling answer, "I do not know. Am I my brother's keeper?"—are by the rendering of the vital, breathing course of speech brought together into a single movement, and thus given their full horror, previously half covered-over by the logical punctuation.[39]

Physical orality here determines only a limit, not a shape. What determines shape is "the inner order of speech," moving in counterpoint with the shapes manifested by punctuation; these Rosenzweig calls "logical," identifying "logic" with the ordinary functioning of syntax in prose.[40] The "inner order" he identifies with the movement of the mind in time from one state of energy to another; and he identifies the task of the translator as the rendering of that movement by all means available, but above all by the physical disposition of the words on the page.

Meschonnic's ideas make the implications of Buber and Rosenzweig's practice clearer and more significant. But their practice does better justice to those ideas than does his own. He himself takes the typographical rhythm of his Bible translations from the *ṭeʿamim*, the cantillation signs.[41] In so doing he makes the translator's task here largely mechanical: learn the signs, find an equivalent, and render accordingly. Buber and Rosenzweig rightly take this aspect of the translator's task to be an interpretive one. Accordingly, they take their *cola* sometimes from the *ṭeʿamim* but sometimes against them, regarding them as an imperfect guide and citing in particular Rashi's interpretation of Gen. 1:1 as an authoritative precedent for looking at them skeptically.[42] Their lineation of the text is their chief work of art, and their chief contribution toward clarifying and thus freeing the translator's task.

---

39. Q.v.

40. English "sentence" sometimes means "sense," and when so used it implies the idea, "the sense of a passage is what you get when you render sentence for sentence but not word for word." I have not seen this connection much discussed explicitly in anglophone translation theory, but it seems to underlie some arguments. If so, Rosenzweig's rejection of "logical punctuation" makes a further point against orienting translation toward the rendering of sense.

41. Meschonnic in fact treats the cantillation signs as if they constituted an authoritative commentary on the meaning of the text. For an authoritative refutation of this long-held view, see Norman Janis' brilliant and regrettably unpublished dissertation, "A Grammar of the Biblical Accents" (Harvard University, 1987). My thanks to Norman for lending me a copy and for some illuminating conversations.

42. See "Scripture and Word."

C: The Collaborative Model

We like consistency between preaching and practice, and we find just that when we turn from the theory of the *cola* to the practical collaboration of the two theorists; their brilliant technical passage around the impasse of sense and word accords precisely with the partnership in which the technical passage was developed.

In anglophone translation, too, there is a match between technique and human relations. In anglophone translation in this century, collaboration has usually meant a philologist working with a poet: Pound with Ernest Fenollosa; W. H. Auden with Paul Taylor; Christopher Logue with Donald Carne-Ross. The new Oxford *Greek Tragedy in New Translations* is founded on collaboration: "collaboration between scholar and poet is... the essential operating principle of the series."[43] Sometimes the scholar is mentioned on the title page, sometimes not; often in any case we forget the scholar's name. But even if the relative prominence of the two roles were reversed, the implied division between them would remain; and that division characterizes translation in this century, recapitulating the battles between Pound and the philologists and reinforcing the notions those battles encouraged: that there can be a poetry separate from philology, and a philology separate from poetry. I do not mean to distort the actual relations between particular poets and particular philologists, nor to disparage the many admirable translations produced in such relations. But the consequences of the structure for our habitual thought remain in place.

Buber and Rosenzweig's collaboration did of course include disputes between the claims of the source language and the claims of the target language; Buber was consistently more inclined than was Rosenzweig to adapt the translation to the genius of German. Buber himself made the point candidly:

> Our interplay was manifested most strikingly . . . around the issue of rendering linguistic peculiarities. In response to my first sketch, Rosenzweig had written, "it's remarkably German; Luther in comparison is almost Yiddish. Maybe now it's *too* German?" He soon began—at first only indirectly, but then more and more emphatically—to combat the "too German." Thus when I had inexactly reproduced the conclusion of Gen. 2:16, he wrote: "I would try to render all these inner infinitives. So, for example: 'you may eat, yes, eat.' But this has to do with the fact that if I were to go beyond Luther I would seek to surpass him in Hebraicizing the

---

43. William Arrowsmith, "Editor's Foreword," as found in Sophocles, *Oedipus the King*, tr. Stephen Berg and Diskin Clay (New York: Oxford, 1988), p. v.

syntax, whereas you, in a dehebraicized syntax, seek to surpass him in excavating the Hebraic context of the individual word."[44]

(Nahum Glatzer told Everett Fox that "Rosenzweig often frustrated Buber's artistic leanings by insisting on a strict reproduction of the Hebrew text."[45]) But Buber in a more polemical moment put the matter differently: "Rosenzweig strove passionately on behalf of his discoveries, sometimes so fanatically that I—here as in other matters—had to function as the admonitory frontier guard of the German language, or as the advocate of the putatively understanding reader."[46]

In some respects, then, Buber and Rosenzweig's conversations resembled the conversations we imagine between philologist and poet. In other respects, however, they did not. For one thing, the two men's roles were determined by character, not by knowledge or talent. Buber knew the Hebrew text at least as well as Rosenzweig did, and had known it longer. Rosenzweig was as great a master of German as was Buber, and as deeply rooted in German literary tradition. Thus freed from their association with an unpoetical philology or an unphilological poetry, the claims of the source and target language became in this collaboration the voices of whole persons speaking in dialogue. Appropriately, they spoke in dialogic order. In the anglophone collaborative model, the philologist must have the first word, and the poet has the higher prestige of having the last. If there was any linear order in Buber and Rosenzweig's collaboration, it was the reverse of this. Buber took the role of first writer, Rosenzweig that of first critic; the claims of German had the first word, those of Hebrew the last. But even this account oversimplifies the facts, in identifying just two stages and in positing a single last word. In fact the collaboration had as many stages as a real dialogue has utterances. Even publication only set in motion a new process of revision, in which both Buber and Rosenzweig participated until Rosenzweig's death in 1929; and only with Buber's death in 1965 did that process come to an end—not finished, to adopt Valéry's remark about poems, only abandoned.

Rosenzweig in a remarkable letter to Buber wrote that his role in the translation would "probably be that of the muse of precision [*gründliche Muse*] (Diotima and Xanthippe united in a single person), as yours was with Judah Halevi. But that role, as you can see from that example, is no small matter."[47] Ordinarily, of course, precision has no muse; and muses only

---

44. See below, "From the Beginnings of Our Bible Translation."
45. Everett Fox, "Technical Aspects of the Translations of Genesis of Martin Buber and Franz Rosenzweig" (Brandeis University, dissertation, 1974), p. 229.
46. See below, "From the Beginnings of Our Bible Translation."
47. Ibid.

inspire, leaving the philological work to laboring mortals. Rosenzweig's oxymoronic phrase restates the exemplary anomaly of the collaboration. He develops the anomaly by doubling his role: Xanthippe and Diotima combined, both Socrates' nagging wife and his inspiring teacher. In the anglophone model the philologist too often plays only Xanthippe. Here, in contrast, the speaker on behalf of the source language not only nags but inspires. Rosenzweig's noting that Buber in his turn had also played the "muse of precision" suggests one last time how this collaboration arose from the necessary dialogue of persons and not from the convenient dialogue between truncated professions.

D: Utopia, Annexation, and the Limits of the Language

We come finally to the most controversial trait of Buber and Rosenzweig's translation, namely its deliberate stretching of the limits of the target language.

In many cases, of course, the best way to judge a stretching of the language is *ad hoc*; does it work or not, and if not how could it be altered? We approve, say, of Tyndale's neologism "scapegoat"; we disapprove of Robert Browning's

> . . . I will no longer teach by riddles.
> And witness, running with me, that of evils
> Done long ago, I nosing track the footstep![48]

But here judgment *ad hoc* is not enough. The dialogue between Buber and Rosenzweig and their reviewers turns around this point again and again, and behind the particular attacks and defenses evidently lie more general questions: What *are* the limits of a language? What does it mean to stretch them? Is stretching them a good thing or a bad?

The anglophone tradition usually treats translations that stretch the limits of the language as translatorese. Thus in *Casablanca* two prospective emigrants to America sit in Rick's cafe and practice their English: "What watch? Six watch," they say, badly translating *Wieviel Uhr? sechs Uhr.* Such translations clearly result from ignorance; they are funny and touching, but not models. We speak of translatorese even as we go higher up the ladder, in discussing, say, some earnest but uninspired version of a Baudelaire poem: "Be good, my pain, and keep yourself more tranquil" for "Sois sage, O ma Douleur, et tiens-toi plus tranquille." And again, such translations are not

---

48. As quoted in Steiner, *After Babel*, p. 313.

models. But we have no way of talking about what happens when, moving still further up the ladder, we reach, say, Hölderlin's translations of Pindar or Sophocles. We do not, that is, ordinarily attempt to discriminate between different stretchings, or between different limits. We find for the most part simply assertions, often eloquent but almost always unsupported, that a translator must, in Robert Bly's words, "ignore the sentence structure of the . . . original, and try to move all sentences bodily into the genius of English."[49] Why this should be the case, or when it should be the case and when not, is not argued.

Probably this linguistic imperialism (Meschonnic suggestively calls it *annexion*[50]) is related to Anglo-American political imperialism. For thinking about Buber and Rosenzweig, however, it is more useful to take it as related to the American linguistic relativism of Benjamin Whorf. Whorf argues in a series of extraordinary essays that languages "divide up reality" in radically different ways, and, therefore, that in certain cases speakers of different languages can really be said to live in different worlds.

> We are inclined to think of language simply as a technique of expression, and not to realize that language first of all is a classification and arrangement of the stream of sensory experience which results in a certain world-order, a certain segment of the world that is easily expressible by the type of symbolic means that language employs [55] . . . the background linguistic system . . . of each language is not merely a reproducing instrument for voicing ideas but rather is itself the shaper of ideas, the program and guide for the individual's mental activity, for his analysis of impressions, for his synthesis of his mental stock in trade. [212][51]

Whorf's work has been controversial; but a simplification of it has passed into our habitual thought, and most of the published remarks of anglophone translators and translation theorists stress the vast and subtle differences between languages and not their common humanity.

The consequence for translation is a license for annexation. Thus Wilbur says, in the passage quoted above, that "if you propose to be thought-for-thought faithful . . . you can chuck particular words that don't have handsome equivalents in your own language." We may be put off by this casual jettisoning. But if we think of Wilbur's remarks in the context of Whorf's conception of language, then what Wilbur calls the lack of "handsome equivalents" is an essential fact about languages; it is inscribed deep in the nature of things that "handsome equivalents" will be lacking. Wilbur's posi-

---

49. Bly, *Eight Stages*, p. 24.
50. *Pour la poétique II*, p. 308.
51. Whorf, *Language, Thought, and Reality*, John B. Carroll, ed. (Cambridge: MIT Press, 1988), pp. 55 and 212.

tion then seems only reasonable: since *no* labor, however strenuous, will produce such equivalents, since languages are *essentially* sundered, cut off, translators must be free to direct their efforts elsewhere.

Buber and Rosenzweig begin from a different conception. In the essays collected here, they do not state that conception but rather make local arguments on its basis. Thus they rightly distinguish between a weak sense of linguistic limit, approximately coextensive with the field of current idiom, and a strong sense, coextensive with the spatial and temporal field of the language as a whole. They point out that Luther, too, was censured for linguistic innovations, but that many of his innovations proved viable. They defend particular stretchings of idiom on the ground that they render a Hebrew idiom, or make possible the retention of a *Leitwort*-pattern, or have a precedent in Goethe or Schiller. Buber asserts but does not argue "that languages exist only provisionally, whereas in the last analysis there is only the one language of *Geist*, 'that simple, universal language' (Goethe)."[52] And in one moving passage of "Scripture and Luther," Rosenzweig writes that

> if we believe that not only a passage called to our attention by a particular circumscribed doctrine but *any human utterance* may conceal the possibility that one day, in his time or in my time, God's word may be revealed in it, then in that case the translator must, so far as his language permits, follow the peculiar turns of that potentially revelation-bearing utterance, whether by direct reconstruction or by implication.[53]

The conception from which all these particular remarks arise had been stated previously, in the essay Rosenzweig wrote to accompany his 1924 Judah Halevi translations:

> That innovation in one language can happen by means of another language presumes of course that just as the language has given birth to each of its speakers, so all human speaking, all other languages ever spoken or to be spoken, are present in that one language at least in embryo. And this is the case. There is only One Language. There is no linguistic peculiarity of one language that cannot be found contained, at least in embryo, in every other language, even if only in idioms, in nurseries, in jargons. The possibility of translating and the necessity of translating, the translator's Can, May, and Shall are all founded on this essential unity of all language and the commandment of universal human communication based on that unity.[54]

---

52. See below, "On Translating the Praisings."
53. See below, "Scripture and Luther."
54. Rosenzweig, *Jehuda Halevi: Fünfundneunzig Hymnen und Gedichte*, Rafael Rosenzweig ed. (The Hague: Nijhoff, 1983), p. 3.
See also the 1921 *Stern der Erlösung* (Frankfurt: Suhrkamp, 1988), sections 98 and 385.

For Whorf, stretching the limits of a language is a little like trying to mate elephants and coyotes; nothing, really, can come of it, so the translator must axiomatically avoid it. For Rosenzweig, stretching the limits of a language makes its potential universality actual—or, in any particular case, makes the potential unity of source and target language manifest—so the translator must axiomatically try it.

Rosenzweig draws here on a conception of language that German tradition has fostered and anglophone tradition has not. He evokes Hölderlin's visionary or hallucinatory sense that German and Greek were one language; he evokes Wilhelm von Humboldt's insight, who in positing for the first time the special character of individual languages also posited their essential unity. He evokes the "pure and true language" posited by his contemporary Walter Benjamin:

> If, however, there is a language of truth, in which the ultimate secrets for which all thinking strives are preserved, tranquil and silent, then this language of truth is—the true language. And precisely this language, in the intuition and description of which lies the only perfection the philosopher can hope for, is concentratedly concealed in translations.[55]

Standing as the heir of this long tradition, Gershom Scholem amplified and clarified Rosenzweig's view in a speech addressed to Buber on the completion of the translation in 1961:

> There was a utopian element in your endeavor. For the language into which you translated was not that of everyday speech nor that of German literature of the 1920's. You aimed at a German which, drawing sustenance from earlier tendencies, was present potentially in the language, and it was just this utopianism which made your translation so very exciting and stimulating. Now whether you consciously so intended it or not, your translation—which came from the association of a Zionist and a non-Zionist—was a kind of *Gastgeschenk* which German Jewry gave to the German people, a symbolic act of gratitude upon departure. And what *Gastgeschenk* of the Jews to Germany could be as historically meaningful as a Bible translation?[56]

Scholem characterizes as "utopian" the translators' aiming at a German "present potentially in the language," and associates this utopian character

---

55. Benjamin, "Die Aufgabe des Übersetzers," in *Illuminationen* (Frankfurt: Suhrkamp, 1980), p. 57.

56. Scholem, "At the Completion of Buber's Translation of the Bible," in *The Messianic Idea in Judaism* (New York: Schocken, 1971), p. 318. Hermann Hesse uses the same phrase of the translation in a review published in Basel in the *Nationalzeitung* for December 31, 1933; I do not know whether Scholem had seen that review.

with the vitality of the translation. It is a surprising word, more surprising than "visionary" or "idealistic" would have been, because "utopian" suggests a general social vision rather than a specifically linguistic one. Scholem suggests, that is, that by stretching the limits of the language Buber and Rosenzweig were pushing not only toward One Language but also toward One World. Or, in von Humboldt's words: "languages do indeed separate nations from one another, but only to link them more profoundly and more beautifully; in this languages resemble the seas, once timidly navigated only near the shores but now become the roads that most link countries together."[57]

By "utopian" Scholem probably means also "impractical," "dreamy," "ethereal"; there is a sardonic tone to the word as he uses it that brings us down from the heights, and reminds us that Buber and Rosenzweig's conception is not after all a falsifiable hypothesis. But neither is Whorf's. Both, rather, are metaphoric rationales to work with. Both, moreover, retain their power to shape our practice even when we acknowledge them as fictions; and even as metaphor, or perhaps especially as metaphor, Buber and Rosenzweig's conception of language opens up new spaces for translators to explore.

---

57. As quoted in Meschonnic, *Pour la poétique V*, p. 205.

SCRIPTURE AND TRANSLATION

FOREWORD

Martin Buber
(February 1936)

This book, which I resolved to publish only recently, after the appearance of *The Book of Praisings*,[1] contains the gist of what Franz Rosenzweig and I have written on the aims and tasks of our Bible translation, and thus on the nature and form of the Hebrew Bible itself. It does not contain discussions of biblical theology[2] or exegeses of individual passages.[3] Whatever bears on theology in this book is stated to clarify our aims; whatever bears on exegesis, to offer examples of our tasks.

In 1926, the second year of our work, we began to give accounts of what we were doing—to ourselves, and also to both a particular and a general public. During Rosenzweig's lifetime, I myself did this almost exclusively in lectures; only after his death did I begin to make extensive written presentations of the material. Whatever is drawn here from those lectures has been taken from shorthand notes, and for the most part only sparingly revised. Accounts of insights or experiences subsequent to the lectures are to be found in the footnotes.

I begin the collection with a discussion of the relation people today have to the Bible, and of how they may approach it; for it is after all to people today that the translation must be directed. Then comes whatever can help readers understand our conception of biblical *unity*; then discussions of the goals we set ourselves, supported by considerations of the history and present state of the work of translation. It was necessary also to include here

---

1. *Die Schrift* ["The Scriptures"] (Schocken Verlag, Berlin), vol. xiv. What Buber calls *The Book of Praisings* is what we ordinarily refer to as the book of Psalms; for an explanation of the characteristically unorthodox term see below, "On Translating the Praisings" [eds.].

2. E.g., Rosenzweig's essays in *Der Morgen* from 1928 and 1929 on the first volumes of the *Encyclopedia Judaica*, or his article in the fourth volume of that encyclopedia on the world-historical significance of the Bible.

3. E.g., my comments on Isaiah in the *Monatsschrift für Geschichte und Wissenschaft des Judentums* from 1930.

some of our encounters with our critics, since a clash of opinions both requires and produces a special clarification. The main part of the book concludes with a few brief accounts of guiding principles, stating once more what is at issue, and with a narrative account of how we actually conducted our work. An appendix then collects various sorts of illustrative material, both general and particular. (It includes essays on the meaning of the tetragrammaton, already available in Rosenzweig's *Letters* and my *The Kingdom of God* but reprinted here because of the importance of the subject, and also Rosenzweig's reply to Josef Carlebach, also available in the *Letters*.[4])

In discussing the goals we set, we chiefly treat two major problems:[5] the problem of word choice, culminating in Rosenzweig's "The Eternal," and the closely related problem of *Leitwort* style. The account of *Leitwort* style adduces a whole series of examples from various contexts, and one example in particular is treated as a paradigm and so given a highly detailed analysis. I decided only reluctantly not to include in that series any examples from the Psalms; even now, in my seminar at the Frankfurt Jewish *Lehrhaus*, I am noting how much the investigation of *Leitwörter* in the Psalms helps to reveal their structure and meaning. But the types there are too numerous, and the method of analysis too singular; both would need to be presented independently, and not merely as examples.

Given the genesis of the various essays it is comprised of, the book had necessarily to contain substantive repetitions. But it seems to me that these repetitions clarify the argument rather than disrupting it.

Here, in this analytical look back at a decade of work, is also the long-sought place to give public thanks—thanks that we stated neither in the volumes of the translation nor in the occasional supplements to them. I know that my thanks to the men who have helped us in our work is spoken in Franz Rosenzweig's name also. Thanks first, then, to the faithful Nahum Glatzer, who from the first volume on would on the arrival of our text in proof-sheets read us the original aloud, so that we could *in hearing* make comparisons and corrections; he would also function himself as a kind of trial reader, expressing his questions and doubts. When death and then distance intervened, he continued his help by reading proofs. Thanks also to Benno Jacob, who during the translation of the Pentateuch provided abundant information and advice, always to our profit and instruction; to Moritz Spitzer, who with devoted and productive zeal read proof of volumes xii–xiv;

---

4. The reply to Jakob Rosenheim, on the other hand, is because of the postscript (printed in *Der Morgen* in 1928 but not in the *Letters*) included in the main part of the book.

5. A third problem, that of biblical rhythm, could be treated here only in passing. I hope to treat that problem adequately in an independent monograph, in the context of an investigation of the rhythm of "oral style" generally.

and specially to Harry Torczyner, who read proofs of volumes xii and xiv and showered upon them an abundance of valuable questions, references, and suggestions. My inability to accede to most of his suggestions was rooted in the difference between our conceptions of word and task; but even when I did not accede, I was enriched. Many others who should be named here for their furthering of our work on this occasion or that I can here thank only generally; but I must single out the name of Jakob Horovitz, who in some of the early volumes fought a moving battle, both for us and against us, on behalf of the absolute primacy of the Masoretic text.

A general thanks only can be offered to the appointed guardians of Hebrew and German, whose continually renewed comfort strengthened our hearts for the "daily continuing of heavy labors."[6]

---

6. From Goethe's *West-östliche Divan*, "Vermächtnis" ("Legacy"), l. 27 [eds.].

PEOPLE TODAY[1] AND THE JEWISH BIBLE: FROM A LECTURE SERIES

Martin Buber
(November 1926)

"The Bible," i.e., *biblia*, i.e., "books": such is the name of a book that is a book of books.[2] But it is in reality One Book. All its stories and songs, all its sayings and prophecies are united by one fundamental theme: the encounter of a group of people with the Nameless Being whom they, hearing his speech and speaking to him in turn, ventured to name; their encounter with him in history, in the course of earthly events. The stories are either explicitly or implicitly accounts of encounters. The songs are laments over exclusion from the grace of encounter, pleas for the return of it, thanksgivings for the gift of it. The prophecies exhort those who have gone astray to return to the place of encounter, and promise the restoration of the bond torn asunder. When we hear cries of doubt in this book, we hear the doubt fated for those who experience distance after closeness, and who learn from distance what it alone can teach. When love songs are found here, we must understand that to see God's love for his world as revealed in the profundities of human love is not a late reinterpretation of the biblical text, but an insight originating with the first development of "biblical" consciousness.

This book has since its beginning encountered one generation after another. Confrontation and reconciliation with it have taken place in every generation. Sometimes it is met with obedience and offered dominion;

---

1. *Der Mensch von heute* is rendered as "People Today" rather than, with Olga Marx in her translation of the first part of this essay (in *Israel and the World* (New York: Schocken, 1963), "The Man of Today," because the German *Mensch* refers equally to men and women, and English "man" does not. We have not in this translation wanted to obscure sexist terminology in the original, but equally we have not wanted to add to it [eds.].

2. The Greek *biblia*, from which English "bible" and German *Bibel* both come, means "books" [eds.].

sometimes with offense and rebellion. But each generation engages it vitally, and faces it in the realm of reality. Even where people have said "no" to it, that "no" has only validated the book's claim upon them—they have borne witness to it even in refusing themselves to it.

It is otherwise with people today. By "people today" I mean "intellectuals," people to whom it seems important that there be intellectual goods and values; people who admit, or even themselves declare, that the reality of these goods and values is bound up with their realization through us; but people also who when probed in inmost truth, where people are ordinarily not probed at all, must then admit that this feeling that *Geist*[3] has obligations is itself for them only an intellectual matter. The intellect's freedom from real obligation is the signature of our time. We proclaim the rights of intellect, we formulate its laws; yet these rights and laws enter not into life but only into books and conversations. They hover in the air above our heads, and do not walk among us on the earth; everything, it seems, is *Geist* except the actual lives we lead. Here we meet with a false idealism, erecting above our life a blue firmament, in the unconstrainingly edifying contemplation of which one recovers from the aridity of earth; there a false realism, which understands *Geist* only as a function of life and dissolves its absolute unconditionality into mere psychological or sociological conditions. In either case a false relation between *Geist* and life is put in place of a real connection between them: in place of a marriage.

People today have, to be sure, noted the disintegrative effects of such a separation of inter-related things—noted, that is, a disintegration that must touch deeper and deeper layers, until the entirely disempowered *Geist* is reduced to the willing and complacent servant of any powers that be. These people have, moreover, had thoughts on how this decline is to be rectified; and they have appealed to religion as the only authority now capable of introducing a new covenant between *Geist* and world. But what is today called "religion" is not capable of that. "Religion" today is itself a thing of unattached *Geist*—one of its departments, a clearly privileged department of the superstructure of life, an especially impressive chamber among the upper rooms. It is not a life-encompassing whole, and cannot on the basis of its present status become one; it cannot lead us to unity, because it has itself fallen into disunity, has accommodated itself to this dichotomy of our existence. Religion would itself have to return to reality before it could have

---

3. German *Geist* means both "intellect" and "spirit." It has two adjectives attached to it, one of which means "intellectual" (as in the first sentence of the present paragraph) and the other of which means "spiritual" (or even sometimes "clerical"). Buber's use of these terms is sometimes crucial to his argument; accordingly, the translation sometimes retains the German terms, and sometimes footnotes passages where his manipulation of the complex of terms is especially intricate. In general, all words referring to "spirit," "intellect," and "mind" in this essay are translations of the complex of terms centered around *Geist* [eds.].

a real effect on people today. But religion has always been reality only when it has been fearless—when it has taken upon itself the whole concreteness of reality, has signed nothing away as belonging by right to some other agent, has embodied *Geist* and at the same time consecrated the quotidian.

The chief document of this reality, however, is Scripture, the so-called Old Testament. This is distinguished from the great books of the other religions of the world by two linked traits. One is that in it, event and word take place entirely within the people, within history, within the world. Nothing happens in the isolated space between God and the individual man; rather the word goes by way of the man to the people, which then must hear and realize it. Events are not raised above the history of the people; rather they are precisely the secret of the people's history made manifest. But the people is in consequence positioned against any national self-centeredness, against any cult of the group, against the "breath of universal history." Rather it must establish the community of God's own as a model for the numerous and diverse peoples of the earth; the historical continuity in "seed" and "land" is bound to the "blessing" (Gen. 12:7ff.), and the blessing is bound to the charge. Holiness enters into history without disenfranchising it.

The other trait of this book is that in it a law speaks that concerns the natural life of human beings. Eating meat and sacrificing animals are linked; marital purity is consecrated monthly in the sanctuary; people in their drives and passions are accepted as they are and included in holiness, lest their drives and passions become obsessions. The desire to possess land is not prohibited, and renunciation of it is not commanded; but the owner of the land is God, and man is merely "a sojourner and settler" with him. God the owner introduces the rhythm of property compensation, so that the growing inequity will not shatter the community existing among its fellows. Holiness enters into nature without raping it.

The living spirit seeks both to spiritualize and to animate; to have *Geist* and life find one another, to have *Geist* shape itself into life and life clarify itself by *Geist*. It seeks to have creation complete itself from itself. The "Old Testament" seeks to bear witness to this striving, and to the command to serve *Geist* in its bond with life. If we take the book as "religious writing," belonging to some department of *Geist* in isolation, then it fails; and we must deny ourselves to it.[4] If we take it as the impression of a life-encompassing reality, then we grasp it; and it grasps us. People today, however, are hardly capable of this. When they still "take an interest" in Scripture at all, it is precisely a "religious" interest—and for the most part the interest is not even that, but is rather "historical" or "cultural" or "aesthetic," or whatever.

---

4. "Fails" and "deny" render various uses of the same German word, *versagen* [eds.].

In any case the interest is that of the detached *Geist*, distributed into independent subjects. People do not in the manner of earlier generations stand before the biblical word in order to hear it or to take offense at it; they do not any longer confront their lives with the word. Rather they store the word in one of the numerous secular warehouses, and rest contented. They thus cripple the power that of all existing powers would most likely suffice to deliver them.[5]

Before, however, I describe more clearly the guiding power of Scripture for people today, and demonstrate that power by means of a few examples, I must deal with the fundamental question that the reflective reader is now posing. Suppose that this reader—suppose that we, in fact—managed to approach with our whole self the totality of this book that you are talking about; would there not, even then, be missing the one thing absolutely indispensable to such an encounter? Would we, that is, be able to *believe* the book? Would we be able to believe *it*? Can we do more than believe that such a belief as this book reports and proclaims once existed?

People today have little access to sure belief, and cannot be given such access. When they are in earnest, they know this and do not let themselves be deceived. But an openness to belief is not denied them. They too can, precisely when they are in earnest, open themselves up to this book and let themselves be struck by its rays wherever they may strike; they can, without anticipation and without reservation, yield themselves and let themselves come to the test; they can receive the text, receive it with all their strength, and await what may happen to them, wait to see whether in connection with this or that passage in the book a new openness will develop in them. For this, of course, they must take up Scripture as if they had never seen it, had never encountered it in school or afterwards in the light of "religious" or "scientific" certainties; as if they had not learned all their lives all sorts of sham concepts and sham propositions claiming to be based on it. They must place themselves anew before the renewed book, hold back nothing of themselves, let everything happen between themselves and it, whatever may happen. They do not know what speech, what image in the book will take hold of them and recast them, from what place the spirit will surge up and pass into them, so as to embody itself anew in their lives; but they are open. They believe nothing *a priori*; they disbelieve nothing *a priori*. They read aloud what is there, they hear the word they speak, and it comes to them; nothing has yet been judged, the river of time flows on, and the contemporaneity of these people becomes itself a receiving vessel.

---

5. This was said nine years ago. Today, Scripture is once again something that people take offense at; and that seems to me a first step toward taking it seriously.

If, however, we wish to understand rightly what is at issue here, we have to visualize clearly the abyss that lies between Scripture and people today.

The claim with which Scripture has approached and still approaches every generation is the claim to be acknowledged as a document of the true history of the world—of the history, that is, in which the world has an origin and a goal. Scripture demands of the human being to embed his or her own life in this true history, so that I may find my origin in the origin of the world and my goal in the world's goal. At the midpoint between origin and goal, however, Scripture puts not something that happened once and in the past; rather it sets there, as a moving, circling, indeterminate center, the moment in which I, the reader, the hearer, the human person, perceive through Scripture the voice that speaks from the origin toward the goal— this moment, my moment, mortal and eternal at once. Creation is the origin, redemption is the goal; but revelation is not a datable, determinate point poised between them. The center is not the revelation at Sinai but the continual possibility of receiving it. *That* is why a psalm or a prophecy is no less "Torah," teaching, than is the story of the exodus from Egypt. The history of the people—accepting and refusing together—points to the history of humanity; but the secret conversation heard in psalm and prophecy points to my own secret.

Scripture as a document in the history of a world hovering between creation and redemption, of a world that in its history encounters revelation— a revelation that encounters me *if I am there:*[6] with this notion in mind we can understand the resistance of people today as a resistance of their innermost being.

People today stand in two relations to history. In the relation *ad libitum*, they accept (and join with) history in the backwards and forwards movement of events, in the rise and fall of struggles for power; history is a muddle, an indiscriminate sequence of processes: the deeds of peoples, the death of peoples, seizings and losings, triumph and misery—a bustle in itself meaningless, to which a sham meaning, unfounded and unstable, can be attributed only by persons themselves. In the dogmatic relation, people determine laws from sequences of events and predict sequences to come, as if the great lines of things were written on a scroll that was just now being unrolled, as if history were not time, time constantly becoming, time constantly and vitally being determined, time into which my time and my decision stream in all force, but a rigid, already present, inescapable space. Both relations are misunderstandings of destiny. Destiny is neither accident nor

---

6. Buber may be alluding to the divine name, which he understands as meaning "I will be there"; see below, "The Eternal" [eds.].

fate; it is nothing that happens and nothing that is there before. In biblical perspective, destiny is the secret reciprocity of the lived moment, the coinciding of over here and over there, the resolution of all time in this particular time. Where there is knowledge of origin and goal, there is no chaos; we are sustained by a meaning that we cannot ourselves devise. We do not, however, receive this meaning to formulate it but to live it; and it is lived in the fearful and magnificent full decisiveness of the moment—of the historical moment, which in its actualities is everywhere a moment of biography, yours and mine no less than Alexander's or Caesar's, but not your moment of yourself but of your encounter. People today know of no beginning—history eddies toward their feet from the whole of cosmically unchronicled time; they know of no ending—history foams past them into cosmically unchronicled time. And what lies between has become so violent and trivial an interval! People no longer know of origins or goals because they no longer wish to know of the midpoint—the midpoint to which they must give themselves in order to perceive it. Only as seen from the presentness of revelation are creation and redemption true. People today resist Scripture because they cannot abide revelation. To abide revelation means to sustain the full decisiveness of the moment, to respond to the moment, to be responsible for it. People today resist Scripture because they are no longer responsive or responsible. They claim to venture much; but the one true venture, the venture of responsibility, they industriously avoid.

Insight into biblical reality begins with distinguishing among creation, revelation, and redemption.[7] Christianity moved away from this insight, and thus from the soil of the "Old Testament," when in its early theology it fused essential revelation and essential redemption in Christ; it was then only a rigorous consistency that led Marcion to devalue creation, now reduced to the status of a postulate, to the tinkering of another and subordinate God. But this was to surrender the essence of *time*, so intimately linked with the essence of *Geist* as being what keeps separate the ideas of having become, taking place, and coming into being—categories that in the biblical notions expand to the full blossoming of their concrete truth. So the faithful *distinction* among the three—not as hypostases or manifestations of God, but as stages, actions, and events in God's intercourse with the world, and thus as fundamental positions in God's movement toward the world—is the necessary gate to biblical reality, to the Bible as reality. But this *distinction* among the three ideas must not extend to a *severance* of them. In the biblical view, revelation is presented as gathered in the middle, cre-

---

7. A fresh presentation of these distinctions to our time is the great accomplishment of Rosenzweig's *Stern der Erlösung*.

ation as gathered in the "beginning," redemption as gathered at the "end"; but the living truth is their present being-together, i.e., that God "daily renews the work of creation" [from the daily morning synagogue service], but also daily anticipates the work of ending. No doubt creation and redemption are true only on the premise of the presentness of revelation; but I could not understand what creation was if it did not happen in me, I could not understand what redemption was if it did not happen in me.

It is from this fact that the recurring question must proceed, the question namely of how the abyss between Scripture and people today is to be bridged. In answering the question of whether people today are capable of belief, we indicated that although certainty of belief is denied them, openness to belief is not. But is the strangeness of the biblical categories not an obstacle to the process of opening oneself up? Has the reality of creation not yielded to the idea of evolution, the reality of revelation to the idea of the unconscious, the reality of redemption to some social or national purpose?

We have to see the massive reality of this biblical strangeness clearly; only then can we attempt to show that there is nonetheless a way in—*the* way in. Again we begin with the center.

What can it mean to us that God accompanied by thunder and trumpets descends in fire to the mountain covered in smoke like a smelting-furnace and there speaks to the people? Three things, it seems to me. First, we can take it as a metaphorical expression for a "spiritual" process. But if the biblical story is not the memory of an event but only metaphor and allegory, then it is no longer biblical, and deserves no better fate than to be handed over to, say, the cultural-historical or aesthetic viewpoint of the modern world. Second, we can say that this is the account of a "supernatural" process, which takes the comprehensible sequence of events—what we call the "natural" sequence—and rends it asunder by the incursion of something incomprehensible. Then, however, people today who may resolve to accept the Bible must, if they are not to lapse into dull familiarity with something they do not genuinely believe in, perform a sacrifice that irreparably severs their life in two; they must, that is, accept not life-encompassing biblical wholeness but detached religion. Or, third, we can say that this is the verbal trace of a natural event, i.e., an event having occurred in the common sensory world of humankind and having fitted into its patterns, which the assemblage that experienced it experienced as God's revelation to it and so preserved it in the inspired and in no way arbitrary formative memory of generations. This experience is no self-delusion of the assemblage, but its vision, its understanding, its observing reason; for natural events are the bearers of revelation, and revelation happens where the witness of the event who has endured the event experiences its revelatory content, and lets himself be told what the voice speaking in the event wished to say to him, to the witness, to his manner of being, his life, his sense of obligation. Only if this is the case can people today, reversing direction but not thereby denying any reality, find a way into biblical reality. And I at any rate believe that this is the case.

We have sometimes a small experience that because it is of the same sort as the great experiences can provide access to them. It happens that we unexpectedly notice a perception in us that was missing just a moment ago, and whose origin nothing can enable us to trace. The explanation of such phenomena on the basis of the celebrated unconscious, arising from the widely diffused superstition that the soul itself does everything, says at bottom nothing else than this: what you are just now experiencing as something coming to you from outside was always inside you, was where everything is and nothing is known. This is only a makeshift explanation; it is useful for psychological orientation, but collapses the moment I actually try to base myself on it. No—what has happened to me was precisely otherness, was being taken hold of by something other. Nietzsche puts it more honestly: "we take and do not ask who it is that gives." I, however, think that what matters above all is to take with precisely the knowledge that *someone is giving.* Those who take what is given to them and do not experience the giver's giving do not really receive, and the gift becomes a theft. If we do experience the giving, however, we know by experience that revelation exists. And we set off on the path on which our life and the world's life will make themselves known by signs—on the path, that is, that leads in. On that path we will have the great experiences that are analogous to these small ones.

On the premise that revelation is perceived, creation and redemption become perceptible. I begin to understand that when I ask about my origin or my end I am asking about something other than myself and something other than the world; but precisely in this manner I begin to understand the origin and goal of the world.

What can it mean to us that God created the world in six days? One thing it cannot mean: that God created the world in six ages, and that "creating" means at bottom here nothing but "becoming," as those would argue who would establish a way into the Bible by harmonizing it with the various views of the natural sciences. But neither can the mystical interpretation serve us, according to which the acts of creation are not acts but emanations. It lies in the nature of mysticism to combat the belief that God accepted for our sake the subordinate position of a personal agent; but if the personal agency of God is torn out of the Bible, then the Bible is trivial, and the empirically derived conceptions of a Heraclitus or a Plato are vastly preferable to the homuncular principles of emanation such an interpretation entails.

So what can the story mean? There is no question of its being the verbal trace of an event, since this event had no witnesses. Does it follow that for those who cannot believe the biblical creation story as the pure "word of God" the way to that story is barred? The saying of traditional Jewish exegesis that the Torah speaks human language[8] hides a deeper truth than one ordinarily assumes; it may be understood to mean that the unsayable *can* only be said as it is here, in human language. The biblical creation story is justified stammering. People do stammer when they arrange what they know of the universe into a temporal sequence of commands and "works" of a divine workshop; but only such stammering can do justice to the task of expressing the secret of how time arises from eternity and world comes from him who is not himself world. Any attempt made by "scientific" cosmology to show intelligibly how everything came into being must be in comparison a hopeless failure.

Suppose, then, that the way into the reality of revelation is opened to people today through the fact that our life is a condition of being-spoken-to. Where then is the opening to the way into the reality of creation? This cannot be found in so immediate a relation to one's own life as can the way to revelation—which can be found in so immediate a relation because, as we saw, any lived moment can itself be the midpoint of that relation. But it can be found, because all human beings know themselves to be both individual and unique. Suppose that it were possible for someone to take a psychosomatic inventory of his or her person in such a way as to dissolve it into a sum of qualities; suppose it were also possible to trace developmentally each of these qualities and the process of their confluence back to their most primitive forms; suppose finally that such a seamless genetic analysis of a given individual, of his derivation and etiology, were in fact to be carried out. At the end of it, the *person*, this unique, incomparable, singular being—the countenance such as was never found, the voice such as was never heard, the bearing such as was never seen—this ensouled body would still be there, the intact remainder, altogether underived and underivable, there and nowhere else but there. At the end of his useless pains, drawing himself up once again to confront the question "where does this come from?" he would find himself in the last analysis finally a created being. With every birth the first person enters the world, because every person is unique. In our own lives, in the manner of children, each of us groping toward our own origin, we learn that origin is—that creation is.

And now for the third matter, the last and the most difficult: what can it mean to us that at "the end of days" there will be accomplished a deliverance and redemption of the world so complete that by it heaven and earth

---

8. Berakhot 31b [eds.].

will, it is said, be created anew? These tidings cannot be made otherworldly; we are talking about this world, its purification into a "kingdom," the completion of creation, and not the nullification of this world for the sake of another. Nor can they be made finite; the promise speaks not of a more just order but of "justice," not of a more peaceable humanity but of "peace." Here too what we hear is warranted stammering. The messenger seized by the divine word can only speak the words of human beings, as one who can only grasp what they are to be redeemed from, and not what they are to be redeemed for. But people today? Will this not inevitably be the strangest of all the things they hear, precisely because it is nearest to their own unfathomably deep longing? They think about change, but have no experience of transformation; they hope that things will go better, if not tomorrow then the day after, but cannot make anything out of the idea that the truth will come; they are familiar with ideas of development and persistence, but understand neither that a power desires to redeem them and the world from contradiction nor that they themselves are required, for the sake and to the end of that desire, to "turn about" with their whole being. How do we mediate between such people and the biblical message? Where is the bridge here?

This is the most difficult matter of all. Lived moments led directly to knowledge of revelation; reflection on birth led indirectly to knowledge of creation. But the essence of redemption is given to us to savor in our personal lives only at their end. Yet here too there is a way in—a dark and still path, the approach to which I cannot show you except by asking you to recall your darkest and stillest hours. I mean by this the hours at the lowest depth, when we lie above the trembling trapdoor that may open at any moment—and it is strange that it has not opened already, opened into destruction, into madness, into the fullness of "suicide." And yet now something touches us, something like a hand, which reaches out to us, which asks to be grasped—ah, it takes such terrible courage to grasp it and to let ourselves be drawn by it up out of the darkness! Redemption is happening. Let us understand rightly what was given us to understand there: that our redeemer lives, who wants to redeem us—but by our *acceptance* of his redemption, in the turning about of our being.

A way in, I said. All this is not yet standing within biblical reality. But it is the way into it, and the beginning.

In what does the guiding power of Scripture for people today consist?

Their real difficulty—it is important here to look beneath the surface, and to understand their ostensible difficulties on the basis of their secret ones—lies in the separation that they make (and indeed which they almost make an article of faith) between *Geist* and life. Now our modern philosophy of life degrades life-suffusing *Geist* by confusing it with isolated intellect; it inverts the relation between procreating *Geist* and conceiving life and thus confuses the fundamental circumstances of our being; it exalts life in the delusion of its sovereignty and thereby brings it near to madness. That philosophy, therefore, has conceptually sharpened this difficulty, has sealed off any possibility of reflection, and has considerably impeded any attempt at deliverance. The "Old Testament" teaches the sacred marriage of *Geist* and life; it accordingly rejects both all enslavement of life to *Geist* and all humbling of *Geist* before life. It has, then, even here and now the power to help people today in their deepest need.

What sort of help this is I will, in accord with the concreteness of the Bible, present in three concrete examples.[9] I draw all three from the connections between the history of creation and the history of revelation; they will then also serve as a suggestion of how the Bible is to be read: in living presence. Sequences of sounds, of words, of groups of words recur in particular relation to various parts of a passage, to various passages, to various books; they recur so as to constitute a discernible continuity, significantly developing one another, clarifying one another, supplementing one another. We are to hear from each recurrence the lesson it teaches. Biblical teaching often does not so much *present* its highest truths as it lets them be *opened up*—opened up not by breaking a code or deciphering an allegory, but by these arcs of significant repetition, linking passage to passage in a manner perceptible to every openmindedly attentive reader.

I have in mind the following three connections: that between the *ruah*[10] of creation and the *ruah* of revelation, that between the creation of the world and the making of the Tent of revelation, and that between God's Sabbath of rest after the creation and the Sabbath commandments of revelation.

The second verse of the Bible says of the *ruah* of God—or the God-*ruah*—that it "hovered," to use Luther's term, above the face of the waters that were not yet divided into those of heaven and those of earth. What sort of "hovering" this was,[11] however, we learn only later (if at all) from the only

---

9. In the original lecture series, I discussed also the account of the divine name, with reference to the *ehyeh* of Exod. 3:12, 14, 4:12, 15. Now, however, I can refer readers to the discussions of this matter in Rosenzweig's "The Eternal" and his letter to Martin Goldner, both in this volume, as well as to the excerpt from my *Königtum Gottes* ["Kingship of God"] (Schocken: Berlin, 1932) also reprinted in this volume (Apprendix I).

10. Usually "wind" or "breath" on the one hand, "spirit" on the other. Buber's insistence on the *union* of these notions in the Hebrew word leads him to retain it in his German text, and the translation accordingly retains it in the English text as well [eds.].

11. In our translation, drawing on the Syriac meaning of the word and on both Jewish and early Christian commentators, we rendered the verb by "brooded." The new version in the Lodge Edition (not yet available) gives the more precise but still not adequate "spread" (understood as an intransitive verb).

passage of the Bible where this rare verb recurs in the same form: Deut. 32:11. God, who takes Israel from among the peoples and bears it into the promised land, is in that passage compared with the eagle, who with softly beating wings hovers over its nest to quicken it, i.e., to agitate its fledgling young to flight, but who then spreads its wings wide, takes up one of its young, and "bears it on its pinions" (cf. Exod. 19:4). We may presume that the waters correspond to the nest and that the creatures (of many of whom it is said that they are to "swarm" forth from the water) whom God calls into being correspond to the eagle's young. But how are we to understand *ruaḥ*? Why *ruaḥ* and not God himself should be the subject becomes clear when we see that the spreading of wings is spoken of here not, as in the song of Moses, metaphorically, but quite literally. What, however, does *ruaḥ mean*? Opinion has been divided from the beginning between "wind"—whether a wind from God or a wind called "Godwind" on the basis of its force—and "spirit"—whether *the* spirit of God or *a* spirit of God. Luther, keeping the question always in motion, has first "wind" and then "spirit." Both interpretations rest on the notion that we have to choose between them. But we do not. The dynamic meaning of *ruaḥ*, which alone enables us to comprehend the passage—a passage, by the way, which even radical source critics have judged "very old" (Gunkel) and "very ancient" (Procksch)—is the meaning of a "breathing," a "blowing," a "surging," a "rushing."[12] It is as such that early biblical man perceives not only wind but spirit also—or rather, what is originally one later divides itself into a natural and a spiritual meaning. But here, in its first appearance, it manifests not the distinction between the two but their association. *Ruaḥ elohim*, the breathing, blowing, surging phenomenon, is neither natural nor spiritual but both in one; it is the creative breathing that brings both nature and spirit into being. The Bible here thinks not lexically but elementally, and would have its readers think in its manner, would have the movement from God that precedes all differentiation undifferentiatedly touch the hearing heart. Here at the beginning of the Bible, *ruaḥ elohim* stands as a great, unformulated, latent theological principle, expressed only by implication: that God is to be assigned neither to the realm of nature nor to the realm of spirit, that God is not nature and is not spirit either, but that both have their origin in him.[13] But even afterwards, where the two meanings of the word appear only in separation, the Bible again and again—in the "naive realism" into which all ideas must be plunged in order to be reborn—seeks to evoke the original dynamic unity,

---

12. Hermann Gunkel (1862-1932), Christian theologian and biblical scholar; Otto Procksch (1874-1947), biblical scholar [eds.].

13. Spinoza, for whom thought and extension are the only two of God's infinitely numerous attributes accessible to us, in this respect sustains the Old Testament vision—in contrast to the Pauline and Johannine pneumatization of God, which in effect amounts to spiritualizing him.

the single happening from God that ferments the heavens into storm and is blown into the essence of earth.

The Bible does this again and again; but its intention is most compellingly presented in the passage of revelation history in which a spiritual manifestation and a natural manifestation adjacent to it are strangely welded together into a single story, namely in Numbers 11. God "takes of" the *ruaḥ* that descends from him to Moses, at Moses' plea—he cannot, he says, alone stand up to his rebellious people—and distributes it to the "elders." And when complaints are brought to Moses regarding individuals who, having been possessed by *ruaḥ* outside the assemblage of elders, are now behaving precisely like those possessed by it inside the assemblage, Moses—who has just wished for his own death on account of his intolerable people—rejects the complaint as follows: "who would give/ that all HIS people were prophets,/ that HE would give his *ruaḥ* over them!"[14] And almost immediately after, without transition—without transition because only thus does what the Bible is saying here become perceptible—there begins the story of the punitive granting of the wishes of precisely the same people: "a *ruaḥ* moved from HIM/ that drove quails from the sea. . . ." Shall we then translate "God's *ruaḥ*" as "God's spirit" and "a *ruaḥ*" as "a wind"? No; that simply will not do. The translation must let us feel how a spiritual divine act and a natural divine act are related to each other: the necessary renderings are rather, "his rushing-of-spirit," "a rushing-of-wind."

But why is this necessary? Because since the time of Luther, who had to choose between *Geist* and *Wind, Geist* has lost its original concreteness—a concreteness it had in company with *ruaḥ*, with *pneuma*, with *spiritus* itself—lost its original sensory character—"a surging and a blowing simultaneously"[15]—the sense that links it with *Gischt* ["spindrift"], the sense that survives today only vestigially, as when Lübeck seamen speak of a certain "dull soughing wind" as a *Geist.* Luther was still within this concreteness, but he felt it dissolving. In Psalm 33, he translates, "by the word of the Lord were the heavens made, and all the host of them by the spirit [*Geist*] of his mouth," and retains this rendering in later editions; but in the 11th chapter of Isaiah, where he had written "with the spirit [*Geist*] of his lips shall he slay the wicked," he later changes this—clearly because a person is being talked about here, and his earlier deconcretization of the word would in consequence be made unmitigatedly clear—into "with the breath of his lips." This splitting of a fundamental word not merely a process in the history of language but also a process in the history of *Geist* and life, namely the incip-

---

14. The recurrence of the verb "to give" is characteristic of biblical emphatic style.
15. Rudolf Hildebrand, in his illuminating article "Geist" in Grimm's *Dictionary.*

ient separation between *Geist* and life. Goethe struggles back toward the biblical unity of *ruaḥ* when he says of God's *Geist* that it lies upon the open field as if it "blew directly upon men";[16] Hölderlin, more powerfully but still no less in vain, and heedful of biblical antiquity still more than of classical, proclaims the kinship of both interpretations of *ruaḥ*, proclaims the secret of the "blowing wind of the spirit" in the call, "O sister of *Geist* who reigns and lives in us all aflame, O holy air!"[17]

We should note that God's *ruaḥ* is named only at the beginning of the creation story—it is the undivided intentional totality of the work of creation that is assigned to *ruaḥ*, not the individual actions in the world's becoming or even the entirety of them. Not even where the divine breath is blown into Adam is *ruaḥ* named, although (as is clear from 6:3) it is *ruaḥ* itself that expands in him into the breath of life—thus prefiguring in the making of the human being all the revelatory inspiriting that will happen to human beings later. Both accounts of creation—the account of the making of the world (1:1-2:4a) and the account of the making of human beings (2:4b-25), the primordial legend of nature and the primordial legend of history, the one narrative that stations the human being as a latecomer at the edge of the cosmos and the other narrative that wants to speak only of this human being and his business and so gathers whatever else it can name in creation around him—both accounts, not cobbled together like essentially dissimilar literary documents, but supplementing each other like the two sides of being that we can know, the outer side and the inner, begin with an action of *ruaḥ*. In the first, *ruaḥ* maternally spreads her[18] wings to shelter the totality of the things that are to be; in the second, unnamed and enigmatic, she is infused into the being destined for existence in history, to be present for his decision and to share his fate. Here, then, the history of creation is joined to the history of revelation; for where personal revelation is accomplished, it will be *ruaḥ* that enters into the person (Judg. 14:6, 19 and 15:14; 1 Sam. 10:6 and 10, 11:6, and 16:13) and "clothes" itself (Judg. 6:34) with him, but precisely thereby makes him into "another man" (1 Sam. 10:6).

This proclamation of unity remains with us still.

I have lingered over this first example in order to show what guiding power can lie in a single biblical word if we will only pursue it earnestly and commit ourselves to it.

---

16. From Johann Peter Eckermann, *Gespräche mit Goethe* (Conversations with Goethe), (Munich: C. H. Beck, 1984), p. 586, March 11, 1828 [eds.].

17. We have consulted the Hölderlin concordance, but have been unable to find the source of this phrase [eds.].

18. Buber's female personification of *ruaḥ* is determined by the feminine gender of the Hebrew word [eds.].

The two other examples can in consequence be grasped more easily and more quickly.

Both examples are taken from the first of the two creation narratives. If, protected by our intention, we manage to overcome our modest reluctance to dissect that narrative, we can, leaving the created world itself for the moment to the side, depict the narrative in terms of the following fundamental motifs, each marked by recurring words. First there are the "days," culminating in the thrice named "seventh day." Then comes the activity of God, comprehended in the word "creating" and, so as not to be misperceived as a subordinate, demiurgic action, again and again depicted as "saying" or introduced by "saying." But for the sake of a connection with human beings and for the importance of the Sabbath, God's activity in the account is also called seven times a "making"; the seventh time this is heightened in the concluding phrase, "which in making God had created," though previously, three times running, the same activity is comprehended in the word "work," a more human word and more appropriate to ordinary human labor. There is also the sevenfold "seeing," with which God assesses his work and recognizes it as "good," and in addition the "here" with which the completed world presents itself to its creator as "exceedingly good"—"and here: it was exceedingly good!"—and thereby restates the "here" with which this same speech that God makes to his last creations begins.[19] There is also the threefold "blessing," and finally the "finishing," which occurs twice, first passive, from the standpoint of the created world—"thus were finished..."—then active, from the viewpoint of the creator, for whom the finishing of what is already finished is itself an act—"and God finished...."

There is however in the revelation story a narrative in which these seven fundamental motifs of the history of creation are significantly repeated: the story of the building of the Tent, the Tent of "Presence," i.e., of God's becoming-present, the Tent in which God presents himself to the people (Exod. 29:43).

"For six days" (Exod. 24:16, cf. 23:12, 31:17, and 35:2),[20] the cloud covers the mountain on which the revelation-form of God, the *kabod*, "takes up its dwelling"—i.e., does not dwell, but on occasion makes its dwelling there— while Moses stands before the cloud. The work is done unwitnessed in the obscurity of the cloud, as it was done unwitnessed above the darkness in the creation story; and Moses is called into the cloud to see the work "on the seventh day" (24:16). The work in question is the "building-pattern" of the Tent and of its implements: "now see and make, according to their building-pattern which

---

19. In the previous editions of our translation this important repetition has not been reproduced.

20. Note that of the last three passages cited the first two frame God's speech on the building of the Tent, the third introduces the account of how the Tent was built.

you are granted to see upon the mountain" (25:40). Marked in the Hebrew by the rhyme characteristic of mnemonic verses, this speech of God's indicates the reason for which Moses is permitted to see the divinely created model in such a way that the sight of it will permeate him and remain fixed within him—such is the meaning of the point made again and again in perpetually varied verbal form (25:9, 40, 26:30, 27:8). For God's creating here differs from his creating of the world; only the building-*pattern* comes into being during the six days, and the Tent itself is to be made later, by the people working under Moses' direction. And the people do indeed *make* it; the word "making" occurs nearly a hundred times in the divine instructions, and more than a hundred times in the account of the execution of the instructions, linked always in the first part of that section with the word "work." And when it is finished, there follow the words "seeing" and "here." What is reported here is not that God sees what has been made but that Moses does, Moses the mediator, who has transmitted his sight of the building-pattern to the people that will build it; and the "here" is linked in this passage not, as in the creation story, to an "it was exceedingly good!"—such praise is not for human work, even when that work is based on a divine model—but only to the indication that what was commanded has taken place: "Now Moshe saw all the work, and here:/ as HE had commanded,/ so had they made" (38:43). The "blessing" must come next: "then Moshe blessed them." But we must have also the double "finished"; here the distinction is that the passive use of the verb concludes the work done by the people, the active the immediately subsequent construction done by Moses: "thus was finished all the service for the Dwelling, the Tent of Presence" (39:32), then "so Moshe finished the work" (40:33).

God makes a world and puts people in it; but the Tent in which he will make his dwelling among them "amidst their pollution" he only shows them, and has them make it themselves. Revelation is history, is history's revealed secret; and though the original stimulus is a solitary word, answered at first only by the dumb genesis of things, history at least is a dialogue. People learn to build; but their hands are not guided. The creation of the world is a primordial revelation, and the secret of creation extends into the cloud of revelation; but there people are called to become "God's fellows in the work of creation"—a Talmudic phrase but a biblical concept. (It should not remain unnoticed that although the builders as bearers of *Geist* are given special trust by God, what we see described as the agent of the building is not individual builders but the community.)

On the "seventh day," when heaven and earth are finished, God rests "from all his work that he had made," and blesses and hallows the day of "ceasing," the day of the Sabbath. Of the seven explicit commandments concerning the Sabbath (Exodus 20, 23, 31, 34, 35; Leviticus 23; Deuteronomy 5), two are especially prominent, and are linked in a peculiar way, one especially characteristic of biblical style: by a very rare verb, occurring outside these two passages only once, a verb meaning something like "to get one's breath back after exertion." Its subject is first "the son of your handmaid and the sojourner": "For six days you are to make your labor,/ but on the seventh day, you are to cease,/ in order that your ox and your ass may rest/ and the son of your handmaid and the sojourner pause-for-breath." Later, however, in the Sabbath commandment that follows God's description of the Tent and precedes the giving of the first tablets (Exod. 31:14ff.), the same pausing for breath that earlier was declared a right of servants or dependents when exhausted is now predicated of God's Sabbath at the time of creation: "the Children of Israel are to keep the Sabbath,/ to make the Sabbath-observance throughout their generations/ as a covenant for the ages;/ between me and the Children of Israel/ a sign is it, for the ages,/ for in six days/ HE made the heavens and the earth,/ but on the seventh day/ he ceased and paused-for-breath" (31:16-17). Such a repetition of so rare a word in two corresponding places is surely not coincidental; rather it establishes a connection between them, so that in reading one we have to recall the other. The knot thus tied between a "social" and a "religious" grounding of the commandment is intended precisely to evoke the divine rest when we are confronted by the claims of the dependent, and to quicken our image of the work-weary slave when we think of God's Sabbath; for *all* of us are to be able to imitate God—to "go in his ways." We have not two diverse justifications but one: God and the "oppressed and needy" belong together. God does not so much love the intermediate degrees of power; rather he dwells in "exaltation and holiness" *and* "also with the crushed and lowly in spirit" (Isa. 57:15). This frank anthropomorphism may offend some—and indeed some translators have softened the first passage and thereby destroyed its connection with the second—but such offendedness is in fact fruitful for the reality of our belief. Indeed God's Sabbath is tied even to the Sabbath of animals. The phrase about pausing for breath links the commandment of chapter 23 to that of 31; but the former is also linked, by the phrase about the resting of the ox and the ass, to the Sabbath commandment of the Decalogue, in which it is said of God, and said with the same verb—a verb that does not occur in the creation story—that on the seventh day he "rested." Without venturing to extrapolate the biblical intention still further, still we are reminded that twice in the biblical story God descends in the form of a "messenger" to an an oppressed creature and speaks to it, or pleads on its behalf with its oppressor, and also that the mistreated creature is on one occasion (Gen. 16:9ff.) an Egyptian maid and on the other (Num. 22:32) a she-ass.

The biblical world of belief is not a higher region in which we can recover from our bad conduct of ordinary life. Biblical belief asks us to do justice to heaven on earth, and nowhere else. We may not turn to God if we have not turned toward the responsibilities of our own daily lives. Those who appease the admonishing heart with the plea that the life around us is only "fate" fall away from God.

The example of *ruah* indicates the power of the Bible for people today in showing that the dichotomy between *Geist* and natural life is a lie and a profanation from the beginning; the example of the Tent, in showing that people must themselves build the dwelling of the holy if the dwelling is to be built at all; the example of the Sabbath, in showing that people's relation to their fellows made dependent on them by destiny is the immovable place of their being tested and of their finding salvation.

It is not a matter of a "return to the Bible." It is a matter of the renewed reception of a genuinely biblical, unified life by our whole time-enmeshed being, with the whole weight of our contemporary many-sidedness lying on our souls, and the incomprehensible material of this historical hour taken into account in full. It is a matter of bearing up responsibly and dialogically against the pressure of our own present situations, in an openness to belief in accord with the biblical vision.

Do we mean a book? We mean the voice. Do we mean that people should learn to read it? We mean that people should learn to hear it. There is no other going back but the turning around that turns us about our own axis until we reach, not an earlier stretch of our path, but the path on which we can hear the voice! We want to go straight through to the spokenness, to the being-spoken, of the word.

THE UNITY OF THE BIBLE: A POSITION PAPER VIS-À-VIS ORTHODOXY AND LIBERALISM[1]

Franz Rosenzweig

Frankfurt, April 21, 1927

My Dear Mr. Rosenheim,

. . . Our difference from orthodoxy lies in the fact that we cannot, on the basis of our belief in the sacred and thus the special status of the Torah, and in its revelatory character, draw any conclusions regarding either the process of its literary genesis or the philological value of the text as it has come down to us. If Wellhausen and all his theories were right, if the Samaritans really had a better text than the Masoretic one, our belief would not be affected at all.[2] This is a sharp opposition between you and us, an opposition that as I see it can be bridged by reciprocal respect, but not by reciprocal understanding—I at any rate simply do not understand the belief underlying Hirsch's commentary or Breuer's essays.[3]

How then does it happen that our translation is consciously more closely related to Hirsch's than to any of its other predecessors? I have recently been thinking this over at length. One reason, but only a superficial one, is that our principled willingness to emend the text on philological grounds is neutralized by an equally principled philological anxiety, and by an ever-

---

1. Published in *Der Morgen*, October 1928.
2. Julius Wellhausen (1844-1918), leading source critic of the Hebrew Bible [eds.].
3. Samson Raphael Hirsch (1808-1888), leader of the modern renewal of orthodox Judaism, author of a noted commentary on the Torah, and an important but not invariably determining influence on Buber and Rosenzweig's biblical thought; "Breuer" without further identification can only probably be identified as Hirsch's grandson Raphael Breuer (1881-1932), author of an introduction to Hirsch's Torah commentary and later of a open letter to Buber complaining of Buber's failure to acknowledge Hirsch's influence on him [eds.].

alert distrust of the necessarily hypothetical element of all *Wissenschaft*. The fundamental reason, however, lies deeper. We too translate the Torah as one book. For us too it is the work of a single mind. We do not know who this mind was; we cannot believe that it was Moses. We name that mind among ourselves by the abbreviation with which the Higher Criticism of the Bible indicates its presumed final redactor of the text: R. We, however, take this R to stand not for redactor but for *rabbenu*.[4] For whoever he was, and whatever text lay before him, he is our teacher, and his theology is our teaching.

An example: let us suppose that Higher Criticism is right, and that Genesis 1 and Genesis 2 are in fact by different writers—though I myself would not like to decide finally in favor of this notion after a man like Benno Jacob has said that he does not believe it. Even in that case, however, it would remain true that what we need to know from the account of creation is not to be learned from either chapter alone but only from the juxtaposition and reconciliation of the two. Indeed, it is to be learned only from the reconciliation of the apparent *contradictions* from which the critical distinction begins: the "cosmological" creation of the first chapter, which leads up to man, and the "anthropological" creation of the second chapter, which begins from man. Only this *sof mas'aseh ba-mahashabah tehillah*[5] is the necessary teaching. Another example: Mount Sinai in smoke and the chapter of the thirteen *middot*[6] are not enough to teach us what revelation is; they must be interwoven with the *mishpatim*[7] and with the Tent of the Presence. And so everywhere.

The other aspect of the deeper reason is our relationship to tradition. Here too, despite a fundamentally different basis of belief, we arrive at a similar result. For Hirsch the oral Torah is a stream parallel to the written, rising from the same spring. For us it is the completion of the unity of the book as written through the unity of the book as read. Both unities are equally miraculous. The historicist vision discovers both in the book as written and in the book as read a multiplicity: of centuries, of writers, of readers. The vision that seeks to regard the book, not from outside, but in inward relatedness and belonging, will find the unity of the book as written and the unity of the book as read equally evident. Such a vision will see in the one the unity of teaching, in the other the unity of learning—the unity, that is, of its own learning with the learning of centuries. Tradition, then,

---

4. Hebrew "our master" or "our teacher," commonly used to refer to Moses [eds.].

5. From [the Friday night hymn] *Lekha Dodi*: the end in deed is the beginning in thought.

6. God's epithets of mercy, Exod. 34:6ff.—which passage together with 33:12-23 has, from antiquity down to the work of Hermann Cohen, offered Jewish religious philosophy its deepest insights concerning the revealed and hidden aspects of God.

7. The so-called "legal texts," Exodus 21ff.

both halakhic and aggadic, becomes itself an element of our translation. Not, as for Hirsch, a *determinant* of the *Peshat*;[8] rather a complement and supplement to it, as befits our different religious position. A halakhic example: we could not bring ourselves to believe that the traditional interpretation of Deut. 23:20 accurately rendered its literal sense;[9] but neither could we bear to eliminate the law based on it, which after all gives a direct glimpse of the inner heart of Judaism. Accordingly we formulated a translation that like the Hebrew permits both interpretations of the passage. An aggadic example: in dealing with Exod. 17:16 we were strongly tempted by the emendation modern critics have generally accepted (*nes*, "banner" for *kes*, "throne"); our final choice of the traditional text was chiefly determined by our desire to leave the great Messianic midrash on the passage with its foundation intact.[10] Here too the material is endless, and the shop talk could go on forever.

The unity of the written Torah and the unity of the oral Torah—or, as we might say, of the read Torah—together create the translator's task: to struggle for verbal exactness in the rendering of biblical terminology. In other translations this struggle is hardly attempted; and it is this struggle that defines what we consider our affinity to the Hirsch translation. By "terminology," to be sure, we understand something both wider and deeper than what is usually called by that name. It is wider in that we concern ourselves not only with concepts like *rahamim*[11] but also with apparently "untheological" words. Thus we consider it of fundamental importance to make evident in translation the threads that lead back and forth between the narrative and the legal parts of the Torah. An example: it is critical to render *reiqam*[12] (Gen. 31:24, Exod. 3:21, Deut. 15:13) with a single consistent expression;

---

8. I.e., the "plain meaning" of the text.

9. "You shall not deal in interest with your brother"; this is traditionally understood as referring not to *receiving* interest but to *paying* it, and not as a non-compulsory exhortation but as a binding legal commitment.

10. The passage reads, "He said,/ It means,/ Hand upon the throne of Yah!/ HE will be at war with Amalek throughout the ages!" [eds.].

The abbreviated word for throne (*kes* for *kisse'* and the abbreviated name of God (*Yah* for *YHWH*) occurring in the same verse are understood by the midrash as the signs of our time, in which the battle against Amalek endures "throughout the ages"; but when once Amalek is bound in captivity, then, the midrash declares, "the throne is perfect, the Name is perfect" [Tanḥuma Buber, *Ki Tetze'*, par. 18].

11. Compassion.

12. I.e., "empty"; here specifically "empty-of-compensation," or, more idiomatically, "interest-free." The traditional explanation of the demanding (not the lending) of the golden utensils as the Israelites leave Egypt is that it represents the payment earned by the centuries of service. B. Jacob, *Monatsschrift für Geschichte und Wissenschaft des Judentums* 68:281ff., has raised this explanation from the level of rationalization to that of scholarly exegesis; the freed servants demand as a gift what according to Jewish law the master was obliged to give his freed servant as the material basis of his freedman's life.

only then can the notorious passage in Exodus be rightly understood. Our notion of terminology is deeper than the usual one in that it must refer not only to words but also the roots of words. In, say, Lev. 19:4, the translation of *'elilim* must reveal the relation both to *'al* and to *'el*.[13] Here too I could no doubt find an example in every verse. But those who know Hebrew will find this unnecessary; they will note on their own the reasons for which we have translated in one way and not in another.

For those who know no Hebrew, ours remains a "creative" translation. This mistaken judgment has accompanied the translation since its first publication, and I have gradually gotten used to it. I am delighted when it is meant in disparagement, not—as is more usual—in praise. It is in any case a comical error. The goal is not beauty but truth; what should be judged is not a "work of art" but a translation, its fidelities and infidelities. And what is to be accepted or discarded, in detail or in the whole, is the belief that stands behind the fidelity, behind its manner and extent. The translation may not compel that sort of judgment; the thing translated surely does.

Sincerely Yours,
Franz Rosenzweig

Postscript

Knowing how printed material is read, I would add a word to the printed version of this letter—a word that, for the reader who wishes to learn from what is read what the writer means, is wholly unnecessary. But such a reader exists only in the presence of a manuscript; printer's ink has the magical power to transform such a reader, indeed all readers, so that they know even from the title—even, indeed, from the name of the writer—precisely what they will read, and will read nothing but what they already know. So this note is necessary after all.

What is said in the letter does *not* imply a distinction between *Wissenschaft* and "religion." This distinction was the penultimate cry of Protestant theology. But now, among our current "irrationalists," with the academic quarter century of delay now obligatory in Judaism, it seems to be on the point of becoming the *dernier cri*. It derives from Kant—so much the worse for Kant! It is in accord with Barth and Gogarten—so much the worse for Barth and Gogarten![14]

---

13. *'Al*, "not," *'el*, "God," *'elilim*, "godnothings."

14. Karl Barth (1886-1968) and Friedrich Gogarten (1887-1931), Christian theologians [eds.].

If *Wissenschaft* and religion seek to know nothing of each other, but do know of each other, then neither is of much use. There is only one Truth. No honest man can pray to a God whom as a scientific scholar he denies. No man who prays can deny God. I do not mean that the scientific scholar perceives God in his test-tube or his notebook. But the contents of test-tube and notebook cannot exist without God. God is not the object of *Wissenschaft*; the world is that. But God made the world that is the object of *Wissenschaft*. He is, then—to put it not in good German, and so incomprehensibly, but in the usual and thus the apparently accessible technical Latinate vocabulary—he is transcendent to *Wissenschaft* but also transcendental to it; *Wissenschaft* does not contain him, but would not exist without him; he is not in it, but it is beneath him.

This has consequences at every level. Helmholtz' remark, that should an optical scientist develop an optical apparatus resembling the eye it would be rejected, could not be the remark of a believing scientist. Such a scientist would have nothing to object to Helmholtz' judgment that the eye was an inadequate optical apparatus; but he would draw from that fact the conclusion that the eye is something different from an—optical apparatus. Or, on the other hand: when Ranke discusses the conflict in Queen Mary between the feelings of a daughter and the feelings of a wife, he says, "I believe in the inward truthfulness of human beings regarding their great inward decisions." Ranke, the founder of the modern critical method, *believes*. And how would an unbelieving historian behave? How else but—unbelievingly?

It is not belief that is opposed to knowledge, but believing knowledge to unbelieving knowledge. Or rather, since it is the legitimation of believing knowledge that it includes unbelieving knowledge, while unbelieving knowledge has no access to believing knowledge: knowledge both believing and unbelieving as opposed to knowledge that is only and restrictedly unbelieving. Or, in the case of the letter printed above: an attention both to the new inquiries (concerning "R") and to the old (concerning "J," "E," and "P") as opposed to an attention restricted to the latter. The word "believing" does not here mean a dogmatic self-commitment but a total obligation embracing the entire person. In this sense, the heretic too can be a believer, and the orthodox an unbeliever. Graetz' national relation to Jewish history is that of a believer; Breuer's juridical perspective on Jewish history ("perspective," because I believe that Breuer's real relation is more that of a believer than is his perspective) that of an unbeliever.

THE LANGUAGE OF *BOTSCHAFT*

Martin Buber
(After a draft from 1926)

The Hebrew Bible is profoundly stamped and ordered by the language of *Botschaft*.[1]

"Prophecy" is only the clearest, the most naked manifestation of *Botschaft*; prophecy proclaims publicly whatever is to be proclaimed. But there is hardly any portion, hardly any style of the Bible that is not directly or indirectly bound to and animated by *Botschaft*. We read the early genealogies, and the apparently random lists of names are revealed in their selection and order as *Botschaft*. We read stories like the story of Gideon's son Abimelech, which seem to belong altogether to secular history until we see how the story presents an image of one of the great concerns of *Botschaft*, namely of what is called "primitive theocracy."[2] We read legal and ritual prescriptions of the driest, the most concrete casuistic precision; and suddenly they breathe out a hidden pathos. We read psalms that seem to be nothing but the cry for help lifted upwards by a man in torment; yet we need only listen carefully to see that the speaker is not just any man but a man standing in the presence of revelation, and witnessing revelation even in his cries and shouts. We read what is ordinarily considered the literature of skeptical wisdom, and in the middle of it great declarations of *Botschaft* blaze out at us.[3] However it fared with certain pieces of the Bible before

---

1. The German term is retained for lack of an adequate equivalent. "Message" most nearly conveys the pertinent sense of *Botschaft*, but "the language of message" doesn't work as an English phrase. "The language of bearing tidings" does, but "bearing tidings" is cumbersome, and feels antiquated as the German term does not. What Buber means by "the language of *Botschaft*" is language when it reveals divine instruction [eds.].

2. See further my *Königtum Gottes*, pp. 26ff. [English edition: *Kingship of God*, 3d ed., Richard Scheimann, tr. (New York: Harper & Row, 1967), pp. 59-65]. A passage from chapter 5 is reprinted in Appendix I [eds.].

3. The deliberately mixed metaphor is Buber's own [eds.].

they entered the sacred text, the Bible as we have it is *Botschaft* in every limb of its body.

If this is the case, then *Botschaft* as it has developed its own particular language in the discourse of the Proclaimers[4] must also have modified biblical language even in many of the passages where it is expressed only indirectly. It would be a fundamental misunderstanding of the nature of the Bible to assume that it tacks on *Botschaft* here and there as morals are tacked on to bad parables. There is no "content" to be smelted from the biblical ore; each biblical content exists in its unitary and indissoluble *Gestalt*, a *Gestalt* at least as indissoluble as that of a true poem; there is no return to an original What that has conceived this How but might have borne another How equally well. Everything in Scripture is genuine spokenness, in comparison with which "content" and "form" seem only the results of a sham analysis; *Botschaft*, then, even where it is expressed indirectly, must not be reduced to annotation or commentary. Rather it enters into the form, helps determine the form, transforms it, transforms itself for it—but without affecting us in the least as distorting, as blurring, as didactic. Narrative retains undisturbed its epic completeness, statute its strict particularity; but within these forms the action of *Botschaft* is accomplished, and does not leave things unchanged.

The principle by which this is accomplished must be, precisely, a formal principle. This formal principle is rhythm—but rhythm both in a broad sense and in a very particular one.

By rhythm here we understand not segmented movement in general, but the auditory connection, manifested in a significant order, of a constant with a variable. The constant can be purely structural—the recurrence of cadence, of tempo, of quantity. Or it can be phonetic—the recurrence of sounds or sequences of sounds, of words or sequences of words.

Accordingly, the formal principle of *Botschaft* is a double principle. Phonetic rhythm—"paranomasia"[5] and the like—is taken directly into its service as such; but structural rhythm becomes an expressive instrument for *Botschaft* only by alterations beginning at a given moment.

And now some examples of both sorts, which I take from the first four books of the Pentateuch. (The fifth book, which in accomplishing its task articulates its *Botschaft* with oratorical directness, offers less in this connection.)

Of the seven revelations made to Abraham, only the fourth is fashioned

4. German *Künder*. Buber refers by the word to what we ordinarily call "prophets"; on his reasons for choosing the word, see "On Word Choice in Translating the Bible" [eds.].

5. By "paronomasia," often used in English merely as a fancy alternative to "pun," Buber means every kind of auditory similarity between one word or word-complex and another [eds.].

in the style of prophetic vision, because only there is the subject a particular future segment of the national history. In that revelation there is a verse (Gen. 15:16),[6] intended to impose itself on the memory—not only on the reader's memory, but also, in the purely oral context of the original narrative, on the hearer's.

> But in the fourth generation they will return here [*hennah*],
> for the punishment of the Amorite has not been paid-in-full
>   heretofore [*'ad hennah*].

What transgression of the Amorite is it that is spoken of so fatefully and at so significant a moment?

In the genealogy, Emori appears as the son of Canaan (10:16). But in the previous story, the story of Noah's drunkenness, Canaan is treated very oddly.

The motif-words of the story are "the nakedness [*'ervah*] of the father" and "Canaan"—though Canaan has nothing to do with the event the story tells of.

> Ham, the father of Canaan, saw his father's nakedness. . . .
> [Shem and Yefet] walked backward, to cover their father's nakedness.
> —Their faces were turned backward, their father's nakedness they did
>   not see. (Gen. 9:22-23)

This is not casual repetition, but the characteristic[7] phonetic-rhythmic or paronomasiastic method of the Bible for imprinting a specially important word or sequence of words (important either within the particular text or beyond it) upon the hearer or reader.

"The nakedness of the father" occurs in only one other context in the Pentateuch, and in that context twice: in the legal passages of Leviticus (chapters 18 and 20) that speak of the *'arayot*, the "nakednesses," i.e., the sexual sins. The first individual prohibition (18:7) begins with the words "the nakedness of your father." The passages from Genesis and those from Leviticus are paronomasiastically related; and it is this relatedness that discloses the actual motivation of the Genesis narrative, of the emphatic account of transgression and the great pathos of the curse toward which the story proceeds and with which the story of Noah concludes.

The sons of Noah are mentioned twice before the Flood and twice after

---

6. The common notion that this verse is only a gloss is a misleading error.

7. I would note in this connection only the thrice-repeated clarion proclamation of triumph over a (historically very disputable) "King of Canaan" at the conclusion of the fourth chapter of Judges (a *prose*-version!).

it; but the third occurrence (9:18) is followed by the phrase, "Now Ham he
is the father of Canaan." No other descendants are named; the rest are
enumerated in the next section, in the genealogy. Only Canaan's name is
thus singled out, though in the genealogy his name comes only fourth. The
hu' ("he") expresses the fact emphatically: this is indeed the father of
Canaan, who is of special concern to us.

Moreover, as the story of his transgression is told, he is again presented
as "the father of Canaan." Elsewhere the Bible joins the son's name to the
father's in this fashion only when the son is the principal person.

And in fact Canaan *is* the principal person for the narrator here, however little he has to do with the event. So much is clear from the wording of
the curse, which mentions the guilty Ham not at all but Canaan three
times: once at the beginning, once in the middle, and once at the end.

The subject is Canaan, the subject is the Canaanites.

The passage introducing the *'arayot* prohibitions begins as follows (Lev.
18:2ff.):

> Speak to the Sons of Israel, say to them:
> I am your God.
> According to the deeds of the land of Egypt, where you were settled, do
>   not do,
> according to the deeds of the land of Canaan, where I am bringing you,
>   do not do,
> in their statutes, do not go.

It concludes similarly:

> Do not go in the statutes of the nation that I am sending out from
>   before you,
> for all this have they done and it was loathsome to me.

Not "in their ways" but "in their statutes." What sort of statutes can be
meant in this context?

In Egypt we would think of dynastic incest, of the official, sacral marriage
of siblings.

In the case of Canaan, all the biblical passages that link "whoring" with
the cult of Baal, and also the Peor story (Numbers 25) with its marvelously
suggestive words and plays on words, establish clearly that what is meant is
the promiscuity of the Canaanite sexual cults, which appear in later traditions (Testament of Judah 12[8]) as "the practice of the Amorites"; the

---

8. The language of the Mishnah blurs the meaning here.

Amorites here as often elsewhere (cf. for example Amos 2:9[9]) are regarded as the representative members of the Canaanite nation's posterity. (It is in this context that we should understand also the striking passages in Ezek. 16:3 and 45, where "the Amorite" is called the "father" of lustful Jerusalem).

The story of "Canaan's father's" *'ervah* sin is, like so much in Genesis, to be understood as an anticipation of the history of the people in the history of the patriarchs. The "transgression" (*'avon*) of the Amorite is explained by this story in connection with the *'arayot* prohibitions. Through that transgression "the land was polluted" (Lev. 18:25, 27), and with God "accounting its transgression (*'avon*)," when it "had been fulfilled," upon the land, so that "the land might vomit out its inhabitants," Israel was able to "possess" their soil (20:24). But the people Israel, "separated from the peoples" (ibid.) as what is polluted is "separated" from the people Israel (v. 25), is subject to the command to be holy (v. 26), and is also subject to the prohibition of what defiles (18:24):

> That the land not vomit you out, when you pollute it,
> as it vomited out the nation that was before you! (18:26)

To hallow sexuality in protest against its being proclaimed intrinsically holy is the deep goal of *Botschaft*, which in the Genesis story has found narrative expression through phonetic rhythm, through audible repetition, and through establishing relations among diverse passages of the story and also relations between passages of the story and passages of the law.

By the "pollution" of humankind—*tum'ah* is not "uncleanness," not something negative, rather something positive, something substantial and contagious—the earth itself teaches the *'arayot* law, becomes defiled. This is common biblical teaching, recurring repeatedly throughout the biblical text. The earth is filled with human wrongdoing in the era before the flood, and the earth thereby "goes to ruin" (Gen. 6:12), and the flood covers the earth as if to purify it. The sinful person "makes sinful the land" he lives upon (Deut. 24:4), and sinfulness destroys both it and him. This destructive effect man exercises upon the earth is ordinarily called *hanufah*, which is normally to be rendered "degeneration." By the "whoring" of the people with idols (Jer. 3:1 and 9), and by the blood-guiltiness of one person toward another (Num. 35:33; Ps. 106:38), the earth likewise is made degenerate. The strongest proclamation of this teaching is probably that in the "apocalyptic" twenty-fourth chapter of

---

9. Note the obvious connection between the attack on promiscuity in verse 7c and the mention of the Amorites.

Isaiah; the earth upon which man's iniquity lies heavy (v. 20) is "fallen and fouled" (v. 4); it "gapes, crumbles, shakes," and finally it falls, to rise no more (vv. 19ff.).

> But the earth was degenerated by its inhabitants,
> for they violated the teachings,
> they slipped past the law,
> they broke the primeval covenant.
> For that the curse devoured the earth . . .

Ḥanefah: degenerated; *ḥalefu*: they transgressed—one of those bitter biblical "puns," in which cause and effect audibly echo each other (*ḥalaf* is used nowhere else in this sense).

The "primeval covenant" is evidently the covenant made with Noah; it follows that the curse, too, is directed to the earth and to humanity, not to the land and people of Israel. And yet the reader of Scripture is reminded of a familiar curse—of the most familiar of all curses, in fact—which does concern the people of Israel and which also binds humanity and the earth together, though of course in an entirely different way: it is not that the land atones for what the people have done, but that the land attains its just claims through its severance from the expelled people.

In the same book in which the *ʿarayot* law derives the pollution of the land from the pollution of its inhabitants, there is, in the twenty-fifth chapter, the command regarding the sabbatical year, the "year of ceasing." Six years the land is to be cultivated, the seventh year it is to cease; seven times the law repeats the words "cease" and "cessation." And just as the commandment of the Sabbath took up all creatures—the servant, the settler, even the domestic animal—in one common rest (Exod. 23:12), so the commandment of the sabbatical year takes up all creatures in the common enjoyment of unharvested aftergrowth (cf. also Exod. 23:11). This "societal" commandment—though "societal" and "religious" cannot be severed in the Torah; the "religious" is the direction, but the "societal" is the *way*—occupies in the legislative context so high a place that failure to obey it is at the center of the great curse concluding the laws of the third book. If the people that has not been willing to observe the Sabbatical year is expelled from its land, if people and land are severed, then the land attains its rightful claim, i.e., its Sabbatical year, which the people had denied it and which is now restored in a long fallow period (cf. the Jeremianic application of the Leviticus text in 2 Chron. 36:21). But just as in the Isaiah chapter the vision of the coming kingdom of God supplants the vision of the fallen earth, so even in the curse itself the promise transcends the denunciation. Here, however, both elements are deeper, and also to an extraordinary degree deeply intertwined, in that the connectedness of man and earth, meaning here the connectedness of people and land, takes on by the repetition of a single word in double meaning a strikingly peculiar linguistic shape. Forms of the verb *ratzah*, which in *qal*-form means, approximately, "to validate an accomplishment through acceptance of it," are used in subtle gradations so that the sabbatical rest of the land, which compensates for its having been neglected, and the expiation of the people, which compensates for its strained relationship to God and in which begins the people's conversion, the "humbling of their heart" (26:41), are comprehended in the same word, and thus held in a stable reciprocal relation.

> Then the land will be made-acceptable according to its years-of-ceasing,
> all the days of its being-silent
> that you are in the land of your foes,
> then the land shall cease,
> it will find-acceptance for its ceasing.
> All the days of its silence it will cease,
> that it did not cease in your practice of ceasing,
> in your being-settled upon it . . .
> When your heart, the foreskinned-one,[10] surrenders,
> when they win-acceptance for their failure,
> I will recall my Yaakov-covenant,
> and also my Yitzḥak-covenant,
> and also my Avraham-covenant will I recall,
> and the land I will recall.
> The land must be abandoned by them,
> that it may find-acceptance for its ceasing, while it is silent,
> and they must win-acceptance from their sin . . . (Leviticus 26).

Here for the seventh time occurs the radical *shabat*; previously, vv. 34ff., in the expression of need, it occurred only six times, and instead of the seventh occurence the text gave, in punning pseudo-replacement of it, the word *be-shibtekhem* (directly after *be-shabbetoteikhem*). But now the restoration has succeeded; and, as in the law of the Sabbatical year itself, the sevenfold naming of the seventh year is completed in the curse that turns into a blessing. Favor, the "accepting validation," *ratzon*—not specifically named in this passage ordered by the rhythms of *ratzah*, but radiating out from the beginning of the book (1:3) and from other passages in it—*ratzon* here triumphs at last.

In this passage, *Botschaft* has said in its own way precisely what it wanted to say about the fated relation between people and land.

---

10. Not "uncircumcised," just as *ṭamei* is not "unclean"; here too reproduction by a *positive* word is indispensable.

In the fourth of the seven revelations to Abraham—from which the first example was taken—verse 10 reads,

> He halved them down the middle, putting each one's half toward its fel-
> low,
> but the birds he did not halve.

The verb rendered by "halve," *batar*, occurs in the Bible only here; the noun *beter* in this sense occurs only in one other place, namely in Jer. 34:18f.

Of the significant verbal repetitions in the Bible this is among the most significant. This can of course be understood as the necessary recurrence of a technical term; but soon it becomes clear that such an explanation only displaces the problem and does not actually deal with it. The ritual of con-cluding a pact by a passage of the partners between pieces of animals is fa-miliar from several traditions.[11] But the Bible knows this ritual only in these two narratives; and it is evidently something special, something common to these two narratives and only to them, that the Bible here specifies. In the first narrative, at least, only one of the partners passes through; in both nar-ratives only one of the partners contracts an obligation to do so. The two cases are fundamentally different; but the obligation is in one respect the same, namely, that servants must leave their servitude and be free.

Through the sign of the fire passing between the pieces, God assures Abraham of the liberation of his lineage from the "oppression" of the Egyptians holding them in servitude; this is the promise that is to preserve Israel during that servitude. When it is fulfilled, God takes the people from the service of their oppressors into his own service: into real freedom. "Be on your guard/ lest you forget HIM/ who brought you out of the land of Egypt, out of the house of servitude!/ HIM your God shall you fear/ him shall you serve" (Deut. 6:12ff.).

But those who in this fashion are taken out of slavery to other men may not themselves make other men their slaves. "You shall not make him serve the service of a serf" (Lev. 25:39) thus lays down the law, and then argues for it on the ground that

> For my servants are you,
> whom I brought out of the land of Egypt,
> they shall not be sold in servant-selling.

If a man falls into another man's debt, and asks for his freedom in the sev-enth year, he is to receive it. But the fiftieth year, the year of Jubilee, for

---

11. On the issues this raises for historians of religion, see my *Königtum Gottes*, pp. 112ff. and 229ff. [English edition *Kingship of God*, pp. 121ff. and 201ff.].

which *deror*, i.e., "going free" or "letting go free," is invoked, restores all the clans to freedom even as it restores them all also to their land.

In the fear of falling into servitude under the besieging Chaldaeans, the lords of Jerusalem take upon themselves and obey the evidently long neglected commandment to free slaves, and engage God in a strange *do ut des* offer of freedom for freedom. No sooner has the enemy army withdrawn, however (in response to an Egyptian attack), than they take their bondsmen back. And now the prophet announces to them the return of the Chaldeans and the coming defeat. But the prophet, who is a man of *Botschaft*, does this in a great, fourfold paronomastic structure of utterance.

The first element of the structure is the quintessentially prophetic word "turning." "Turning" is what all depends on, even in the hour of greatest need; not, however, on particular and therefore inconstant turning, but on true and faithful turning. "You, however," says the prophet, "no doubt *turned back* today" (v. 15), "but then once more you *turned away* and let your servants *return*" (v. 16)—"and so I bid its enemies *return* against this city" (v. 22). Often the turning of men is associated with the turning away of God "from the fire of his anger"; so here a response is given from above that *corresponds* to the human action. But the *Leitwort* language also reveals man's actual malady: that he turns away from his own returning.

The prophet draws the second element of the structure from the account of the vision-revelation to Abraham. At the beginning of the divine message, to be sure, the pact that the people have made and broken is compared not to the pact with Abraham but to the pact at Sinai: "I myself concluded the covenant with your fathers/ on the day that I brought them out of the land of Egypt, out of the house of servitude" (v. 13). Nor can this be otherwise, since from this comparison alone is it possible to introduce the law cited in v. 14 from Deut. 15:12; what is at issue is the previously transpiring moment of the deliverance of all Israel, which ought thenceforth to have preserved itself free in its totality. But linguistically Jeremiah reaches back to the Genesis narrative, in two ways. He gives the *karat berit*, the "cutting of the covenant" (a phrase that of course evokes Greek and Latin metaphors), a concrete meaning based on no other biblical passage than Genesis 15. The prophet's meaning does not appear to be the original one; he identifies the original meaning of the metaphor with the accomplishment of the ritual: the lords "cut" the covenant by "splitting" the calf (v. 18). Note the remarkable and deliberately complicated syntax; we are supposed to perceive it with astonishment, are to think of that appalling image of primordial history! But this is not all; the prophet has also adduced the *ʿavar* from Gen. 15:17—not merely to be used, as would be only appropriate in the situation, but to be explained concretely in a bold pun: the lords have indeed "gone through" the halves (*betarim*) of the calf, as is said twice,

again in explicit circumstantial discourse (vv. 18ff.); but then they have also
"gone against my covenant" (v. 18); again one and the same word encompasses the opposed ideas of returning and turning away.

The third and fourth elements of his structure the prophet takes from the
law. His "from the house of servitude" states through the most powerful of
all historical reminders what is at stake here: the people delivered from service to the peoples and taken into the service of God is betraying its freedom—a freedom based on the freedom of all people—and betraying its
service; now it must pass out of freedom into service to the peoples, into a
new house of servitude. And from the law—not now the law of the seventh
year that is being spoken of here, but the law of the year of Jubilee—the
prophet draws the rare and exquisite word *deror*, and thereby paranomasti-
cally augments the sharpness of the terror he is instilling. Directly after the
twofold anticipation of the word—in the introduction, v. 8, and in the
speech itself, v. 15—follows in v. 17 the call of the overpowering divine
response: "You, you have not hearkened to me,/ to call out Release, each
man for his brother, each man for his fellow,/ so then, I will call out Release
for you.../ sword, pestilence, famine." Those who *crave* freedom but do not
will it are delivered over by God to the unhindered course of destiny.

Even in its proper domain, then, even in prophecy, *Botschaft* practices its
peculiar linguistic work.

The preceding examples illustrate the principle of repetition; to them I
now want to add some examples illustrating the structural variation that
the power of *Botschaft* brings about.

In the instruction "on the seventh day" that God issues to Moses in the
cloud at Sinai concerning the building of the Tent and all its apparatus we
find (Exod. 28:13-30) the description of the *ḥoshen mishpaṭ*, the "breastpiece of judgment," which contains the enigmatic *urim* and *tummim*. A sanc-
tified, matter-of-fact precision marks the enumeration of the materials, the
gems, and the remaining components of the breastpiece, and also the
account of their preparation and assembly. But then, after the words "the
breastpiece is not to slip from the *efod*," there is a change. The change does
not disrupt the continuity or the compositional unity of the passage; rather
the change in diction, style, and rhythm gives both continuity and unity a
last validation and consecration. The final command, saturated with significant repetitions, is as follows:

> So *Aharon is to bear*
> the names of the children of Israel
> on *the breastpiece of Judgment*
> *over his heart,*
> *whenever he comes* into the Holy-Place,

for remembrance *before ME*
regularly.
And you are to put
into the *breastpiece of Judgment*
the shining-things and the planing-things
that they may be *over the heart* of Aharon,
whenever he comes before ME.
So Aharon is to bear
the Judgment of the children of Israel
over his heart
before ME
regularly.

This final instruction is formed *in se* in strict phonetic rhythm. Not oratori-
cally but in the utmost purity of form does *Botschaft* offer its secret here: the
act of bearing, the heart, the breastplate, Judgment, entrance, before
YHWH, regularly. The whole sacral anthropology of the Bible lies in the
connections among these emphasized words.

We find similar things, though on a smaller scale, at the conclusion of
numerous other passages of the great series of teachings. One, however, is
conspicuous among the others: the prescription for the daily "highbringing" (29:38-46).[12] This passage too begins with concrete precision in diction and sound. But when mention is made of the "Tent of the Presence,"
the tone changes, and *Botschaft* expresses the meaning of the whole teaching, though this utterance too is pure imagery:

at the entrance to the *Tent of Presence*, before ME,
where *I will present myself* to you
to speak to you there.
So *I will present myself*
to the Children of Israel,
and it will be hallowed
by my Glory.
I will hallow
the *Tent of Presence*,
and the altar,
and Aharon and his sons *I will hallow*,
to be-priests for me.
And I will *dwell amidst* the Children of Israel
and I will be a God for them,
that they may know
that *I am their God*

---

12. On this and related terms and on the English renderings of them see below, "On Word
Choice in Translating the Bible" [eds.].

who brought them out of the land of Egypt
to *dwell*, myself, in their *midst*,
_I_, their God.

Each fundamental word occurs twice, and the body of meaning is knit
together by the rhythm of the verbal repetitions. Theological holiness has
found its language here as anthropological holiness found its language in
the passage discussed previously.

The rhythmic changes here have been prepared for earlier, in the chief
commandment among the laws of the year of the Jubilee (Lev. 25:8-12).
The pattern is already signaled in the beginning, by the alliterations among
the numbers and dates: *sheva'*, *shabbetot, shanim.* And once the proclamation of *deror* has been commanded, then there follows, in a closed ring-
pattern:

A homebringing let it be for you,
when you return,
each to his holding,
each to his clan
shall you return.
A homebringing let it be, this year. . . .
In this Year of homebringing
return,
each to his holding.

Surely this form resembles the great communal restoration itself, in which
"every man" is "brought home" to his original condition.

But the poetic power of *Botschaft* works still more strikingly in another
passage. Here again the beginning of the passage (Num. 15:1-16) offers a
prescription for sacrificing, one concerning the gifts of grain accompanying the major sacrifices. But at the conclusion we find this pattern, growing
in logical consequence out of what precedes and yet as different from that
as a flower is from its stem:

And if a sojourner sojourns with you,
or whoever is among you, for your generations,
and prepares an offering of fire, scent of assenting, for ME:
as you prepare it, so shall he prepare it.
Assembly!
One kind of rule let there be for you and for the sojourner that
    sojourns,
a rule for the ages, for your generations:
like you, like the sojourner before ME,

one kind of instruction and one kind of judgment
let there be for you and for the sojourner that sojourns with you.

As the unimposing youngest son of Jesse was chosen king, so here *Botschaft* has chosen an improbable place to express one of its chief concerns: the equal status in law of that man with whom *Botschaft* is so concerned that it remembers him again and again with strong adjurations, the only man of whom it is said (Deut. 10:18) that God "loves" him, the unprotected man away from home. The rising rhythmic pathos proclaims that the decreed "equality" of all men before God and and "all-oneness" of their rights is valid not for a single situation or by a single ordnance but everywhere in human communal life.

SCRIPTURE AND WORD:
ON THE NEW BIBLE TRANSLATION

Franz Rosenzweig
(Late 1925)[1]

Every word is a spoken word. The book originally served the word, whether declaimed, sung, or spoken; it sometimes still serves it today, as in theatrically living drama or opera. Opera people talk of the score and theater people talk of the script as something technical, instrumental, provisional; once, that was how people characterized the rank and condition of books generally, vis-à-vis the spoken word. But technique has a dangerous power over those who wield it; all unintentionally the means becomes an end, the provisional becomes the permanent, the technical becomes a magic spell. The book no longer serves the word. It becomes the word's ruler and hindrance; it becomes Holy Scripture. And with Holy Scripture, with letter-by-letter commentaries on the soundless and dumb word—the Alexandrians' Homer, the Neoplatonists' Plato, the Jewish and the Christian Bibles—we have the end of the book subservient to the word, the book unproblematically read aloud, as it was known everywhere in antiquity and is known even today where ancient tradition still lives, e.g., in the orthodox study of the Talmud. Holy Scriptures are the precursors of the modern book—dumb, and because dumb detached from man, full of unlimited possibility, but therefore damned to exile in space and time. Scripture in the charged sense of the term, Holy Scripture, opens up the unsurveyable territory of *Schrifttum*,[2] no longer bound to any human receptive power. This native word *Schrifttum* has an apparently (but only apparently) nobler tone than

---

1. Published in *Die Kreatur*, first year.
2. The German *Schrifttum* is often translated "literature"; but it is, as Rosenzweig goes on to suggest, simply an extension of *Schrift*; if *Schrift* is "writing," *Schrifttum* is "writingness." "Writingness," however, transgresses what Rosenzweig calls the "boundaries of linguistic possibility"; so the translation retains the German term.

the foreign import "literature," whose place it takes here; in reality both mirror in their abstract suffixes our hopeless despair of ever coming to the end of the accumulated heap of books.

Where there is a curse, people necessarily seek to be delivered from it. When what is written becomes Scripture, at once there arises everywhere an oral teaching joined to it. This teaching—however dubious in itself, like the *pilpul* of the Talmud, the dialectic of the scholastics, the lecturing at modern universities, the administrative control of the word in Protestant preaching—offers through the very fact of its orality the deliverance of humankind. However merciless a mouth may be, it is still of flesh and blood and not of paper; it becomes weary, and so accepts the alternation of day and night; it must eat, and at least then it will find a moment to chat. But the book is indefatigable, cares nothing for day and night, has no sense of the human need for relaxation and change. True, the mouth may "say nothing but what is in the book"; the "holy spirit" of Mephistophelean mockery, the spirit of spiritual grace may flow from it only tricklingly. But the genuine holy spirit, the spirit of mankind, is nonetheless delivered by it. Even elegant party-talk about the newest novel, indeed even the newspaper *feuilleton*, however shrunk to fit the capacities of the breakfast hour, has something of the blessed oral power to banish this curse of literature: its timelessness.

But one book—and precisely the book from which in our Judeo-Christian culture this fateful scripturalization and literarization of the word had its beginning, and in connection with which the antidotes of oral teaching and of tradition were first tried out—one book alone among all the books of our cultural horizon cannot content itself with this antidote of an oral tradition to complement it. This book alone must not, even *qua* book, enter entirely into *Schrifttum*, into literature. Its unique content forbids it to become wholly *Schrift*. It must remain word. It cannot attain the autonomous, aesthetic value of *Schrift* because it cannot attain the distance that is the precondition of this value. Its content, the essential part of its content, refuses displacement into the objectivity, the separatedness, the *madeness* that characterize all that becomes literature. Only its accessories are capable of becoming literature, and it is these accessories that a literary consideration must content itself with. But the essential content is precisely what escapes the specifying and distancing power of *Schrift*: the word of God to man, the word of man to God, the word of men before God. We have only to consider the letter—the most legitimate form of writing, the form

---

Readers should be reminded of the multiple meanings of *Schrift*: "Scripture," "writing," "literature." When those various terms appear in the translation they most often render the one German term; when the precise term is crucial to the argument the translation retains the German [eds.].

always addressed to an immediate need and necessity,[3] the form from which all other forms borrow whatever legitimacy they have—to see that this legitimation of writing can never pertain to the word of and to and before God; God is *present*, and if he acts through messengers, they are not postmen bringing yesterday's news, which perhaps in the meantime has already been overtaken by the intervening events; rather in this moment of theirs God is what acts immediately in them and speaks immediately through them.

It is, accordingly, a vital question for Scripture, for this one *Schrift*, whether the word is to be merely adjacent to it or within it. The word of God cannot dispense with the word of man—the true, spoken, sounding word of man. The Bible alone, among all books of the literary epoch, whether literary or pre-literary, demands a pre-literary mode of reading— demands, that is, what the Hebrew expression for reading means, which is familiar in the west from the Koran and which has also yielded what words pertaining to writing have not yielded, namely the most familiar term denoting the Old Testament: the *qeri'ah*, the "calling out." It is in response to this command that in all worship Scripture is customarily read aloud; it is in the service of this command that Luther in his translation has recourse to the spoken language of the people. The crucial question to ask of any new translation is whether this command has been fulfilled at a given time and for a given people.

The fetters that today hold all written German mute are constituted by the semantic system in which the words are embedded: punctuation. Even when a thoughtful and self-willed writer like Hermann Grimm has broken free of the purely logical framework of this system—and almost all German writers transgress more or less against their former schoolteachers on this point—even then the most we get is an approximation to the French punctuation system, which is based on a musical principle rather than on a logical one, but which is not suited to the contours of the German sentence, kept by the relatively free placing of words in German from falling easily into consistently recurring melodies. Where, therefore, these fetters must be loosed at any cost—as they must be in the German Bible, for today's reading public, which public has in reading been read off, read wrong, and read under—we need more drastic measures. Martin Buber has found these measures. The bond of the tongue must be loosed by the eye. We must free from beneath the logical punctuation that is sometimes its ally and sometimes its foe the fundamental principle of natural, oral punctuation: the act of breathing.

---

3. There's a crucial pun here: because, Rosenzweig writes, the letter comes in aid of an immediate need (*Not*, "need"), it is truly necessary (*not-wendig*, "necessary"). Now *wendig* means "averting" or "turning"; so by separating the two components of the word Rosenzweig suggests that that is necessary which averts our need, or which we turn to in our need [eds.].

Breath is the stuff of speech; the drawing of breath is accordingly the natural segmenting of speech. It is subject to its own law: that we cannot speak more than twenty, at most thirty words without taking a deep breath (and not just a catch-breath)—often indeed we can say only five to ten words. But within this boundary the distribution of breath-renewing silences follows the inner order of speech, which is only occasionally determined by its logical structure, and which for the most part mirrors directly the movements and arousals of the soul itself in its gradations of energy and above all in its gradations of time.

Thus the movement of speech is segmented into units of equal value, temporally equal breaths, so to speak (but *only* so to speak)—from the isolated "Yes" of God's confirmation of human disobedience (Gen. 3:22) to the elaborate naming of the five kings against whom the four went out (Gen. 14:2). Sentences that in unambiguous logic are distinct and so separated by periods—say, Cain's appalling answer, "I do not know. Am I my brother's keeper?"—are by the rendering of the vital, breathing course of speech brought together into a single movement, and thus given their full horror, previously half covered-over by the logical punctuation. Commas retain their logical function as subordinate distinctions; but through the added modulation of breathing they acquire a quiet resonance which in the press of adjacent clauses and the throng of subordinate clauses would otherwise get lost.

But this segmentation can only arise from the text itself. It remains, in the final analysis, like so much in translation, "arbitrary," an "experiment." In the New Testament, where the division of verses is a late addition of the sixteenth century (and where also the distinction into breathing units has been advocated from various standpoints[4]), it is clear that no traditional basis for these distinctions exists. The situation for the Old Testament is only apparently different. Here there is indeed a received system of punctuation, established more than a thousand years ago, on which the usual verse-divisions are based. It is an extremely fine-grained system; it does not make evident the structure of the sentences, but by pressing into all the chinks of the individual sentence it directly indicates the relation of each individual word to its successor, and only indirectly and as a consequence explains the connections among the sentence-components. But it is chiefly a comprehensive logical analysis of the text—a work, by the way, of philological interpretation to which all later philological work on this text must do homage. It does of course have a musical significance as well; but the

_____

4. See Norden, *Agnostos Theos,* p. 361; Roland Schütz, "Die Bedeutung der Kolometrie für das Neue Testament" (*Zeitschrift für die neutestamentliche Wissenschaft,* 1922, 161ff.); and Roman Woerner's translations of the Gospels and Revelations.

musical significance is almost entirely—aside from certain individual passages, like the recitative-like phrasings of numerous sequences of names—a functional expression of the logical element. The apparent singsong of Talmud study, i.e., the musical "setting" of the sentence as read, sets up the logical understanding of it; Hermann Cohen similarly "set" difficult sentences of Plato and Kant even in reading them aloud. Those who comprehend such experiences will understand how logical meaning can be based on musical value in the biblical punctuation as well.

But these signs, the so-called accents—for they *are* accents, as well as marks of punctuation and musical notes, or rather note-groups—have never been, not at any rate before the violently reactionary orthodoxy of the Emancipation, anything more than the accomplishment of great and honorable predecessors, whom the later-born follow cheerfully and trustingly, but from whom they may and must in all modesty be permitted to diverge. When the classical Jewish commentator, whose almost nine-centuries-old commentary accompanies almost every Jewish Bible ever printed—when Rashi, that is, with his incomparable balance of childlike absorption in the popular tradition and clear-eyed independent insight into the text, interprets the very first sentence of the Bible in clear contradiction to the traditional punctuation, he gives direction and measure for all interpreters who come after.

In the Old Testament, then, the traditional punctuation is, for the translator who recognizes the obligation to let Scripture be suffused once again with the breath of the word, not so helpful as at first it seemed to be. The punctuation thus fares differently than does the traditional vocalization (and indeed consonantization) of the Hebrew text, which to an extent surprising to us today with our scholarly prejudices turns out to be almost entirely reliable—or, more prudently put, almost entirely usable. Remember that our task in making the lineation is not the task of those who placed the accents in the first place: that task was simply not present for them, since for them the orality of the *miqra'*, the "calling out," was assured by the laws of worship, and they needed accordingly to attend only *within* this assured orality to the need for comprehensibility. In the matter of the received verbal text, on the other hand, today's Old Testament scholar is in a tricky situation; with all his charismatic professional expertise, with all his knowledge of biblical Hebrew, developed beyond that of the ancient Jews for more than a millennium, he nonetheless has before him the *same* task as did his ancient predecessors, and must like them substitute in the most vexed passages of the text what is at best probable for what was at least possible.

The obligation of freedom that accrues to the translator in connection with this point, the obligation of hearing the breathing movement of the word from the pen-strokes of the Scripture, is clearest when the passage is not only segmented according to its content, but also obeys a self-imposed formal law in the metrical rhythms of poetry.[5] The metrical linkage generates of itself—at least in a poetry that like the poetic parts of the Bible eschews the charms of cross-relations between verse-ending and thought-ending—an upper limit for the length of the "breathing-colon"; when the line ends, the reader breathes. Now in other cases this upper limit is also the lower limit; the metrical pattern is thus immediately legible from the typography, and the poetic structure has as many lines as it does verses. But in our translation this is only preponderantly the case, and not systematically. For us the respiratory movement of natural speech must sometimes break the metrical dance-step of the poetry. So, for example, in the dying Jacob's proclamations to his twelve tribal sons (Genesis 49). In each case there, the first two *cola* of the translation correspond only to a single verse of the meter, most strikingly in the prophecy to Judah. The inwardly rhythmic speech of the word wins out over the discrete pulses of the song; prose wins out over poetry.

For poetry is indeed the mother tongue of the human race; we need not reject here the insights of Hamann and Herder. But *only* of the race. Even today the language of every child is originally lyrical and magical, the enraptured outburst of feeling and the powerful instrument of desire, both often in the same sound, and if in the same word then only, precisely, in sounding that word. But the child only becomes an adult when through his *Ursprache* there breaks the unlyrical and unmagical fullness of the word, equally alien to song and proverbial saying alike—a breakthrough that like every genuine revelation is perceived only in retrospect, and avoids being assigned to a particular moment of the past. Just so, one day—and afterwards no one knows what day it has been—through the original language of the human race breaks the language of humanity in the human being, the language of the word. The Bible is the hoard of this language of the human being because it is prose, prose in the enraptured song of the prophecy and in the powerful declaration of the law. It is as Scripture supplementary, a deposit, a deposition of that breaking through of the word which occurs in the history of the race just where it occurs in the history of the individual: at the moment of becoming human. The word that cannot tolerate meter because in it the soul breaks free of measure is spoken into it, and speaks out from it. There was prose before and outside the Bible:

---

5. One technical adjective for referring to metrical verse, and one which Rosenzweig likes a lot, is *gebunden*, "bound." Some of the meaning of the ensuing passage depends on the association that word implies between metricality and enslavement. English, of course, has "free verse"; but it has no technical term to indicate the enslaved metricality to which "free verse" is opposed [eds.].

unpoetry, not freed speech but only unbound, not measureless but only unmeasured. All poetry that has been written in the Bible's light—and indeed poetry more than prose, Judah Halevi more than Maimonides, Dante more than Aquinas, Goethe more than Kant—has been animated by the Bible's spirit of prose. Henceforth the gate into the nocturnal silence that enveloped the human race in its origins, dividing each from each other, and all from what was outside and what was beyond—henceforth the gate is broken and cannot altogether be closed again: the gate of the word.

SCRIPTURE AND LUTHER[1]

Franz Rosenzweig
(July 1926)

Translating means serving two masters. It follows that no one can do it. But it follows also that it is, like everything that no one can do in theory, everyone's task in practice. Everyone must translate, and everyone does. When we speak, we translate from our intention into the understanding we expect in the other—not, moreover, some absent and general other, but *this particular* other whom we see before us, and whose eyes, as we translate, either open or shut. When we hear, we translate words that sound in our ears into our understanding—or, more concretely, into the language of our mouth. We all have our own individual speech. Or rather: we all would have our own individual speech, if there were in truth such a thing as monologic speaking (as logicians, those would-be-monologists, characteristically postulate) and all speaking were not already dialogic speaking and thus—translation.

If all speaking is translating, then the theoretical impossibility of translating, which we recognize and acknowledge, can have for us only the significance that all such theoretical impossibilities, as perceived from the stork's pond perspective of the man standing at the gateway to life,[2] afterwards have in life itself; it will, in the succession of "impossible" and necessary compromises we ordinarily call life, give us the courage of modesty, which asks of itself not what is recognized as impossible but what is given as necessary. So, for example: in speaking and hearing, what is asked is not that

---

1. Published separately.
2. In German as in English, the stork delivers babies, and the "stork's pond perspective" is the view one would have just before being born [eds].

the other possess our ears or our mouth—in that case translation would be of course unnecessary, as indeed would be speaking and hearing as well. And in speaking and hearing between peoples it is not asked that the translation be either the old original—in which case the hearing people would be superfluous—or a new original—in which case the speaking people would be annihilated. Only a mad egoism could desire either of these, mad enough to imagine itself satisfied with its own personal or national being, and to long for empty desert all around it. But the world was not made an empty desert,[3] but rich in distinctions and kinds; and there is no room in it for such an attitude.

Schleiermacher, himself one of the great translators in his version of Plato, once wittily divided translations into two groups: those that leave the writer in peace and move the reader in his direction, and those that leave the reader in peace and move the writer.[4] It is clear that this dazzling antithesis was, insofar as it was genuinely intended *qua* antithesis, dazzling and nothing more. If it were more than the antithetically clarifying illumination of a diversely intertwined and never antithetically divided reality, then the ideal Plato translation would have to be either the Teubner text or the *Critique of Pure Reason*. Taken sensibly, however, i.e., not as an either-or but as a means of sorting out the mix of reality, Schleiermacher's phrase can help us in our investigation and accompany us for a while. It can teach us to ask about the proper proportion of the two procedures; and when we have answered this question, which like all quantitative questions is very important but also only preparatory, it can lead us to the real question: *at what points* the reader is to be moved, and *at what points* the original. Simply to name the pertinent impulses says, here as always, almost nothing; the determination of the quantitative relationship among the impulses says, here as always, something but not very much; it is only an account of the points where the one impulse or the other takes effect that can give us a useful picture.

II

Of Luther's comments on his translation, the most widely known are those articulating his desire to make his translation *German*, generally comprehensible German: "to produce clear language, comprehensible to everyone, with an undistorted sense and meaning."[5] Such comments are in fact

---

3. An allusion to Isa. 45:18 [eds.].
4. Schleiermacher, *Sämtliche Werke* III, II, p. 218.
5. Preface to the Book of Job, editions of 1524 and 1525.

predominant in his work; and the great advance he made over previous Bible translations was most striking for his contemporaries in precisely this respect.

But he was also altogether conscious of the other side of his work, of the movement of the German reader in the direction of the alien original, the genius of the alien language. The separate preface to the German Psalter is the most instructive of all Luther's writings on translation; in the course of it, in connection with a whole series of examples, Luther provides for the reader and for himself an account of his method and also of the most thorough and far-reaching revision he has given to any section of his work. In so doing, he finds occasion to speak explicitly of this other side of his task, and presents this as the rule he has discovered and followed: "sometimes to hold rigidly to the words, and sometimes only to give the meaning."[6]

The reasons, or reason rather, for which Luther sometimes asks his reader to "give the Hebrew some room" and to "put up with such words" are stated by him in a passage that despite its length I must reproduce in full:

> But we have also sometimes translated word for word, though we could have done it otherwise and more clearly, and for this reason: the words have something important in them. Psalm 68:18, for example: "Thou art gone up on high, and hast led captivity captive." An idiomatic translation would be, "hast freed the prisoners." But that is too weak and does not yield the rich, subtle sense of the Hebrew. "Thou hast led captivity captive"—that is, not only has Christ released the prisoners, but he has in the process taken away the prison, taken it captive, so that it can never again take us prisoner, and our redemption is eternal. St. Paul speaks in this way when he says, "by the law I died to the law." Again: "Christ has condemned sin by sin." Again: "death is put to death by Christ." These are the captivities that Christ has taken captive and annihilated, so that death has no further hold on us, and sin cannot accuse us, the law can no longer chastise our conscience; and such rich, exalted, comforting teaching does St. Paul provide everywhere. To honor such teaching, and for the comfort of our souls, we must retain such words, must put up with them, and so give the Hebrew some room where it does better than German can.

It is perfectly clear here how the realms of the two principles, that of moving the text and that of moving the reader, are bounded. The former principle is ordinarily the dominant one, for Luther as for every other translator—all translation is after all into the language of the reader and not into the language of the original—and that Luther speaks at such

---

6. Luther is referring to Psalm 68.

length of this self-evident side of his work becomes intelligible only when
we understand that he may well have felt himself the first competent prac-
titioner of the translator's art. The translations of his predecessors swarmed
with Latinisms—not, however, in adherence to the latter principle, but simply from bungling.

The latter principle is for Luther, as for every translator, the exception. It
occupies us more today because when once the rule is secure the exception
becomes more controversial and problematic, and therefore more instructive and interesting. But where, according to Luther, does the necessity
arise "to give the Hebrew some room"? Where the statement is very important, directed to us, "to our souls"—that is, where for Luther, for the living
Christian, the Scriptures are the immediately compelling word of God, living truth and living consolation. The "analogy of faith"[7] was for him the
unerring divining rod, which quivered wherever the Old Testament "prac-
ticed Christ." Where for him, the Christian, it was the living word of God—
there and only there, but there necessarily, it had to be taken word for
word, and translated in "rigid" literalness. Elsewhere—and for Luther in
the Old Testament "elsewhere" was the chief part of the text—where, in the
language of the wonderful passage in the preface to the Old Testament, the
text was only a picture and pattern of governing and living, of "how things
happen when life is on the move," the translator "sends the Hebrew words
packing, and speaks the meaning of them in the best German he can."

Luther's belief, then, determines at every level how the work of mediation is to proceed—that is, where to leave the word in peace and where the
hearer. But Luther's belief implies Luther's concept of a delimitable
(because limited) religious content. Our time has lost his notion of revelation; whether in greater clarity or in greater confusion, it seeks the revelation of what it considers worthy of belief in the whole range of what Luther,
considering it merely a picture and pattern of life, had excluded from the
firmly, visibly, and eternally circumscribed religious kernel of the Book.
Our time, then, must in translating be permitted to ask the book the essential religious question all over again, as firmly and assuredly as it can. For no
other European people and language would this question be a question at
all. In Germany it is a question of utmost gravity, and for the following reason. For Luther himself his work always remained in flux; at the end of his
life he regretted that he would have no further opportunity to rework his
translation further, and hoped that posterity would "extend and improve
it."[8] For Luther's people, however, the Luther Bible broke free of its mak-

---

7. I.e., the notion that the Hebrew Bible is the foreshadowing of the New Testament [eds.].
8. In Hopf, *Würdigung der Lutherschen Bibelübersetzung* ["An Assessment of Luther's Bible
Translation"], p. 126.

er's religious life, and became the fundamental book not only of a particular church but of the national language itself. In Germany, then, the project of revision that Luther boldly allowed and earnestly commanded strikes at the locked door of the impossible.

III

Languages can be accompanied by writing for hundreds of years without there arising what we call, oddly enough, a *Schriftsprache*.[9] Writing does of course everywhere shape turns of oral expression in accord with[10] its own formality; but outside the spheres of experience where writing reigns, the language remains free and productively powerful. So, for example, children at school forget even how to speak, but at home chatter on regardless. Only later, when they get the itch for reading—at the latest when they begin to read newspapers—is their linguistic[11] energy finally tamed and yoked. From then on they require a special stimulus if they are not to speak as they write—or rather, as *one* writes.

So also in the life of a people: a moment comes when writing ceases to be a handmaiden of language and becomes its mistress. This moment comes when a matter encompassing the whole life of the people has been cast into writing, i.e., when there is for the first time a book that everyone simply "must have read." As of this moment, language can no longer proceed spontaneously, can no longer take its course exclusively in response to what it encounters along the way; rather it must in its progress look about constantly, lest it lose sight of this point of orientation. Moreover, it will, looking back as it moves forward, move forward more slowly than it has done before; the developmental tempo of the language becomes from that moment on more ponderous. Thus we can generally understand Luther's German if we modernize its spelling—though of course spelling is always

---

9. Ordinarily this is translated "literary language," and ordinarily that is what Rosenzweig means by it. But the *Schrift*-component of the word means not only "literary" but also "written" and "scriptural." For Rosenzweig, writing, scripture, and literature are in some sense equivalent; so *Schriftsprache* has been retained throughout, as a crucial term of art [eds.].

10. German *ent-sprechen*. This ordinarily means "correspond," "to be in accord with," but component by component means "to speak away." Rosenzweig separates the two components with a hyphen to emphasize that these "turns of oral expression" corresponding to literary formality are "spoken away" from speech itself [eds.].

11. "Linguistic" is used to render the *Sprach*-component of several of Rosenzweig's compounds, and of course *Sprache* is often translated as "language." These choices are almost inevitable, but they are also falsifications, concealing what for Rosenzweig is the vital connection between *Sprache*, language, and *sprechen*, speaking. A language is a thing *spoken*; "linguistic energy" is the energy of the *spoken* language [eds.].

the product of a purposeful will. If, on the other hand, we take the literature contemporary with Luther, insofar as it is not the product of his influence—say the final, 1518 print of the pre-Lutheran Bible translation, or Dürer's Dutch travel journal—we encounter considerable difficulties. Here we would have to modernize more than the spelling—at the very least the morphology. And Meister Eckhart we have to translate as from a foreign language, let alone Berthold von Regensburg or the *Nibelungenlied*. Yet Italians read Eckhart's contemporary, Dante, as we read Luther; and if we can read an Italian newspaper, then Dante's poem presents few difficulties other than those that were already perplexing to the fourteenth and fifteenth centuries. Here the origin of a *Schriftsprache*, and the regulation of a previously unchecked and ever-widening flow of language, lie fully six centuries past; yet we can find an origin more than twice as ancient in classical Arabic. The classical Arabic text is of course the Koran. Like *Hochdeutsch* today in Switzerland, or for that matter like *Hochdeutsch* in the whole domain of Low German since the triumph of the Luther Bible in the middle of the seventeenth century, the language of the Koran has become among all dialects the language of cultivated expression; it is made use of not only in literature and in journalism, but also in the theater, in political and ceremonial oratory. A celebrated Berlin orientalist tells us that the call to holy battle made during the last war might have come from the time of the Omayyads.

That a book thus reigns over a language does not of course mean that the language ceases to develop. Rather its development is vastly slowed; and just as, for the individual, development becomes dependent upon the leverage of charged moments, so for the language, development becomes dependent upon the equally haphazard and equally necessary appearance of language-shaping genius. From this time on, moreover, neither these language-renewing moments of individual need, nor these bearers and deliverers of national need, must invariably point toward the linguistic future; rather they are often born of the linguistic past. Just as for the individual a word read once long ago may come at need to his lips, a word that he would otherwise have shunned the use of but that now nonetheless becomes the true word for this moment, so the public speaker, in the urgency of his task, is no longer restricted to the vague, hovering realm of the linguistically possible, but often will conjure up the shades of the linguistic underworld, and, with the blood of his imminent need, bring them to speech.[12] On the other hand: the individual, even in these momentary expansions of his linguistic circle, will nonetheless remain bound within

---

12. Rosenzweig alludes here to Odysseus' visit to Hades in book XI of the Odyssey; Odysseus too conjures up the ghosts of the dead with blood [eds.].

the circle of what his time is reading; and the language as a whole, and thus the speaker entrusted by the language with a task, will most likely not, even in conjuring up the dead, reach past the time of the work that has founded the *Schriftsprache*. What is written in the Luther Bible is, though antiquated, still mostly subject to rejuvenation; if we look, say, in the cogent work of the Berlin Enlightenment writer Teller,[13] to see what he in his time found antiquated in the Luther Bible, we find chiefly words and expression that in 1794 had already been brought again into living use by the classical writers, and some others that in the decades following were pressed once again into common speech—and we think, perhaps, that no linguistic resurrection is impossible. But from the linguistic eras preceding the Luther Bible it is only seldom, and in very special circumstances, that any word can be reinstated in its full civic status.

The question of the classical text, i.e., of the text by which the *Schriftsprache* is founded, is here sharpened by the fact of its being a translation. There applies to translations a law of uniqueness that here joins with the law governing the uniqueness of the classical moment of linguistic history: every great work of one language can in a certain sense be translated into another language only once. There is a characteristic sequence in the history of translation. At the beginning there are on the one hand humble trots, seeking only to be of help in the reading of the original, and on the other free adaptations and imitations, seeking somehow to convey to the reader the meaning of the original, or at any rate what they presume the meaning to be. (There is no more striking proof that for, say, Dante in Germany this first period is not yet past than the fact that Geisow's "translation" and even Trenck's have found not only publishers but readers.[14]) Then, one day, there occurs a miracle, and the genii of the two languages are wedded. The time for this *hieros gamos*, this sacred marriage, is strictly determined; it is the time when the receiving people comes forth of its own desire and in its own utterance to meet the wingbeat of the foreign work— the time, that is, when the act of reception is motivated not by curiosity, by interest, by edification, not even by aesthetic pleasure, but by the whole range of a historical movement. Thus Schlegel's Shakespeare appears only when Schiller is creating an authentic German theater, Voss' Homer only when Goethe is investigating classical form. (For Dante in Germany the right time is not the age of "world literature," of exquisite or despairing Romantic conversions, but will probably be—so much we can prophesy— an age that without being Catholic nonetheless seeks to be truly catholic,

---

13. Vollständige Darstellung und Beurteilung der deutschen Sprache in Luthers Bibelübersetzung ["A Complete Depiction and Assessment of the German Language in Luther's Bible Translation"], 1794 and 1795.

14. Hans Geisow (1879-1939) and Siegfried von der Trenck (1882-1951) [eds.].

universal, encyclopedic. The translator whom the foreign work finds at such a moment will exhibit neither a modestly timid "philological" limitedness nor the naive insolence that can impose itself upon Dante even in our time; he will be led by the honorable belief that the more faithfully the original enters his language, the more abundantly the needs of this great national hour will be fulfilled.

As of this moment, the foreign book has become one's own. That means, concretely, that young people—it is, after all, the young for whom all that is written is intended, adults having other things to do, both better and worse—can experience their own developmental needs and torments in this foreign book. (There are as of this moment a good many Germans for whom Homer or Shakespeare means more than he has to most Greeks or Englishmen.) Now this astonishing stride toward the union of the Babel of peoples is not owed to the individual translator, but is the fruit that the national life has brought to ripeness in the circumstances of an altogether unique historical moment. Accordingly, it cannot be repeated. The historical moment does not return, because it does not need to return; it is, within the boundaries that are pertinent here, i.e., those of the horizon of the present national moment, immortal. It remains immortal as long as the connection between this moment and the past is not catastrophically ruptured. Now catastrophic ruptures happen only seldom; it is not a rupture when a fashion simply becomes outmoded, as happens to the rococo coiffure around 1770, and there was no rupture in the partial catastrophe we underwent in 1918. We can, on the other hand, speak of catastrophic rupture in describing the death of medieval German culture, in which, of that culture's great poems, still being abundantly copied in 1400, only *Parzifal* and *Titurel* were printed, and even they only once. But in the absence of such a rupture—and it would be as senseless to try to anticipate this sort of catastrophe as it would be, for the individual, to attempt a depiction of what awaits him after death—Voss remains the German Homer, and Luther the German Bible. No new translation can attain a comparable national significance; it will be restricted in its effects to parts of the people and to isolated individuals, and only through this partial effect will it influence the whole. The unique, classic translation influences the whole simply through its presence, through a mythical concept emanating from it—"biblical," "homeric"—which is grasped even by, or rather especially by, those who never open the book. A new Homer translation can be of course much better than that of Voss; but it is not and cannot become a world-historical event. It can strive only for the laurels the genius of its own people awards, and not for the already and forever awarded laurel of the world spirit, which can only be awarded once because the world tournament can only be enacted once—and cannot, unlike the trial matches of countries and peoples, be enacted any year or any day.

To this twofold national uniqueness of the Luther Bible is to be added its institutional uniqueness. This latter is of course narrower in its effects than the others; the Luther Bible considered as a German classic and as the archetype of the "biblical" has taken hold not only of Protestants but also of Catholics, and even of Jews. For the Protestant churches, however, Luther's translation has become what the Catholic church articulates in a complex system of institutions: the bearer of its visible presence. In this respect, Protestants are and have long been "Catholic," from Luther's death till the present day. The Luther Bible would thus have been fatal for Protestantism had Protestantism not had, and here also from the beginning, something to oppose to this inclination toward an idolatry of the book: the administrative control of the word. The Protestant pastor prepared his sermon in consultation with the original text; and even where this was not the case, at least the preparation of the preparation, so to speak, did take place in the presence of that text: the professors with whom the country pastor studied taught him the Bible in the original. This resulted, of course, in a separation between clergy and laity; but the separation was bridged precisely by the sermon itself. And what the sermon accomplished every Sunday has been brought about over the long sweep of history since Luther's death by the never entirely suspended efforts at revising him, which both at the turn of the seventeenth century and in the second half of the nineteenth century were drawn together into a great work, first the Cantstein Bible and now our present "Revised Luther Bible," both nurtured by the Germanic scholarship of their time,[15] both repeatedly returning to Luther's original wording, but both animated by the desire to keep Luther's work usable in the church and readable for the congregation. Both succeeded. The Cantstein Bible formed the text from which the German classical writers learned their German, and through which the language was preserved from the threat of Latinity. The revised Luther Bible produced at the end of the nineteenth century is considered by everyone except philologists to be Luther's authentic text; and this fact alone refutes the critique of Paul de Lagarde, that strange mixture of genius and pedantry, who reproached the authors of that translation, notably the brilliant Franz Delitzsch, for what was in fact their chief accomplishment. Lagarde argued, that is, that not only had the revisers not rewritten Luther according to the "state of current schol-

---

15. This is carefully demonstrated for the Cantstein Bible in Burdach, *Die nationale Aneignung der Bibel und die Anfänge der germanischen Philologie* ["The National Appropriation of the Bible and the Beginnings of German Philology"], published in 1924.

arship" (in 1885), in particular according to the discoveries of Paul de Lagarde—discoveries, as Lagarde noted, accepted even by Olshausen!— they had also for the most part repressed much of their own better insight, as recorded in Delitzsch's more scholarly translations.[16]

Today, then, and for as much of time to come as a heart and mind rooted in this Germany of ours has the inclination or the authority to see, those who would undertake a new Bible translation encounter a threefold obstacle in their way, composed of these three singular aspects of the Luther Bible. Prospective translators must, that is, encounter at once the book by which the church is made visible, the book by which the German *Schriftsprache* was founded, and the book by which the world spirit has been mediated. This threefold entanglement we neither can nor should dismantle. But we can leap over it, can and should and must. Must—if only that we may be free then to stand still, and not be in danger.

IV

For the voice of the Bible is not to be enclosed in any space—not in the inner sanctum of a church, not in the linguistic sanctum of a people, not in the circle of the heavenly images moving above a nation's sky. Rather this voice seeks again and again to resound from outside—from outside this church, this people, this heaven. It does not keep its sound from echoing in this or that restricted space, but it wants itself to remain free. If somewhere it has become a familiar, customary possession, it must again and anew, as a foreign and unfamiliar sound, stir up the complacent satedness of its alleged possessor from outside. This book and this book alone among all the books of humankind must not find its end in the treasure-house of human culture—because, precisely, it must not find an end in the first place. In the library of this treasure house lie all the books ever written. Most are dusty, forgotten, seldom paged even once; some are requested daily. The Bible, too, lies in these stacks, in many hundreds of languages— the languages of peoples, of arts, of sciences, of institutions, of programs. It is borrowed more often than is any other book, and yet there are always more copies available. Then some reader approaches the desk and requests the book. The attendant comes back: no copies left. The librarians are appalled, desperate, bewildered; just now, when Frau Professor Day-Before-

---

16. Paul Anton de Lagarde (1827-1891), renowned both as scholar of oriental languages and as nationalist and anti-Semite; Franz Delitzsch (1813-1890); Justus Olshausen (1800-1882) [eds.].

Yesterday picked up a copy for her husband, all the shelves were full. The Bible is written for the sake of the reader who has been denied it.[17]

The Luther Bible was when first written what the Bible should be, was the thing through which, as often as the Bible becomes it, it establishes itself as unique among all human, i.e., merely human books: a sensation. This is clear both from the publication figures printed by Hans Lufft and from the price,[18] as also from the numerous reprints. It is clear also negatively from the outrage of "Mr. Cleverling," that "tedious man," who though "greatly envious" at being incapable "of making anything good himself, yet wishes to pursue honor and become a master by abusing and slandering the good work of others,"[19]—this comic character that Luther in his Bible prefaces has cobbled together from the figures of his critics, without respect of persons. Mr. Cleverling knows perfectly well what the Bible is, and is furious that Luther's book is "an altogether different book from the Latin Bible";[20] he has his "received text,"[21] and why is Luther diverging from it? This "troublemaker"[22] doesn't even print the names[23] in their familiar Latinate form, but approximates the unfamiliar forms of the Hebrew! He, Mr. Cleverling, rightly seeks to have translated the Bible as it has always been "sung, read, used, and received from the holy Latin church, and not to be troubled by how it may sound in Hebrew, Greek, or Chaldaean."[24]

The Luther Bible was, then, a trumpet-call in the ear of those who had fallen asleep happy in their possession of the "received and certified text."[25] But it did not remain that; it became itself a possession, a national possession. It could remain a historical and trans-historical sensation only in the first decades after its appearance; afterwards the great historical effects radiating out from it are effects upon the individual streams of the cultural system—effects, that is, upon the religious portion of the culture, but precisely upon a part and not the whole. Thus from the end of the sixteenth century to the beginning of the eighteenth and the lofty accomplishments of the Bach Passions it animates Protestant hymnody; from the eighteenth

---

17. Note the similarity here between Rosenzweig's implied parable and the end of Kafka's parable of the Law; to the dying countryman who has spent most of his life trying to gain admittance to the Law, and who wishes to know why no one but himself has come on the same errand, the doorkeeper of the Law says, just at the moment of the countryman's death, "no one else could ever be admitted here, since this gate was made only for you. I am now going to shut it" [eds.].

18. The New Testament of 1522 cost one and a half guilders: "as much as a horse."

19. Preface to the German Psalter.

20. Preface to Job (1524 and 1525).

21. Cochlaeus and Dietenberger (in Hopf, pp. 132ff.).

22. Cochlaeus, in Hopf, p. 132.

23. Emser and Eck, in Hopf, p. 172.

24. Eck in the Preface to his own translation of the Bible, undertaken at the command of the Bavarian nobility (in Hopf, p. 134).

25. Cochlaeus, in Hopf, p. 132.

to the nineteenth century it animates the poetic diction of classical and romantic writers, as far as Goethe's *Faust*. But only once was it a storm churning up the waters of the national life before these were gathered and channeled into their individual channels; and having been that once it could not be that again, since it was now a possession and thus safely chained up again. Even the individual can today claim possession of it, institutional or national or cultural possession; that is why he has a right to it— though not, to be sure, a power over it.

It is, historically considered, no accident that at least until well into the eighteenth century the inner church history of German Protestantism played itself out on the Luther Bible. Since the middle of the eighteenth century there appear, chiefly at first in grotesque guise, efforts to replace it, efforts that we may characterize as caricatures adorning the margin of a significant historical text, i.e., the tottering of the old, precisely circumscribed religious concept, which, as noted earlier, was the all-controlling impetus of the Luther translation. Today this process, at least in its negative aspects, has been completed; though the various orthodoxies profess in public an obligation to take into consideration their connection with their particular Middle Ages and with all the late flowerings of these, they do not in private found their belief on medieval grounds. In its positive aspects, however, though the development of these aspects commences as early as does that of the other, the process has only begun. This too is clearest among the orthodoxies, namely in their constant devotion to counter-argument. The man who seeks to make a positive statement now makes it on his own; though there may be many to join his confession, he does not see them, and the individual voices do not join in chorus. And yet what he has to say, if it is shaped, word by word, from genuine experience and perception, is not at all "subjective"; and the so-called psychology of religion—that favorite study of today's scholarly Chelmites, who with Chelmish[26] earnestness disassembles the telescope in the hope of finding the stars among the parts—simply cannot make sense of such a man.

This man is no believer, but no unbeliever either. He believes and doubts. He is, then, nothing; but he is alive. Better: he has neither belief nor unbelief, but both belief and unbelief happen to him. His only obligation is not to run away from what happens, and, once it has happened, to pay it heed. Both of these sound easy, if we are far from the shot; but they are difficult, and probably no one alive has consistently—indeed, has accomplished them more than a few times altogether.

A person leading such a life can bring to the Bible only a readiness both

---

26. German *Schilda* and *schildbürgerlich*, referring to a proverbial city and population of wise fools; the translation takes the liberty of substituting an equivalent more familiar to its likely readers [eds.].

for belief and for unbelief, not a circumscribable belief that he finds the Bible confirming. Even his readiness is uncircumscribed and unlimited. Everything can become credible for him, even the incredible. What is believable is for him not interspersed within what is unbelievable—i.e., what merits unbelief—like veins of metal in stone, nor linked with its opposite like the kernel of the ear of corn with its dry husk. Rather, as a spotlight brings one sector of the landscape out of darkness, then another, then is dimmed, so for this person the days of his life illuminate Scripture, and let him see sometimes, amidst Scripture's human traits, also what is more than human—today here, tomorrow there, but with today's event implying no guarantee of tomorrow's. Yet everywhere these human traits can, in the light of a lived day, become transparent, so that suddenly they are written into the center of his own heart, and the divinity in what has been humanly written is, for the duration of this heartbeat, as clear and certain as a voice calling in this moment into his heart and being heard. Not everything in Scripture belongs to him, not today and not ever. But he knows that he belongs to all of it. This readiness and this readiness alone is, as applied to Scripture, his belief.

Is it not clear that on the basis of such a belief Scripture must be read differently and transmitted differently than Luther read and transmitted it? Luther had his reasons for sometimes giving the Hebrew some room, for expanding German till it accustomed itself to the Hebrew, namely that on occasion the text spoke of "teaching" and the "comfort of our souls." We do not know from what words teaching and comfort may come; we believe that the hidden springs of teaching and comfort may someday break through to us from every word of this book. Ought not Luther's reasons incline us to a new reverence toward the word, to a reverence that necessarily must renew our reading, our understanding, and our translating?

V

Every new thing has its history, at least its negative history, the legacy once Goethe spoke of to Eckermann.[27] Since the middle of the eighteenth century, an entire *Wissenschaft*[28] has attempted to humanize Scripture. To be

---

27. Probably the passage Rosenzweig has in mind is Eckermann, *Conversations with Goethe,* May 2, 1824 [eds.].

28. The German term means both "scholarship" and "science." The particular *Wissenschaft* Rosenzweig is referring to here is biblical criticism, of course; we would normally call this a branch of scholarship, and "scholarship" would then be the right translation. But what Rosenzweig wants to criticize about biblical criticism is precisely its claims to *Wissenschaftlichkeit,* to scientific accuracy; and since we do not ordinarily regard scholarship as making such claims, Rosenzweig's attack on it for making them would seem misguided. To avoid confusion, the translation uses either the German term itself or the phrase "scientific scholarship" where this is not too cumbersome [eds.].

sure, the attempt was caught in a striking confusion of two questions: what does that say? and, what did the writer want to say by that?—a confusion that these same scientific scholars would as, say, reviewers, plausibly and enthusiastically castigate. But the movement has attained at least its crucial goal: the aura of sanctity once surrounding the Bible like some golden orb or circlet surrounds it no longer. To conclude from this that the book is no longer sacred would be naive, as naive as to think the old painters imagined that St. Francis really went about with a circlet of metal around his head. What legend taken from eyewitness testimony reported about the phenomena of radiance was translated by artists into the general and local forms of their art. If today an artist paints an aura differently, if he does not paint it at all, he does not need on that account to believe any the less in the saint's holiness; binding a belief to the expressive forms of a past time is the cheap evasion of people troubled by the thought that someone "in our time" could have a belief at all.

Now the critical study of the Bible has not been guilty of this error; it has, more or less consciously, sought from the beginning to determine a new concept of the holiness of Scripture. It has, to be sure, regularly arrived at a fixed, partitioned notion of revelation characteristic of the old dogma. This is not, perhaps, as Jews like to think, due to religious prejudice so much as it is due to the confusion just described between what has been written into the book and what speaks out from it. A historical investigation is necessarily the product of a historiographical purpose, and can when directed to something genuinely *present* to us too easily write into it the lines of the historian's own purpose, which then become lines of separation and demarcation—thus Goethe's *Faust* as he sketched it and as the literary historian teaches it in class is simply not the poem he wrote, which is rather what the student with glowing cheeks reads from the paperback text.

The scholarly battle for a new, human sanctification of Scripture is mirrored in the translational enterprises that it, like all philological study, brings in its wake. One of these, the translation undertaken by Kautzsch and ten other scholars, has in its unannotated edition, prepared "for the edification of the Bible reader,"[29] been distributed in tens of thousands of copies, and rightly claims to offer the result of one and a half centuries of Old Testament *Wissenschaft*. Rightly; it is in fact an entire *Wissenschaft* that is expressed in it. If in what follows we shall show that this translation is simply not *wissenschaftlich* enough to attain its own declared end, this criticism does not refer to the individual translators but in fact to the *Wissenschaft* itself, of which the individual translator is only an exponent, and thus to the

---

29. Foreword to the *Textbibel*.

scholarly claim to precise accuracy, i.e., to *Wissenschaftlichkeit*, which *Wissenschaft* sets itself.

Kautzsch's translation announces its purpose as follows: "to offer readers of every sort the content of the Old Testament, with the means of current biblical research, in clear contemporary German."[30] This formulation alone expresses clearly what the translational activity of this sort of *Wissenschaft*— and not this sort alone, but indeed the translational conscience in all branches of philology—lacks in conscientiousness. For—it is almost embarrassing to state such truisms, but also necessary—it is impossible to transmit the content without at the same time transmitting the form. How something is said is not peripheral to what is said. The melody makes the music. The command: "attention!" is, as regards "content," identical with the "your attention, please" of a cultivated art historian or desk lieutenant, and also with the substantially irreproachable syntactic reworking, "I order you to pay attention"; but it is not the same thing as either. Yet *wissenschaftlich* translations are based on precisely this sort of "identity." This sounds exaggerated, but it is an exact description of what is happening when, say, in the story of what happens at the Sea of Reeds (Exodus 14)—I take all my examples from the second book of Moses, which in the edition in question has been translated by two scholars in turn and then recently revised by a third,[31] and is thus a good sample of what is common to them all—when in that story, in the course of a few sentences (14:19ff.) we get "altered his position," "brought . . . to yield," "took up the pursuit," "brought . . . to confusion" in place of the simple "went away," "drove back," "followed after," "frightened away" of the original. Perhaps there are, in a book as stylistically diverse as the Bible, passages for which this provincial bureaucratic diction is precisely right. But diffused equally over the whole story, it falsifies the tone and thus the "music." True, scientific translation lets the waters "flood back"; but for this particular piece of "strong sensual realism" the original is not responsible, as here it has only the pedestrian "return." And it is a fal-

---

30. Foreword to the scholarly edition, quoted in the Foreword to the *Textbibel.*

31. I quote the revision of the scholarly edition of 1922, because no revision of the *Textbibel* is as yet available; but for those passages which the scholarly edition, presuming corruption of the text, does not venture to translate, I quote the bolder *Textbibel.* The scholarly edition too addresses itself to the wider public; and the revision paves its way to that public with high-minded phrases in the Foreword about "an approximation to the *Urtext,* which does not shy away at the strong sensual realism characteristic of the Hebrew linguistic character," and makes a promise to the god of "living scholarship," the *dernier cri* of 1922, "to improve infelicitous turns of speech, and in general to make the translation not only photographically exact but also pictorially alive, so as to bring it closer to the ideal of an artistically valid image of the original." For those who on hearing the phrase "living scholarship," that product of a gallows-repentance, feel their hair stand on end, clearly a good photograph is better than a bad painting. What matters in translation is only and exclusively "exactness"; we need not concern ourselves with the "artistic."

sification in reverse when the original avails itself of a formally ornate phrase, as in the peculiarly unnarrated account of God's descent to the mountain of revelation. "The sound of the trumpet became continually more and more strengthened," says the Hebrew; and the translation gives only a flat "became louder and louder." When Luther translates in this mode, he is obeying his own injunction. When modern scholarship claims in this manner to have reproduced the context of the text, it reveals only the limitations inherent in scholarly modesty.

This sort of superficial translation does ordinarily permit itself a slightly greater degree of exactness in dealing with a poetic passage, like the song of triumph in chapter 15; here even scientific scholarship knows that the means of expression is not altogether irrelevant to the thing expressed. But ballad tone (13:21ff. and 32:17ff.) and dithyrambic exaltation are unerringly cooked down to the ubiquitous German of the police blotter.

What has been superficial becomes devastating, however, at the climax of the book, which is also perhaps the high point of the whole five books together: the account of the Tent. The powerful divine speech of chapters 25 through 31, the word concerning the vision vouchsafed to Moses, explaining to what end, to what "service of labor" his people are to be led after their "service of bondage," is in the translation under discussion transposed from its austere, concrete sublimity to a relentlessly chatty idiom that scribbles over all the original clarity of line. It is as if a sergeant attempted in his giving orders to "explicate" the classical commands of field duty ordnance. An evident example: these chapters are shot through with the word "made," which is as it were the theme of this great fugue. The Kautzsch translation, no doubt to keep the reader from boredom, undertakes to render the word in charmingly diverse guises—sometimes as "erected," sometimes as "produced," sometimes as "put up," sometimes as "worked." It has not the least suspicion that what happens in consequence is the loss not "only" of the form but also of the entire meaning of the vision, which in fact looks toward the original model of the "Dwelling"[32] created on Sinai in the six days of cloudy darkness (24:16), to behold which Moses is called up into the clouds on the seventh day, and which is then completed by the people as a human replica of the divine act of creation (Exod. 39:32 and 40:33 reproduce Gen. 2:1ff.; Exod. 39:43 reproduces Gen. 1:31 and 2:3). The six days and the seventh recur here, as does the word of completion, and the approving and validating "Indeed," and the concluding blessing—and also, as noted, the simplest of all words for creation, the simplest and also the

---

32. On this and on the Tabernacle generally see Benno Jacob, *Der Pentateuch.* Among living scholars, both Christian and Jewish, Jacob is probably the acutest student of the Hebrew Bible.

most comprehensive, which compares divine action with human, human with divine: the word "made."

Again: this argument is not at all aimed at the disparagement of individual translators, who surely gave this translation their best efforts. Rather it is aimed at *Wissenschaft* itself, which in translating is simply not *wissenschaftlich* enough. It has shaken many persons' trust in the Luther translation; but it has not put in place of that translation the translation of contemporary belief and its expressive forms—which is, after all, consciously or unconsciously, what all its work is meant to serve. It has indeed corrected various details; but it is also true that many of Luther's "errors" can be defended even by the judgment of modern scholarship, which credits the ancient translations Luther was often working with a reliable witness even against the received Hebrew text. Aside, then, from its correction of particular errors, the modern translation offers even in a scholarly sense very little that is better, and much that is worse, than Luther.

VI

Luther himself saw the scholarly significance of his work as lying in his return to the original text. Even his antagonists found that return to be the revolutionary element, though they acknowledged it with the bad conscience characteristic of a resistance to the needs of the historical moment. Luther the revolutionary, however, was still inwardly linked to what he was overthrowing. The Vulgate was indeed, as is clear even from the previously quoted utterances of "Master Cleverling," for educated persons of the sixteenth century much what today the Luther Bible itself is: a genuinely or apparently familiar possession, and in either case (today preponderantly the latter) a soothing pillow for the conscience and a padding for the door of the cultivated man's study against disruptive noises from outside. The Vulgate lived even in Luther's flesh and blood. His German Psalter is perhaps the summit of his translational accomplishment; but in his later years, when he, the "great psalmsayer," withdrew from inner or outer conflict to renew his strength in prayer through the recitation of a series of psalms, what he chanted was the Latin text his long years as monk had made so familiar to him. This alone, even if we had no other evidence,[33] and if the text of his translation did not reveal as much continually, would lead us to see that the inner and often the outer point of departure for his translation

---

33. See, for example, for the earlier years, his remark in 1514 that the Hebrew text is the letter, the Latin the spirit (quoted in Scheel, *Martin Luther*, II: 228 and 408); for the later years we have Mathesius' celebrated description of Luther revising his translation, "with his old Latin Bible and his new German one ready beside him, and the Hebrew text always there as well."

was in spite of everything the Vulgate, with the received Hebrew text serving only as the corrective to it, though of course used extensively for that purpose. In other words: when Luther investigated the meaning of the Hebrew text, he was not thinking Hebraically; nor was he, as he later did in rendering the investigated meaning into German, thinking Germanically; he was thinking Latinately.

Now Jerome's work is today recognized even by Protestants as the masterpiece which it is, and which Luther himself judged it to be. So it was no bad guide to whom Luther entrusted himself for his first steps. Above all, the Vulgate was the heir, though at some distance, of the logical-rhetorical linguistic tradition of antiquity, and often develops the sense of the sentence as a whole surprisingly well—and it was after all the sense that was for Luther, given the relation described earlier in his translation between the two fundamental directions translation can take, the thing that predominantly mattered. The classical example is, "thou hast led captivity captive," classical because explicated by Luther himself as typical—and where, as it happens, Luther is led to an unduly dogmatic conception of the text precisely through the wording of the Vulgate at that point. But precisely that example shows what profound views, albeit sometimes too profound, an intimate connection with Hebrew idiom can reveal. And if we believe that not only a passage called to our attention by a particular circumscribed doctrine but *any human utterance* may conceal the possibility that one day, in his time or in my time, God's word may be revealed in it, then in that case the translator must, so far as his language permits, follow the peculiar turns of that potentially revelation-bearing utterance, whether by direct reconstruction or by implication.

To linger over this same example: in the Semitic languages—though not only in them, but in all strongly pictorial languages—we find verbs having what we may call exponential powers,[34] even when these are not, as in Luther's classical case, activated by means of a noun but, as is most often the case, simply by an infinitive. In the Hebrew these various powers have on each occasion an altogether distinct meaning, even if this meaning is only a pronounced emphasis of the verb in question. So, for example—and here also all examples are drawn from Exodus—the seven daughters of Jethro (2:19) let their answer to their father's question come repetitively tripping forth: "he drew, yes drew [water] for us"; and again, Moses (5:23) returning to God after the first failure, reproaches him, "yet rescued—res-

---

34. German *Potenzierungen*. The word is used both mathematically and pharmacologically; in the former case it indicates exponential powers, in the latter case it indicates the varying effects of dilutions or intensifications of the same substance, as in homeopathy. Rosenzweig liked mathematical metaphors, and is probably using the word in the first sense; but he had also passed his medical boards, and the second sense cannot be ruled out [eds.].

cued your people you have not." The lively emphasis of the answering verb and the expressive energy of the reproach emerge in the translation only when the translation reproduces the doubling of the original. This is all the more true when, as in the language of the law, the doubling has an altogether precise legal sense, usually that of normative legality: compensatory recompense, expiatory expiation, payment paid.

The boundaries of linguistic possibility are of course not to be transgressed. Even the rendering of a Hebraically idiomatic expression by a Germanically unidiomatic expression is inadmissible—a shallow phrase ought not to be deepened, a smooth one not roughened, a plain one not beautified. But the reverse is true as well. Thus the terrible, wonderful conclusion of the second chapter is with its fourfold-repeated subject "God" surely no normal German, as Luther felt. But neither is it normal Hebrew! Only the closest attachment to the original text allows the German to articulate the transcendence of one "anthropomorphism" by the next—in truth, of course, God's so-called "anthropomorphisms" are human theomorphisms—until the last, untranscendable, "God knew." What is linguistically possible for the Bible in German is then not to be determined by any individual's sense of language, member though he be of the professionally infallible professions; nor is the translator to limit himself to his own idiolect. The translator here is not an individual facing an individual or the work of a particular epoch; rather, from a literary point of view, he is facing the anthology of a millennium. Even the Bible's *vocabulary* is incomparably greater than that of other equally voluminous books. And in this matter of linguistic possibility even great men sometimes err—in the 1523 preface to the Old Testament Luther gives as examples of impermissible neologisms *beherzigen, behaendigen, erspriesslich*![35] Witness the dangers of schoolteaching —even for men of genius. But if Luther doubted for a while whether German *Sprachgefühl* could manage the concrete pictoriality of "a mighty hand" (Exod. 3:19), and accordingly replaced that phrase in editions eight through twelve with "mighty wonders," nonetheless he rightly restored the authentic "mighty hand" in the thirteenth; only that phrase can lead to the following "I will stretch out my hand" (3:20), and indeed is clarified by that continuation. (The Kautzsch translation in all editions from 1894 to 1922 persistently gives "force"; but by this point the reader will hardly be surprised at that.)

What lay beyond Luther's understanding—though it had sometimes been grasped by Jerome—was the most important means of transplanting the living growth of Hebrew idiom into a western language. I have elsewhere[36] dealt at length with the importance of breathing-units. Here I need

---

35. All words to be found in any German dictionary today [eds.].
36. In "Scripture and Word."

say only this: first, they do not by their divisions make prose into poetry—a common misunderstanding, but not on that account any less foolish. Nor by their overlapping and intersecting with poetic meter do they make poetry into prose. Rather to the poetical and prosaic parts of the Bible alike they restore the free, oral breathing of the word, previously enmeshed precisely in the *writtenness* of Scripture. Consider the vast distance between, say, in the first book, the unarticulated and articleless stammering description of the original creation in the second verse of the creation chapter, and the fluid narration of the Joseph story; or, in the second book, among the grotesquery of the plague of frogs, the exultation of the Song of the Sea, Moses' speech to God with its weighing out of word upon word on the scale of deep emotion, the sublime account of the Tabernacle, and the precise circumstances and conditions of the legal propositions. It is only when it is freed from the monotonous gray of the usual piano reduction that this whole wealth of voices and tonal colors becomes, precisely through this notation of it in full score, audible, legible—and audibly legible.

VII

Neither Luther's translation nor any of those that have followed it has felt any obligation to reproduce this last, overarching characteristic of Hebrew discourse as a totality. The same is true as regards the other pole of language, its minimal component: the word. Here also it was Luther, perhaps more than any later translator, who saw the problem—as in the wonderful remarks of another Psalter preface[37] on the Hebrew words for kindness, truth, and fidelity or faith; or still more pertinently at the end of the preface to the German Psalter, in the earnestly meant joke by which he promises fifty guilders to all masters and "Cleverlings" if they will only translate the one word *ḥen* "throughout the Scriptures, idiomatically and accurately." It is his word, the most Lutheran word of the whole Hebraic lexicon, the word for grace. This alone, as well as the three words named previously, shows us again what this whole investigation has shown: the religious compulsion that directs all real translation of Scripture in every detail. Again: a different religious hope, to which all that is profane in Scripture—and what is *not* profane!—is only a shell beneath which one day something holy, something holy for me, may be revealed—such a hope must consider this problem of verbal literalness[38] otherwise and more comprehensively. It

---

37. In "The Third Part of the Old Testament," 1524 and 1525.

38. German *Wörtlichkeit des Worts.* Our "literalness" refers to the letter; German *Wörtlichkeit* refers to the word. Taken component by component, Rosenzweig's phrase means, irreproducibly, "the wordishness/literality of the word" [eds.].

must in principle acknowledge the task of translating a word "through Scripture, idiomatically and accurately" as pertaining to *every* word; and at least where to such a hope the awaited revealing of the *presence* of a word has already occurred, this task acknowledged in principle becomes also inevitable, and must be performed with all possible strength.

There is only One language—I have by this paradox, in another account of the problem of translation,[39] attempted to understand both the goal and path of such a task. The unity of all languages lies more deeply hidden as regards the element of the word than as regards the totality of the sentence. The sentence presents itself even to the superficial glance as a form, and so as both formable and transformable. Grammar, then, both in syntax and in morphology—which after all refers the individual word to its environing sentence—habitually sets up simple analogies between languages. But the aerial view of a language's *verbal* landscape seems at first glance severed and radically diverse from that of every other language; and even the maps of these landscapes, the dictionaries with their enumerations of various senses, only construct for each word in the one language an environing circle of a certain diameter that intersects several circles surrounding words of the other language. There come into being a certain number of common areas—which all, however, apparently lie apart, unrelated and unconnected. The picture alters only through a more geological approach. In the roots of words the severed areas lie together; and still deeper, at the roots of meaning, the roots of physicality, there is, apart from questions regarding some possible original relatedness of languages, that unity of all human speech which the surfaces of words only let us dimly intuit. The translator must dare to descend to these lower layers. How else is he to locate for the words composing a conceptual circle in the source language an analogous group in the target language? And find it he must, find it composing an equally coherent conceptual and pictorial circle, even if the two groups of words seem superficially or lexically far removed from one another.

He will need for his expedition the miner's lamp of scientific etymology; but he must not then arrogantly disdain to regard the glimmer emanating from the veins of the text itself. Indeed, these latter connections, intended, felt, and willed by the speakers and writers of the text, must be more important for his work than the verbal relationships verified, rejected, or revealed by comparative philology.[40]

Thus the text begins again and again by saying that in the Tent of the *moʿed* God will *hivvaʿed* himself to man above the ark of the *ʿedut.* The mean-

---

39. In the Afterword to the Judah Halevi translations.

40. It may not be altogether clear that what Rosenzweig is defending here is what is often called "folk etymology," i.e., the scientifically untenable etymological connections that the biblical text itself offers, as in, say, its explanations of the names of people and places [eds.].

ing of this is not exactly made clear when Kautzsch writes that God reveals himself in the Tent of revelation above the chest of the law, nor when Luther writes that God bears witness to himself in the Tent of meeting above the chest of witness, nor yet, though more nearly, when Luther in earlier editions writes that God bears witness to himself in the Tent of attestation above the chest of witness. The text speaks of none of these things. The lexically related meanings are here of no help to the translator, if at any rate he believes in the significance of the connection that Scripture makes so emphatic. Here he must descend to the depths, where in the components ʿ*ad*, "until," and ʿ*od*, "still," the concrete sense of the verbal group is revealed: spatial and temporal *presence*. God makes himself *present* in the Tent of the *Presence* above the ark of the recalling-to-*presence* of the covenant made at Sinai. Also the *haʿed*, the "arouse" and "warn" of Kautzsch, the "attest" and "proclaim" of Luther (Exod. 19:21 and 23, 21:29) is now clarified as meaning "make present to." Only the ʿ*ed*, the man-present-in-the-action, must still be translated "witness"; and the ʿ*edah*, those-then-composing-the-presence-of-the-people, must still be translated "community"—for in these words the translator reaches the boundary of linguistic possibility, which the root meaning permits him to see beyond but not to walk across.

The boundary of linguistic possibility is also and unconditionally to be maintained regarding the injunction to translate a word "everywhere consistently in Scripture." Consider the almost casual, multivalent interjection that Luther renders "*siehe* [see, behold]," lacking a similarly multivalent interjection in German—though Italian has one in *ecco*, the descendant of the *ecce* with which the Vulgate rendered the Hebrew term. This simply cannot be consistently translated by a single German word, however much of the charm of the "biblical" the loss of "behold" may entail. But the boundary of linguistic possibility is no defense for rendering arcane Hebrew with familiar German. In any case, German today, with its ease of word-construction, has considerable resources in this matter, which the translator must exploit wherever the excavation of verbal roots leads to no practically usable result. Take for example the verbal equivalence of the two sorts of "service," the slave service done in Egypt and the devout service of labor to be performed in the Tent. This equivalence frames and unites the whole book. In the middle of the book, in the Ten Commandments (chapter 20), it is further woven into the book's texture through the reminder of the house of bondage and the command to "serve" only the one God; and it lies still deeper, beneath the historical surface, in the command to rest on the seventh day, through the use of one and the same word for the servant and the six days' "service" of the servant's master. A reverent fidelity to the words of Scripture will honor such connections as well—whether they are, as in the first example of the account of the Tent, demonstrably intended by the text, or, as perhaps in this last example, put into the mouth of (or dictated to the pen of) the text only by and from the unconscious depths of the language itself. This mute deeper meaning of the words becomes language upon being spoken. The dictum that the language of Scripture seals fidelity and truth in a single word, and then makes these sealed words burst out into belief, is a dictum spoken among others to the translator.

VIII

When Luther in 1523 published the first part of his Old Testament, he addressed himself not only to the "Cleverlings" of his time, nor only to the seventeen editions of the German Bible that the next twenty years were to produce; he addressed himself also, across a historical divide of eleven centuries, in bold independent homage, to his great predecessor Jerome:

> The mud will cling to the wheel; and no one will be too coarse to wish to lord it over me and find fault with me here and there. All such I bid fare well! I have known from the beginning that I would sooner find ten thousand to find fault with me than one to imitate even the twentieth part of my work. I too, in fact, wanted to seem very learned and to show my art masterfully when I sought to find fault with St. Jerome's Vulgate. But he might well throw it in my face that I was only his imitator, after all.

Such are the stretches of time this book extends over. I said at the beginning that all speaking is translation. The conversation of humanity began with this book. In this conversation, statement and response are separated by centuries and millennia. Paul sought to answer the question of the third chapter of Genesis by questioning the words of the twentieth chapter of Exodus. His answer was repeated by Augustine and Luther, but to his questioning each in his turn gave a different answer: Augustine his city of God, Luther his injunction to the councilors to set up Christian schools. Before every new sentence of the conversation is a translation: into the language of tragedy, into the language of law, into the language of the phenomenology of spirit. No one knows when the conversation will be over; and no one knew when it began. So no human reluctance, impudence, or prudence can put an end to it, but only the will, the knowledge, the wisdom of Him who began it.

THE HEBREW BIBLE'S DIRECT INFLUENCE ON GOETHE'S LANGUAGE

Franz Rosenzweig
(July 1927)

It is generally known that our Bible has through Luther's translation of it exerted a profound influence upon our German language. It has recently been shown, to be sure, that the claim that Luther created our written language is in a strict sense untenable. More important, however, is the fact that only Luther's Bible made possible the *rebirth* of our language in the second half of the eighteenth century, a rebirth without which German today would be what English is: an inner and outer hybrid, part German and part Romance. Goethe himself recognized often enough how deeply his use of his mother tongue—in the strictest sense of that phrase, i.e., of his language that was his mother—drew from that source; to get a sense of that we have only to read the Balt Victor Hehn's perceptive essay, "Goethe and the Language of the Bible."

All these influences were exerted through the medium of Luther's Bible. Luther's Bible is of course rich in Hebraisms—to an extent hard to fathom today, precisely because through Luther the Hebrew idioms have become German—and Luther was fully conscious of "giving Hebrew room where it can do better than our German can," especially in places that seemed to him theologically and religiously crucial. The immediate influence of the Hebrew text on our classical language, however, the influence not mediated by Luther, is hardly known at all. All the more so, then, does the following case of that influence deserve the attention that any rare thing demands.

Rudolf Hildebrand's immensely fruitful entry on *Geist* in the Grimm *Dictionary* quotes (p. 2686) two passages from Goethe in which *Geist* "broods"—in a clear allusion, which Hildebrand then himself explains, to the second verse of the Bible. Hildebrand adds, "this activity of brooding must here be imagined as hovering above its object." First, in 1784, in his remarkable essay "On Granite," Goethe writes, "when this peak still stood as a sea-girt island in the ancient waters, the *Geist* that brooded above the waters was still blowing around it." And again, in the late essay on universal philosophical history, "Epochs of *Geist* According to Hermann's Most Recent Communications," he writes, "at first an empty wasteland occupies all space; but *Geist* is already brooding over animate and ordered substance." To these two passages we might add other allusions, more distant but equally certain: *Natürliche Tochter* 3:4: "When before, above what was about to grow,/ the fathermind hovered, brooding with delight"; *Wilhelm Meister's Apprenticeship*, 1:6 (and correspondingly in the *Urmeister*): "my imagination brooded over this small world, which very soon took on a different shape"; and the essay on Justus Möser: "the power of imagination broods above the desert of physicality."

We have then to consider the surprising fact that in widely diverse periods of his life Goethe was accustomed, in alluding to the usual text of the Luther Bible, "and the *Geist* of God hovered above the water," to replace "hovered" with "brooded." (When we read in "To His Brother-in-Law Kronos" that "from peak to peak/ the eternal *Geist* hovers," this is, despite the words *Geist* and "hovers," precisely *not* an allusion to the scene of Genesis 1.) Now even the phrase, "the *Geist* that brooded above the waters was still blowing around it," of the first-quoted and in the strictest sense quotable sentence makes clear that Goethe understood very well the nature of *ruaḥ* in this passage, in which it means not *Geist* in the current abstract sense of that word, but in the physical and meta-physical sense it still had in Luther's time: Godblowing, Godsurging. And clearly "brooding" too derives from the Hebrew studies that Goethe had undertaken as a boy, and of which the fourth book of *Dichtung und Wahrheit* gives an account.

The meaning of the rare and difficult verb is rendered by the classic Jewish medieval commentator Rashi, in his characteristic French, as *couver*, i.e., "brood over." (Rashi here follows an ancient tradition known also to the patriarch Jerome.) And most recent scholars, including Franz Delitzsch, Dillmann, Gunkel, and Holzinger, follow Rashi; the most recent commentary on Genesis, the 1924 second edition of Proksch, translates the word by "brood." The interpretation was common in the eighteenth century also. The elder Buxtorf, the reviver of Jewish studies, gives in his extraordinarily brief pocket-lexicon "to move back and forth in the manner of a bird; to brood." And in the German translation of the English biblical work to which the young Goethe's Hebrew teacher referred him for the assuaging of all his "old questions and doubts," Goethe found at least the clear suggestion that the word referred to "the action of a bird." How he then arrived at his choice of "brood" I do not know. He could not have taken it from Herder's inspired explanation of the creation chapter in his "The Oldest Document of Humankind," since Herder consistently says "hover" or even by preference "move about," like Mendelssohn later. But he could have heard in Herder's essay the blowing of the God*geist* above the waves. For Herder spares nothing in depicting how "the *Geist* of heaven, the breath of God, casts itself down from above, burrows among the billows and weaves its way above them; where it passes it entwines a heavenly presence, and everything is awe!" He writes of "the blowing air of God," the "weaving storm," the "nocturnal scene of the strongly surging awe of the night wind . . . where expression contends with night and sea." He is nonetheless far removed from the sober folly of those ancient and modern commentators who seek to explain this surging Godstorm as a "mere strong wind." And Goethe then, grasping with bold intuition the meaning of the passage in which the dynamic tension of the moment of primordial creation still holds together irreconcilable opposites, fuses together the "surging" and the "brooding" into the "blowing wind that broods above the waves."

ON WORD CHOICE IN
TRANSLATING THE BIBLE[1]:
IN MEMORIAM FRANZ ROSENZWEIG

Martin Buber
(Summer 1930)

The special obligation to create a new version of the Bible, which came alive in our own time and led to our undertaking, resulted from the discovery that the passage of time had largely turned the Bible into a palimpsest. The original traits of the Bible, the original meanings and words, had been overlaid by a familiar abstraction, in origin partly theological and partly literary. What people today ordinarily read when they open "the Book" is so unlike the attentive speaking that is registered there, that we might reasonably prefer to such a sham reception of the text a shoulder-shrugging rejection of it, on the part of those who "just don't know what to do with it." This applies, moreover, not only to reading in translations but also to reading in the original; the Hebrew sounds themselves have lost their immediacy for a reader who is no longer a listener; they are suffused by a voiceless, theologically and literarily determined rhetoric, and are compelled by that rhetoric to speak not the spirit that attained its voice in them but a compromise among the spiritualities of two thousand years. The Hebrew Bible itself is read as a translation—as a bad translation, as a translation into a smoothed-over conceptual language, into what is apparently well known but in reality only familiar. The Bible asks us for a reverent intimacy with its meaning and its sensory concreteness; but that has been replaced by a mix of uncomprehending respect and unthinking familiarity. This pseudo-Bible is the object of the shoulder-shrugging dismissal noted above; and its relation to the real Bible resembles the relation of the murdered God of our time—that is, the familiar and diffuse concept of God—to the living God of reality.

To seek to affect this situation through a new version of the Bible may seem hopeless; and it would in fact be hopeless, if the Bible had already been translated rigorously, and its translation widely disseminated. In that

---

1. Published separately.

case, it would be the textual truth itself and not a paraphrase of it that had ossified; in that case the plasticity, the emotionality, the corporeality of biblical discourse would already have entered western consciousness, and would there have fallen victim to trivialization—a trivialization from which it might be rescued by the new illumination of new religious events, but surely not by one additional rendering into one of the western languages. But that is not the case. Even the most significant translations of the Bible that we possess—the Greek Septuagint, the Latin Vulgate, the German of Luther—do not aim principally at maintaining the original character of the book as manifested in word choice, in syntax, and in rhythmical articulation.[2] They aim rather at transmitting to the translators' actual community—the Jewish diaspora of Hellenism, the early Christian *oikumene*, the faithful adherents of the Reformation—a reliable foundational document. They accordingly carry over the "content" of the text into another language. They do not *a priori* ignore the peculiarities of its constituent elements, of its structure, of its dynamic; but they easily enough sacrifice those peculiarities when stubborn "form" seems to hinder the rendering of "content." It is for them as if genuine tidings, genuine speech, genuine song contained a What easily detached from their How; as if the spirit of the language could be found elsewhere than in its concrete linguistic configuration, and could be delivered to other times and places otherwise than by a faithful and unprejudiced imitation of that configuration; as if the general understanding acquired at the expense of that initial linguistic concreteness would not necessarily entail a general misunderstanding, later if not sooner. The great translators were of course possessed by the inspired insight that God's word must hold for all times and places; they did not see, however, that such an insight does not diminish but rather increases the importance of viewpoint, of There and Then in all their national, personal, corporeal conditionality. Revelation is accomplished in the human body and the human voice, i.e., in *this* body and *this* voice, in the mystery of their uniqueness. The prophet's proclamation consists not only of its symbols and parables, but also of the fundamental sensory concreteness of even the subtlest Hebrew concepts, of the taut stretching in the architecture of the ancient Hebrew sentence, of the Hebrew manner of relating adjacent or even widely separated words through similarity of verbal root or similarity of sound, of the powerful movement of Hebrew rhythm that goes beyond all meter. To understand all this is of course to indicate to the translator a theoretically impossible task; what is special to a language is after all special, and cannot be "reproduced." Imagery differs from one language to another, as do concepts and the means of elaborating them, as do impulses

---

2. See on this also Rosenzweig, "Scripture and Luther."

and motions, passions and music. *Theoretically* speaking, the biblical messages cannot be rendered in their fusion of meaning and sound; but practically speaking, they can. Can, that is, approximately—as approximately as one is allowed by the boundaries of the language one translates into. But the translator must press toward these boundaries again and again—to the real boundaries, that is—and must accept instruction as to what is permitted him and what is not only from the mouths of the supreme watchmen of language. *Theoretically* we cannot even meet the necesssary precondition of translation, namely, the discovery of the fundamental text; for what was primarily meant by a biblical word cannot be known but only inferred, and often inferred only conjecturally—often we have to be content with conjecturing what the "Redactor" may have meant by it, meaning by that term the single consciousness that built the halls of the Bible from the constructs and fragments passed down to it. Yet even this may well satisfy us in our act of approximation; for not in sources but in that consciousness do we in truth find the *Bible*, i.e., what supplements testimonies and documents to join them into books and a book—in, that is, a faith in reception and transmission that fuses diverse times together, in the comprehensive vision of all transformations embodied in the repose of the word.

The relation of our translation to the text is determined by this knowledge of living unity. Analytic scholarship has the right to substitute as it judges appropriate new and apter characters for the ones already written; we however have the right to abide in the givenness of the fixed letter of the text as long as it allows us to do so. Scholarship may dissolve a story, a song, a sentence into genuinely or supposedly independent components; we however may consider and imitate the forged work of the totality—meaning by "imitate" not the stupefying attempt to repeat an established form in different matter, but the striving to create for that form, in the differently ordered language into which we translate, a correspondence or a series of correspondences. The auditory patterns of German can never *reproduce* the auditory forms of Hebrew; but they can, in growing from an analogous impulse and in exercising an analogous effect, *correspond to* them Germanically, can *Germanize* them.

To meet the demands of such a task, the translator must elicit from the letter of the Hebrew text its actual auditory form; he must understand the writtenness of Scripture as for the most part the record of its spokenness— which spokenness, as the actual *reality* of the Bible, is awakened anew wherever an ear biblically hears the word or a mouth biblically speaks it. Prophecy, psalm, and saying were originally born not of the pen but of the tongue; but the same is true of report and law. The holy text is for all uninterrupted antiquity an orally transmitted text—transmitted orally even where it coexists with a highly cultivated secular repository of writing. It is recorded only when its uncorrupted preservation has, despite the mnemonic imprints of its rhythm and the strict stipulations regarding its memorization have become difficult, or when special needs have arisen. But what originates in speaking can live again only in speaking, indeed can only in speaking be purely perceived and received. In Jewish tradition, Scripture is to be recited. The so-called system of accents that accompanies each word of the text furthers a return to its rightful spokenness; even the Hebrew term for "reading" means "to call out." The traditional name of the Bible is "the reading," i.e., "the calling out"; God says to Joshua [1.8] that the book of the Torah is never to depart, not from his eyes, but from "his mouth," that Joshua is to "murmur" in it (that is what the following verse actually means), i.e., to form the intonation patterns in a low voice.

The auditory form of the German translation should then correspond to spokenness thus understood—not for silent reading but for accurate recitation, drawing out the full auditory value. The Germanization of the Bible must also be "called out." Only then will its unfamiliarity not become merely an alienating oddness. But its unfamiliarity is itself necessary, is indeed the one necessity, if, with all our false expertise about the Bible, all our condescending solidarity with it, a translation is to produce an encounter between the Bible and people today. Only a false, superficial, dubious, late-Romantic unfamiliarity could arise from aesthetic or literary reflections—if, say, the diction were to be wholly or even partially determined by taste (no matter whether a taste for archaism or a taste for neologism) and not by the demands of the text, its commanding being-as-it-is, its peculiar powers and intimacies. To create a western equivalent of this, a German equivalent, we have to reach past the present verbal repertory toward the defamiliarized—indeed toward the obsolete and forgotten, if well-attested obsolete words have no synonym and their reintroduction into the language is therefore both legitimate and desirable. Sometimes the translator must venture new formations, if he can find in the established German vocabulary no exact equivalent for a biblical institution or concept; it will in that case depend on the scrupulousness of his linguistic conscience, on the certainty of his linguistic tact, on his whole relation to the laws of the target language—a relation that must be simultaneously venturesome and obedient—whether the new word will be confirmed and assimilated by future generations even if only as a designation for an element of the biblical world. Readers openmindedly looking for the way to the Bible will encounter words of the new version at odds with what they are used to; but then they will seek to pass from those words to the realities that are expressed in them, will consider whether the usual rendering does justice to the special character of these realities, will measure the distance between the two, and will consider how the new rendering holds up in comparison. For such readers the biblical world will in their reading be revealed, sector by sector; its otherness in comparison with much that is familiar will become clear, but so will the importance of our receiving this otherness into the structure of our own life. No doubt the biblical world will seem to such readers in many ways linguistically sharper and more vivid than it did to those who inhabited it; concepts will in the translation be distanced from the familiar, and will accordingly present their concrete fundamental significance more emphatically than they do in the original, in which the concrete, pictorial aspect sounded only as an overtone in the use of a concept, though often very powerfully. But that is precisely why readers who read in earnest will have to face the task of working themselves—living themselves—into the text, a task that will inevitably bear fruit. The same task, moreover, confronts the readers of the original in another guise, when they seek to free the living There and Then—and thereby the corporeality of the biblical spirit—from the verbal conventionality that at once overspreads the reading of any current student of Hebrew, regardless of whether the student's sense of what the words ostensibly mean is derived from a dictionary or from the casual talk of instructional conversation.

Let us look closely at some concepts relating to the sacrificial cult, and to related matters; these permit us to see most clearly how the reality meant by the biblical terms has been attenuated or replaced by other notions. (In what follows I quote for comparison both Luther's version [L] and the scholarly Kautzsch-Bertholet version in the edition of 1922 [K-B].)

The word generally rendered in German by *Opfer* ("offering"), *qorban*, has little to do with the associations the German word evokes. *Opfer* has long since lost its connection with the Latin *offerre* ("to offer," "to present," "to bring before"); it evokes chiefly ideas of renunciation and abandoning. The Indo-European notion of *Opfer* does not presume a being to whom sacrifice is made; *qorban*, on the other hand, is a term of relation, and implies the existence of two persons, in particular two persons one of whom seeks to diminish the distance between himself and the other in approaching it by means of the *qorban*, which he "brings near" the other. *Qorban* is not *Opfer* but *Darnahung* ["nearbringing," "forebringing," "therebringing"]. If we read, say, the story of the Korach's rebellion (Numbers 16), and see the importance to that story of terms of "nearing" and "allowing near," we can measure what effect the resonances of distance and approach have had for the biblical concept of offering.

The case is the same for the terms for the types of offering, e.g., the so-called "burnt-offering," *'olah*, and the so-called "meal-offering," *minhah*; the words have nothing to do with burning or meals. *'Olah* is "the ascending": "that is what ascends in its glowing-embers on the slaughter-site,/ for the whole night until morning," we read in the often misunderstood passage of verbal explanation in Lev. 6:2. *'Olah* is what the man who makes the sacrifice, who brings it forward and sets it aflame, causes to rise toward heaven in smoke, i.e., his "highbringing" or "highgiving." *Minhah* has a disputed etymology; but within the framework of biblical thought, our understanding of which is often aided more by popular etymology than by scholarly, it can be understood as "the brought-in," i.e., the contribution that is brought in or the inbringings; the word always points to a dealing between man and God, or at least to the bringing forward of this dealing by man. It is important in any case that something in the translator's equivalent refer expressly to the *direction* of the sacrificial act.

The offering is offered on the *mizbeah*, the "slaughtersite," so called because slaughtering takes place there. This notion will seem harsh to contemporary readers; but it must remain the central notion of the translator's equivalent for the word, because precisely the "slaughtering of the slaughter-meal" is the heart of the biblical matter. What happens in the Bible is not that slaughter takes place at the altar but that offering is made at the slaughtersite. The scent of offering-smoke is called *reah nihoah*, a recurring idiom almost like a refrain, whose assonance is characteristically so crucial to the imprint it makes on the mind of the hearer that the translator must seek to create an equivalent to it. *Reah* is scent or smell; *nihoah*, however, is a very particular term. It is used *only* of the scent of offering-smoke, and accordingly cannot be rendered by "pleasing." It is connected with the ideas of rest and respose; but "calming," too, would be imprecise, since it would exclude the idea of pleasing. So let us take all the factors together, and we have the *Ruch des Geruhens*.[3]

The Hebrew word *kipper* is ordinarily rendered by the theological terms "expiate" or "atone." Several derivations of the word are possible; but in the biblical sense, as is clear from a precise investigation of all relevant passages, it means "to cover," "to cover over," to "protect." Thus in Exod. 30:12, in the mustering—or rather, from the biblical viewpoint, in the putting-in-order—of the host, all those put in order are to give half a shekel (or half a "weight") of silver as a "covering over" of their lives. That is: during the passage through the desert, they are isolated, and thus in a special way exposed to the risk of a sudden stroke, against which they protect themselves by this holy tax "covering over their lives"—a tax everywhere equal, since the rich "are not to pay-more and the poor are not to pay-less than half a shekel." The tax does not expiate, because there is nothing *to* expiate; the census

---

3. The German means "the scent of *Geruhen*"; *Geruhen* means the action taken by, say, a king: "his majesty *was pleased to* receive the messenger." But it is etymologically connected with *Ruhe*, "rest" or "calm," and echoes *Ruch* as *nihoah* does *reah*. "The scent of assenting" or "the savor of favoring" would get the assonance but not the particular etymological connection. [eds.]

that God commands here cannot, unlike the arbitrary census undertaken by David in 2 Sam. 24, be regarded as "displeasing." The ransom similarly named *kofer* can similarly protect those who pay it in some cases of capital punishment (Exod. 21:30). K-B of course gives here "protection," as if here the idea were different from, say, Lev. 17:11, where we find in fact precisely the same phrase: "to cover over your souls [or lives]." In the latter passage K-B offers "to make expiation for you"; but in both cases the Bible has the same image and the same meaning.

The Hebrew word *negef,* translated above as "stroke," together with the related word *maggefah,* which we translate as "a striking down," are further documents to show the blurring of meaning the usual translations entail. The first is usually translated "plague"; the second, similar but not identical to it, is translated by Lebenfalls[4] as "plague," by K-B variously as "plague," "sudden death," "destruction," and "pestilence." But the word always means the same thing: God *strikes down* the guilty, whether a person or a people, whether directly or indirectly.

The consequences of misunderstanding the character of a Hebrew word can be very extensive. Consider as an example the renderings of the word *qodesh*—for which translations ordinarily give "holy"—and the phrase *qodesh ha-qodashim*—for which Luther gives "the all-holiest" and K-B gives "highly holy." The noun *qodesh* denotes not a static but a dynamic concept, not a condition but a process: the process, that is, of hallowing, of making holy and being made holy (only the article or the possessive suffix can give the word the meaning of "holiness" or "sanctuary"). Moses stands before the Burning Bush not on holy ground but on the ground of hallowing. Aaron in being consecrated a priest is clothed in garments of hallowing and anointed with the oil of hallowing, the Sabbath is a festival of hallowing, and the children of Israel are summoned by God to become a people of hallowing. The presents brought before God are called not "holy gifts" but "forehallowings," the priests' portions are called "outhallowings"; in both terms the dominant concept is the process of ritual exclusion. Hence the priests' portions of the offerings are called "outhallowings of forehallowings"; they should not, therefore, be characterized as "highly holy" or "all holy." Exod. 30:29 says of the consecration of the objects in the sanctuary, "you are to hallow [*qiddashta*] them [not, with K-B, "you are to consecrate them thus"] that they may become a means of hallowing for the forehallowings." Not "the all holiest" and not "highly holy," but simply objects that separate out all that touches them for ritual exclusion, as the remainder of the verse explains; "whatever touches them is made holy [*yiqdash*, not "consecrated" as in Luther, and not "becomes the possession of holiness," as in

---

4. A scholar we have not been able to identify [eds.].

K-B, which is merely a paraphrase]." The innermost part of the sanctuary itself is not "all-holiest" but that from which, i.e., from the cover above the shrine there that bears the Cherubim, everything in the sanctuary receives its becoming holy: "the hallowing of the holinesses."

The opposite of *qodesh* is *ḥol*. It means neither Luther's "unholy" nor K-B's "not-holy," both of which are, unlike the Hebrew, negative characterizations. Rather it means "the surrendered," i.e., what has been surrendered to ordinary use rather than been subjected to ritual exclusion. The first use of a vineyard after the years of obligatory consecration following its planting is accordingly called an "abandoning" or a surrendering of it. Similarly, *ṭameiʾ*, the opposite of *ṭahor*, "pure," is not to be rendered by "impure" but by a positive concept, for which we give "stained." "Stain" is not simply an absence of purity but a force in action, like a miasma.

The Pentateuch most often calls the movable sanctuary of the desert wandering *ohel moʿed*. *Ohel* is unambiguously "tent," "dwelling," but the second word has over a long time been rendered in various ways. The Septuagint gives the clearly wrong "of witness." Jerome in his turn gives the equally wrong "of the covenant." Luther has "tabernacle of the foundation," melodious but neither clear nor warranted. Modern biblical scholarship finally comes near to the meaning, with "tent of revelation" (K-B). But even this rendering does not really grasp the meaning. The Hebrew word meaning "to become apparent," "to be revealed," is *niglah*, which K-B accordingly in, say, Gen. 35:7 or Deut. 29:29 translates as "reveal." The basis of *moʿed*, on the other hand, is the reflexive form of the verb *yaʿad*. When used of more than one person, *yaʿad* means an encounter of those persons at a determined place; when used of a single person—and in the Bible the only single person the word is applied to is God—it means to be present for an encounter at a determined place (but not at a determined time). "Where I shall go to present myself to you [either plural or singular]" is God's recurring declaration, by which the biblical meaning of *moʿed* is explained. (This biblical intention is altogether misunderstood by the ancient translators. The Septuagint gives "where I make myself known to you"; Jerome, still worse, gives "where I shall speak to you." Luther comes closer to the intention, but his "from which place I shall bear witness to you" is also a misunderstanding.) *Ohel moʿed* is then the tent of divine presentation, the Tent of Presence. But this is only a piece, although an important piece, of the translational problem here; the depth and complexity of that problem become apparent only if we juxtapose to *ohel moʿed* the other epithet of the movable sanctuary, namely *ohel* (or sometimes *mishkan*, "dwelling") *haʿedut*. This second epithet is similar to the first but also different from it; it too occurs often and without any nuanced variation in its general meaning. By the ancient translators this is rendered by "tent [or "dwelling"] of witness"; it is, then, treated as if *mo'ed* and *'edut* were the same. But they are so little the same that modern philologists mostly attribute them to different roots. For reasons I cannot articulate here, I believe that we can trace beneath these two roots a single root in common, encompassing the whole semantic territory of being-present, becoming-present, being-made-present, remaining-present. (Thus *'edah*, which we had no choice but to translate as "community," means by etymology "the generation of the people *present* at a given occasion.") *'Edut* is the making-present, is what can make something present to someone, is what is supposed to make it always present anew; in our context, the tablets of the covenant are given this name because they have received revelation as writing inscribed upon them, and are to make that revelation "present" to all later generations not themselves present for it. Hence they are preserved in the inmost region of the tent, in the "ark of the covenant," whose upper part, the "cover" with the two Cherubim, is the place where God "presents" himself to the people: "before the presentation into the Tent of Presence, where I will go to present myself to you" (Exod. 30:36; similarly Num. 17:19). (The cover with the cherubim is *kapporet*, related by root to the expiating "covering over," *kipper*; it is significantly juxtaposed to that word once, in the passage that deals with the so-called Day of Atonement, *yom ha-kippurim*, i.e., the day of covering over, Lev. 3:15ff.) It has been one of the strongest confirmations of our method that we have been able to reproduce such verbal patterns in both their breadth of manifestation and in their unity.

This same verbal pattern furnishes also a striking example of the other question to be asked about word choice. We have so far discussed what I would call *absolute* word choice; let us now add to that the question of *relative* word choice. Absolute word choice is aimed at grasping the meaning of the individual word, at liberating its original concreteness from the encrustation of ordinary abstraction. Relative word choice is aimed at preserving the biblically intended relation between two or more words related by their roots, or sometimes merely by their sounds. I have already shown how important "paronomasia" is for biblical style, i.e., the use of several words of similar construction or sound in sequence, or at any rate in so close a succession that when we encounter the second or the third occurrence in the series we still hear the sound or echo of the first. Such words are thereby removed from their immediate environment and put in a special relation; in that relation, something expressed in the text is, as it were, strengthened in its acoustical effect and made more striking in its impression. Sometimes, indeed, something is expressed in this way that the text wishes to express *only* in this way. In the Bible, then, alliteration and assonance, and to a still greater degree repetitions of words, phrases, and sentences cannot be understood in aesthetic terms alone; rather such patterns belong for the most part to the matter and character of the biblical message itself, and rendering them rightly is one of the central tasks of the translation. Extremely important connections are being made when we attempt within a passage—and sometimes within a larger portion, within a whole book, within a sequence of books—to reproduce a single Hebrew root with a single German one.

Mo'ed also means "set-time." At first it means this only in the sense of the annual return of the same day or days; its regular return is regarded from the standpoint of its present occurrence as a continually recurring presence. Then it means this in the sense of the annual return of the festivals. In the end, however, under the influence of the verbal content, the idea of encounter is peculiarly linked to the concept of the holiday encounters of the people with one another, and of the people with God. These two nuances of meaning can occur together (Lev. 23:4):

> These are the meeting-times [*mo 'adei*; Luther, "festivals"; K- B, "festival
>   times"] for HIM,
> callings-out of holiness [*miqra'ei qodesh*; Luther, "sacred festivals"; K-B,
>   "assemblies at the sanctuary],
> that you shall call out [*tiqre'u*; Luther, "proclaim"; K-B, rightly, "call out,"
>   but the word that K-B translate with "assemblies" is the same verb!],
> at their set-time [*be-mo'adam*; Luther, "when you come together"; K-B,
>   "at their determined time"].

Ḥag, the actual word for festival, undergoes an altogether different shift in meaning; its original concrete meaning—"round-dance," and then "festive assemblies" (or, as a verb, "to assemble the festive assemblies")—gradually fades, and the translator has to reproduce this blurring of meaning; similarly the translator must throughout the Pentateuch render *hitpallel*, usually rendered consistently by "pray," with the more specific and evidently more ancient meaning of "stake something" (i.e., stake one's own person with God for someone with whom God is angry). *Ḥodesh*, on the other hand, means "new moon" and "renewal" generally; it is never to be rendered "month," since it indicates not the temporal interval as such but either the whole sequence of the new moon or the new moon as the beginning of that sequence, and because the dynamic of this concept is indispensable to the psychology of biblical temporalization. Still more important is preserving the verbal dynamicism in Hebrew terms like *shabbat* and *pessah*. These are normally left untranslated, but must not be. *Pessah* must not become a technical term; rather its living associations must remain vivid, and the holiday remain the festival of remembering the great passing or leaping over (Exod. 12:13). A German Bible must also absolutely deliver *shabbat* from the rigidity of "Sabbath" and restore it to the vitality of *Feier* and *Feiern*[5]—indeed the word in some places, e.g., Lev. 23:15, indicates not the weekly day of rest but another festival day altogether—must restore it, that is, to that conception in which people in the *Feier* they celebrate in resting from the "work" they have "made" in the week understand themselves as imitating God, who on the seventh day of the week of creation also celebrated in resting from the "work" that he had "made." It follows that we should reject the usual distinction between God's "works" in the creation story and humans' "work" or "labor" in the Sabbath laws, as well as that between the divine "making" in the Creation story and the human "doing" of the Sabbath laws. Rather we must use the same words for both, as the original does—except in the anomalous cases where the Sabbath commandments do not refer to the creation.

The seventh year, the year of *shemiṭṭah*, is wrongly called the "Year of Remission"; during it, debts are not remitted but rather may not be exacted; they are to be "eased" or "loosed," and *shemiṭṭah* is "easing" or "loosing." The fiftieth year, the year of Jubilee, is wrongly called "the sounding year," and would have to be called the year of the ram, or of the ram's horn, if in fact *yobel* originally meant that animal. But despite Phoenician parallels and Talmudic tradition, the biblical usage does not suggest that meaning; rams are never called by that name. Rather the word always—always, that is, except, precisely, in the laws for the Year of Jubilee, where the charged pathos with which the word is linked speaks still more strongly against linking it with a ram—denotes a special sort of horn or horn sound. The etymology, then, rather evokes the thought that these things are called by this name because it was their purpose to assemble and guide a host of people; the ram, then, might be called by this name in its capacity of leader of flocks. But Lev. 25:10ff. makes clear enough what idea biblical consciousness associated with the Jubilee Year: it is the year that leads the return, that leads home and brings home, that restores impoverished original owners of land to their original land and people fallen into bondage to their families: "a homebringing let it be for you,/ when you return,/ each to his holding,/ each to his clan/ shall you return." The horn of jubilee calls and fetches us home.

Two words deriving from different roots, like *tzedeq* and *mishpaṭ*, are not to be translated by two words deriving from similar roots, e.g., "justice" and "jurisprudence." This is true on theoretical grounds, but also because in that case the distinction of meaning between such important concepts would be lost. *Mishpaṭ* is from *shafaṭ*, i.e., "to judge." It covers areas of

---

5. The German verb *feiern*, and the associated noun *Feier*, can denote both "celebration" and "cessation" [eds.].

jurisprudence, of legal judgment, of law and legality. *Tzedeq* is the objectively accurate expression of judgment, the "verdict."[6] It denotes the concordance of an utterance or an action with the postulated reality, denotes
"truth" and "truthfulness." *Tzedaqah* is the manifestation of that concordance in the personal conduct of life: "verification."[7] *Tzaddiq* is the man
living in that concordance, "the verified-one." *Hatzdeq* is to reveal someone
in the truth of his person or action, is to "verify" him.[8] On the other hand:
emet and *emunah* in the Bible almost never indicate truth in this absolute
sense, but rather the attitude and certitude of confidence between one
being and another—"troth" and "trust." *Emet* is more objective, *emunah*
more subjective, so that the verb *aman* is almost always to be understood
not as "to believe" (a splendid word but theologically loaded) but as "to
trust."

To translate *paqad* as "to visit" or "provide for" is most often misleading.
Paqad is the activity of accounting and recounting, of taking into account,
of giving an account of—hence also God's authority that orders human
fate, his supplying in need, his deliverance from oppression, but also his
taskmasterly activity of balancing deed and consequence. Sarah becomes
pregnant in old age because God has taken account of her, not because he
"visited" her (Gen. 21:1; Luther and K-B). God "counts out" deliverance for
Israel in Egyptian bondage: e.g., Gen. 50:24ff., where K-B gives "God will
accept of you," or Exod. 3:16, where K-B gives "I attend carefully," though
this is precisely the same divine action previously recounted in Genesis. The
distortion of meaning is especially disastrous in the passages where God
proclaims his punitive "calling-to-account" (Exod. 20:5 and 34:7, Num.
14:18). These much discussed passages—some time ago an apologist for
Judaism went so far as to seek license from the scholars of the Roman curia
to claim that *paqad* here meant not "visit" but "take thought for"—are after
all almost identical in diction, yet both the Septuagint and the Vulgate have
chosen to render the one word *poqed* with two different ones; even K-B gives
for the one phrase "who visits the guilt of the fathers upon the children,"
and for the other "avenges fathers' guilt on children." But in fact the translation should read (I choose the third, most complete passage), "but clear-
of-punishment he does not clear him, calling to account the fathers' sin for
them (the dative should be supplied to clarify the sense[9]) on sons and sons'

6. German *Wahrspruch.* Both *Wahrspruch* and "verdict" etymologically mean "true-saying,"
but German readers can see this in the German word, whereas English readers for the most
part cannot see it in the English, whose root is Latin [eds.].

7. German *Bewährung;* see previous note [eds.].

8. German *bewahrheiten;* see previous note [eds.].

9. "For them" is Buber's, as is the claim that the interpolation clarifies the meaning. Many
readers of the Hebrew text would argue that the interpolation does not clarify the meaning so
much as it blurs and softens it [eds.].

sons, to the third and fourth member," i.e., God makes sinners feel how their sons and grandsons must suffer from their transgression precisely as long as the original transgressors are alive. (There is no thought here of a punishment counted up for the posterity of the sinner after the sinner's death.)

A few more examples of wrong associations evoked by imprecise renderings: *torah* is not "law" but always "instruction" or "teaching"; *nabi'* is not "prophet." Despite the meaning of the Greek word from which it derives[10] (a meaning quite close to that of the Hebrew word), "prophet" all too easily evokes the common notion of "prophesying," i.e., predicting. A *nabi'* is properly "proclaimer," one who proclaims or expresses the divine word spoken to him, the "mouth" of God. *Mal'akh* is not "angel," is not, that is, a being of a particular sort, concerning whom one knows at least that there exists such a sort of being, but in general (and in accord with the Greek *angelos* from which "angel" comes) a messenger, who exists for our biblical sense only in his message, and whose nature *aggadah* rightly indicates in speaking of his emerging from fire and afterwards returning to it—ultimately the word *mal'akh* so precisely overlaps, at least in the historical portions of the Bible, God's various interventions into human affairs that the messenger can speak God's "I" just as God can at any point take up the messenger's speech in his own person.

In these cases we can get at the biblical intention by returning to the simple meanings of the words. But a word like *kabod*—"honor" when used of people, "glory" when used of God—reveals the insurmountable obstacles to even the most scrupulous translator's verbal choices. No western equivalent exists for the actual meaning of this Semitic word. It means the "force," the "weight," the substance and power of a being—not, however, *in se*, but in manifestation, in radiating out, in *appearing*. God's *kabod* should rather be called his "appearing" than his "majesty,"[11] but only to the extent that the reader can take the word "appearing" concretely enough and visually enough, can understand it as the manifestation of invisible *majestas*, its *becoming-apparent*—glory, but glory as the radiation of "force." Presuming, or at least appealing to, this immediacy of linguistic perception in the reader, the translator may well in dealing with *ekkabed* or *ikkabedah* in passages like Exod. 14:4 and 14:17f. and Lev. 10:3 want to reject Luther's "I will get me honor upon Pharaoh" and "I will be glorified" (as well as K-B's "I will

10. The Greek *prophêtês* means chiefly someone who speaks for a god and interprets that god's will to human beings; the fact that such speaking and interpreting sometimes involves making assertions about the future is secondary [eds.].

11. German *Herrlichkeit*, etymologically "lordliness." Buber notes in parentheses here that one of the problems with *Herrlichkeit* is that it often gets used in close proximity to *Herr*, "lord," though the Hebrew words these two German terms translate are unrelated [eds.].

show myself superior" and "I will glorify myself"), and in their place, renewing a good old German word, have God say, "Ich erscheinige mich."[12]

More immediately accessible to German than the idea of God's *kabod* is the idea of God's *ruah*, which in the beginning of creation hovers above the face of the waters, spreading its wings as the eagle spreads its wings above its children in their nest. ("Hover," however, does not by itself render the Hebrew *merahefet*, because, unlike the Hebrew word, "hover" does not necessarily evoke the image of a bird, in particular a bird holding steady in the air with gently beating wings; and it is important also here to consider the significant assonance.) Previously people were satisfied with opting for one of the two fundamental meanings of *ruah*, namely, "wind" or "spirit." Most often the second was chosen, in Luther's case after a severe struggle to ascertain the right meaning. But clearly Luther too postulated that the meaning was to be found in one of the two possibilities, not in a third meaning encompassing them both. In this passage, however, *ruah* denotes not one of the two meanings but both together and undivided: the primordial surging from God, which takes on a natural form in "wind," a psychological form in "spirit." In the Greek *pneuma* this connection of the primordially spiritual with the primordially sensory lives on, though not so strongly as in *ruah* because *pneuma* does not so intimately contain the meaning "wind"; the same meaning can be felt still more weakly in the Latin *spiritus*. In the German *Geist*, that meaning was however so strong before Luther's time that writers, e.g., Meister Eckhart, could translate the phrase in Jesus' conversation with Nicodemus, *to pneuma pnei*, not, with Luther, "the wind blows where it will," but "the spirit spiritizes where it will."[13] The dynamic character of the word *Geist*, its connection with *Gischt* ("foam") was in the German middle ages still clear. By Luther's time, however, *Geist* had nearly been transformed from a process to an object. In the Bible, *ruah* always denotes a process; even where we are compelled to translate it by *Geist*, the reader should think rather of a *Geist*-ing taking place than of a fixed spiritual entity. But also, again and again—and most strikingly in the story of God's pouring out of *Geist* upon the elders and the sending out from God of the quail-blowing wind (Numbers 11), where both meanings of the word are significantly and intentionally juxtaposed—the Bible attempts on the basis of the unity of the word to imprint upon our thought the original unity of the concept. A word of this sort, with a "natural" meaning and a "spiritual"

---

12. Grimm does not cite this "good old German word"; an English approximation of it would be, "I beshow myself" [eds.].

13. Luther in the third chapter of John translates *pneuma* in v. 6 with "spirit," in the first half of v. 8 with "wind," and in the second half of the same verse with "spirit." The result is that the unifying sense of the passage—namely, the ontological equivalence between the one reborn from *pneuma* and *pneuma* itself, and the consequence that we can therefore know of neither entity where it comes from or where it is going to—is disrupted.

meaning, is not for us to split unbridgeably into two, as most translations do. Rather we must consider that the spiritual meaning is falsified when it loses its connection with concrete physicality. Here, with *ruaḥ*, the bridge between the two meanings is supplied for us precisely through the primordial surging at the beginning of creation, by the "rushing of God." Our rendering speaks of *Geistbraus* ("spiritsurge"), not of *Geist* ("spirit"); *ruaḥ* appears as the "Godstorm," seizing the human being and clothing itself with him (Judg. 6:34 is to be similarly understood, though later the concept blurs), transforming him, animating him. Correspondingly, our rendering speaks of "windsurge" and not of "wind," in which case we note of the text that it seeks to make the divine origin of the wind inwardly felt.

The difficulty of translation rises to the level of paradox when the question is how to render the divine epithets. For the tetragrammaton, the name YHWH, I refer the reader to Rosenzweig's important essay "The Eternal."[14] That name alone among the divine epithets in the Bible is entirely a name and not a concept; but it is a name in which biblical consciousness perceives a meaning, or rather *the* meaning, the meaning that is disclosed in revelation, in the Burning Bush. God says *ehyeh*, which expresses in the first person what the name conceals in the third, and thereby makes no theological statement about his being *in se*, or his immutability, or his eternality, but rather says to his creature what it is necessary for it to know: that he is there with it, is present to it, but in continually new and never predictable forms, in the forms appropriate to the situations in which his creature is found, and that what is important is simply to recognize him again and again in whatever form he takes. The name is thus both secret and revealed; it is no longer exempt from revelation, but its being revealed does not deprive it of its mystery. It cannot, however, even though it has been disclosed, be rendered by an idea. The Septuagint, the Vulgate, and Luther all render it "the Lord," and thus replace the reality with a fiction. Calvin and Mendelssohn render it "the Eternal," and thus misread the disclosure. The scholarly translations, offering only a transcription (and a highly questionable one), ignore it, and thereby transform the name of God into a name of idols. The name might be rendered "the one-who-is-there," or "the-one-who-is-present," and such a rendering would indeed be founded on a right understanding of the disclosure; but it would also betray that disclosure, in that the certainty that those who trust in revelation feel welling up from every naming of the name would be impaired by a rigid conceptual knowledge capable of grasping in the disclosure only the idea of constancy—the *ehyeh*: I shall be there—but not the idea of continual and unpredictable renewal—the *asher ehyeh*: as whoever I shall be. We

---

14. See below, "'The Eternal': Mendelssohn and the Name of God."

had, therefore, to find in our western language an equivalent that would for the hearing reader create a feeling similar to the certainty issuing from the name, would, that is, not express God's being-with-me, being-with-you, being-with-us conceptually but would embody it in full presence. That is what is done in our translation by the pronouns: the I and MY when God is speaking; the YOU and YOUR when God is spoken to; the HE and HIS when God is spoken of. (Rendering the "abbreviated form" of the name, the YAH, presented a special difficulty; we decided to use a typographically more ordinary "he" and "you," but to precede these where appropriate with an "oh," in order to preserve the original exclamatory character of that epithet, which occurs chiefly in hymns and songs.)

The difficulty with *El* and *Elohim* is of a different sort. These two terms ought not both to be translated "God," as they usually are; but it is impossible to establish a *fixed* distinction between them. It would seem plausible from the nature of the words *in se* to translate *El* with "God" and *Elohim*, which is actually a plural, with "godhead." In fact, however, *Elohim* became more of a name, more of an epithet for the one God than did *El*; to *El* there is rather attached the general idea of "power" and "powers," though not so that we could translate it as "power" and thereby sever it from the verbal root "God." (I cannot here discuss the vexed question of the etymological relation between the two words; it is clear at least that in biblical consciousness they are associated.) In general, then, *Elohim* is to be translated as "God," *El* variously as "God in might," "God the lord," "divinity," "God our shield"—the nuance of the word varies, and the rendering of it has to take into consideration the environment in which it appears. (There are, however, passages, e.g., Balaam's speeches, where the relation between the two terms is precisely the reverse.) "God," by the way, has to be a component of the translation where the verbal component *el* is understood as such by popular etymology. Thus with *elah*, where the component denotes a holy tree, we give "God-ash." *Elil* means a nothingness, a nothing, but above all, precisely, the nothingness of an idol; and because that epithet must resonate among other things of God, the *elilim* become in our translation "godnothings."

It will not do, then, to translate the tetragrammatic name of God into a concept of God. But it is equally unacceptable to transform concepts like *ba'al* and *molekh* into names. Of *molekh* the old translations make an idol named Moloch. But *molekh* is in fact only a euphemistic revocalization, made according to the pattern of the word *boshet*, "shame," of the word *melekh*, i.e., "king";[15] it denotes the idea common to numerous Semitic

15. I discuss Eissfeldt's recent arguments against this position in the second edition of my *Kingship of God*.

tribes of a kingship of the tribal god, to whom one prays for the increase of the tribe and to whom one therefore brings offerings of children as payment in kind. *Baʿal* too is not a proper name; it indicates the possessor, the "master" of an object or being. The possession or mastery in question is never one-sided but always reciprocal. A man is the *baʿal* of his wife, who is *beʿulah*, matrimonially mastered, by him; he is not, however, her lord, even if she calls him that. As an epithet of God, *baʿal* means the god of a place (the name of which place is always juxtaposed to the word *baʿal*): an oasis, a mountainous region, a city.[16] In particular it means a god for whom, unlike the *molekh*, it is essential to be allied to a goddess; the marriage between the local god of heaven and the local goddess of earth, the fructifying power of the rain together with the bearing and generating powers of the soil maintain and renew the fertility of the place. As offerings of children are brought to the *molekh*, so sexual rituals are performed for the *baʿal* and his consort. The most severe defection of the people, the defection the prophets warn of with the greatest horror and speak of as the greatest abomination, is precisely to serve the god of the patriarchs *as a molekh*, by offering him children—Jer. 32:35, "as I have not commanded them"—or *as a baʿal*, by performing sexual rituals for him—Hos. 2:18, "on that day you will call me, My Husband! and will not any more call me, My Master [*baʿali*]!" We accordingly translate the epithet *baʿal* as "overmaster" (to distinguish it from human "masters"), and the epithet *melekh* as "shamking" when accompanied by the euphemistic vocalization, as "overking" when not.

Our work illuminates the palimpsest; it gets beneath the waxen surface upon which nations have inscribed the "Bible" of their religious needs and expressive forms, and the original text appears. The great work of the human mind and spirit inscribed upon the waxen surface is named *history*; but the name of the original text is *the book*. To the former belongs the honor of having gathered humanity around the book; to the latter, however, belongs the right, in a late and necessarily reflective moment of that history, to be discovered and contemplated by that humanity. It will be harder to live with the book than to live with history; the book will not conceal from us that it is as contradictory and vexatious as the world itself. But even its contradictions and vexations have something to teach us.

---

16. Compare with Baudissin's concept of baʿal as a tribal god (in his great, posthumous *Kyrios als Gottesname* ["Kyrios as a Divine Name"]), the third section of my *Kingship of God*.

ON TRANSLATING THE PRAISINGS[1]

Martin Buber
(1935)

The translator of the Bible is presented by the form and style of the Praisings with several new tasks; we have then an occasion for presenting the reader with information on certain important points.

The text here being translated is the traditional Masoretic text. The inevitable task of the translator is to grasp this text. To that text is attributed a solid stability in comparison with which even the most tempting conjecture must seem arbitrary. Since there simply is no reliable method of getting "behind" the text to a "more original" reading, the rendering that *represents* the original—unlike commentaries, which brightly adorn it—must preserve and transmit what is in it. Only in the rare borderline cases, where meaning and continuity are severely vitiated but can be remedied by a small emendation of the text, will the translator consider himself authorized and obligated to adopt that alteration, in consequence of the special responsibility of his office.

This attempt to preserve the Masoretic text is based on the view that we cannot reach behind what is already there without replacing an actuality by numerous and contradictory possibilities; that we have to try to understand what the "Redactor," the person responsible for the shape of the text, meant by the given reading; that we have to try to understand this final consciousness, since we cannot really find our way to any earlier one. The same view bears on the word choice in this translation, a translation that has set itself the goal of translating not the Bible as national literature but the Bible

---

1. First printed as a supplement to the *Buch der Preisungen* ["Book of Praisings"] (vol. xiv of *Die Schrift*); here somewhat abridged.

Buber's note does not explain that what he calls the *Buch der Preisungen* ("Book of Praisings") refers to what is ordinarily called the Book of Psalms. Buber chooses this term because *Preisungen* ("Praisings") renders the etymological sense of the Hebrew word *tehillim*, traditionally translated by the etymologically opaque word *Psalmen* ("Psalms") [eds.].

itself, a translation whose business is the comprehension of a whole that has become a genuine unity—regardless of how many and how diverse pieces it has grown from.

The Bible seeks to be read as One Book, so that no one of its parts remains self-contained; rather every part is held open to every other. The Bible seeks to be present as One Book for its readers so intensely that in reading or reciting an important passage they recall all the passages connected to it, and in particular those connected to it by linguistic identity, resemblance, or affinity; so intensely that all these passages illuminate and explain one another, that they cohere into a unity of meaning, into a theological doctrine not taught explicitly but immanent in the text and emerging from its connections and correspondences. These linkages are not introduced by interpretation *ex post facto*; rather the canonical text came into being under the influence of precisely this principle, and we can legitimately presume that this principle was a factor in the choice of what the canonical text was to include and of which versions were to go into it. But clearly the same principle controls even the composition of individual portions. The repetition of homonymous or near homonymous words and word sequences within a passage, within a book, within a sequence of books exercises a quiet power that nonetheless overwhelms the reader prepared to hear. To consider in this light the linguistic connections between, say, the Prophets and the Pentateuch, between the Psalms and the Pentateuch, between the Psalms and the Prophets is to perceive anew the Bible's powerfully comprehensive vision.

I have elsewhere[2] adduced characteristic examples of conscious repetitions. The structure and meaning of many Psalms become clear only on the basis of such repetitions. But the recurrence of fundamental words *without* any particular intention is equally subject to this same objective principle of the interrelatedness of diverse passages. Fundamental positive words like *ḥesed, tzedeq, emet,* fundamental negative words like *aven* or *shav'* do not reveal their breadth and depth of meaning in a single passage; rather the passages supplement and support one another. Messages come perpetually surging from between them, and the reader possessed of an integral biblical memory reads the individual sequence not in itself but as enmeshed in the full abundance of all sequences together. The latent theology of the Bible exerts a direct effect where the content of individual fundamental terms is thus revealed in diverse sentences, diverse genres, diverse levels of discourse as the same. No doubt the sentence and not the word is the natural unit of living speech, and the word in comparison emerges only as the

---

2. See also "People Today and the Jewish Bible," "The Language of *Botschaft*," "*Leitwort* Style in Pentateuch Narrative," "*Leitwort* and Discourse Type."

product of an analysis; but the biblical sentence must be understood biblically, i.e., in the atmosphere produced by the recurrence of the fundamental words. Only the fact that these words lead their own strongly influential
life can make comprehensible the continuity of the book of Psalms, or artistic configurations like the litany-like Psalm 119.

The translator is assigned the task of making this inner link visible. The
translator knows the power of indolence, of casualness, of superficial reading in Hebrew and German alike; he knows how easily lifelong readers of
the Bible fall victim to those powers; he must summon all his forces to
counter them. It follows that where necessary and appropriate he will
choose the pregnant, striking word, the word that when it recurs is immediately recognized; he will not shun an unusual word when the language
freely offers it from one of its forgotten chambers. It follows that where necessary and appropriate he will reproduce a single Hebrew word-family by a
single German one, not one by many or many by one. "Where necessary,"
since with words given little or no mental emphasis, this principle may be
eased or annulled—to the extent, that is, that the task common to all translators is not at issue, namely, to keep synonyms sharply differentiated in
meaning rather than jumbling them all together.[3] And "where appropriate," since often the special conditions of a passage will impose the obligation to treat it as an exception. Every translator is subject to two laws, which
seem on occasion to contradict each other: the law of the one language and
the law of the other. Translators of the Bible are subject to a second pair of
laws: the law speaking from the peculiar claim of the individual passage and
the law speaking from the biblical totality. The two former laws, to be sure,
are reconciled, indeed are brought into alliance, by the fact that languages
exist only provisionally, whereas in the last analysis there is only the one language of *Geist*, "that simple, universal language" (Goethe).[4] The conflict
between the claims of the sentence and the claims of the book, however, is
overcome again and again by the fact that both sentence and book draw
their meaning from the single dialogic encounter between them, which in
the one case concerns the human person and the particular moment, in
the other the people and the age—the people incorporating the
autonomous person, the age incorporating the autonomous moment.
What the translator is inclined on a given occasion to see as a compromise
can in fact derive from something else than his human frailty.

Such a particular right vis-à-vis the whole can accrue also to the individual biblical book or group of books, so that within such a unit certain words

---

3. This axiom the translators of the Old Testament neglect even today; even so important a
translation of the Psalms as Gunkel's renders four different Hebrew roots by "scorn," and five
by "cry."

4. From "Zwo biblische Fragen" ("Two Biblical Questions") [eds.].

may and must be translated otherwise than in other units—because the manner and style of this unit of the Bible require that, because, say, this or that word in this unit has become more abstract, or because, precisely, it is by means of a variation from the ordinary rendering that we can achieve in the individual book a single, unified meaning with its own specific significance. In every case we ask about what will produce the higher value for the intention of the rendering, and make our decision accordingly.

I want here to show first, in connection with the five fundamental words previously mentioned, the strict method, then the looser method in connection with a few other examples.

Of the five words, the three positive ones are translated as uniformly in the *Praisings* as in previous books, the two negative ones still more so.

Ḥesed, tzedeq, and *emet* are central concepts of biblical theology; they celebrate divine virtues, and portray them for imitation to those who are to go "in God's ways." All three are concepts of concordance and trustworthiness. *Ḥesed* is trustworthiness between beings, especially trustworthiness in the covenantal relation between the liege lord and his vassals, above all the covenantal fidelity of the lord who sustains and protects his servants, and so also that of the servants faithfully committed to their lord. The word corresponding to this notion of reciprocity is *hold* ["gracious"]: both the adjective and the noun, *Huld* ["grace"], originally indicate also fidelity from below to above ("to be gracious and watchful for the lord, in sincerity of heart," says Niebuhr[5]). In middle high German, *Holde* was a vassal, and that aspect of the concept is preserved in *huldig* ["showing homage"]. There is also an independent aesthetic aspect to the word, required by Isa. 40:6; that is supplied by German *Holdheit* ["gracefulness"]. In the Psalms, God's *ḥasidim* are his *Holde,* his faithful followers. *Tzedeq* is the broader and more manifold conception; it indicates the trustworthiness of an action in relation both to outer and inner states of affairs. In relation to an outer state of affairs in authorizing it, creating room for it, granting its rights; in relation to an inner in realizing it, in bringing it out of the soul and into the world. The only German root adequate to both meanings—*recht* ["right"], equivalent to the Hebrew root *shafaṭ,* accounts only for the first—is *wahr* ["true," "veritable"]: *Wahrheit* ["truth"], *Wahrhaftigkeit* ["truthfulness"], *Bewahrheitung* ["verification"] (of the innocent in trial), *Wahrspruch* ["verdict"], *Wahrbrauch* ["fair dealing"] (the usage performed with honest intention), *Bewährung* ["verification"] lay out the range of the concept. *Emet,* finally, indicates trustworthiness generally, innermost trustworthiness included; like the associated *emunah,* it can only be grasped by the root *trau* ["trust"]; *emet* is essentially *Treue* ["fidelity" "troth"], and *emunah* often

---

5. Probably but not certainly Barthold Niebuhr (1776-1831), classical historian [eds.].

occurs so near to it that it cannot then be translated by *Vertrauen* ["putting trust"], but rather, anomalously (I tried for some time to resist this, but failed) by the same word *Treue*.

For these three positive concepts I had in translating the Psalms simply to maintain the previously established regularity of the rendering. The two negative terms, however, had to be dealt with more strictly here than elsewhere. In the case of *aven* the reason is evident. We do not, perhaps, presume with Mowinckel[6] that the word indicates black magic; but we have to acknowledge the appalling force the word has here. It indicates evil as a power, denoting most often the activity of evil, but sometimes also the enduring of that activity. I know no word as adequate here as *Harm* ["hurt"]. In other parts of the Bible the translation of the Hebrew term has been irregular; but here it must be uniform, in order to make clear, from the confluence of all pertinent passages together, the envisioned power of evil in its action and in the suffering its action creates.

The uniformity necessary in the rendering of *shav²* has a qualitatively different reason, based on the relation of the text to another biblical book. *Shav²* is "the fictitious"—and unlike, for example, *hebel*, "vapor" or "trifle," *shav²* means in particular the fictitious thing that is credited with reality, which accordingly can become a counter-reality or counter-divinity. Words like "vain," "empty," "false" are not strong enough to denote this vast power of idols; the only word in German capable of that is *Wahn* ["delusion," "madness"]. Hence we render the central *shav²* passage, namely the Decalogue, as follows: "you are not to take up the name of HIM your God to a delusion" (Exod. 20:7). (Not "you are not to speak the name irresponsibly": *nassa²* without *qol* can mean "take up" but not "speak out"). That is: do not give a puffed-up fiction the name of the highest reality. This passage concerns *shav²* in relation to God; soon after it (Exod. 23:1) comes a passage using the same verb concerning *shav²* in relation to other people:[7] "you are not to take up a delusive rumor." *Shav²* pertains not only to those who speak on the basis of delusion but also to those who speak or act toward the goal of delusion; not only those who sustain delusion but also those who create it. In the Psalms, the meaning of *shav²* as the suggestiveness of the fictitious, the sacrilegious playing on the delusion created in others (or about to be created in them), false or delusive play, occurs in 12:3, 26:4, 41:7, and 144:8 and 11. But the Decalogue usage also occurs twice in Psalms, and these occurrences are, with the exception of the passages of the Pentateuch

---

6. Sigmund Olaf Plytt Mowinckel (1884-1965), Norwegian biblical scholar [eds.].

7. A corresponding passage has been incorporated into the Deuteronomy version of the Decalogue (5:18); the *sheqer* of the Exodus version is replaced by *shav²*, clearly to supplement here also the utterance concerning *shav²* in relation to God with an utterance concerning it in relation to other human beings.

discussed previously, the only occurrences in the Bible of the phrase *nassa'
la-shav'*. In one, 139:20, it is said of "God's adversaries" that they "talk about
him in their cabals," and "lift it," i.e., their talk, "up to delusion." In the
other, praise is given to "the man pure of heart," who "has not lifted up his
soul to delusion," i.e., who has not surrendered his soul to this fiction of vast
power. (Hence the impossibility of the usual renderings "express," "speak
forth.") These two passages must be seen—and heard—in combination
with the statement of the Decalogue. Something of their pathos is diffused
into all the psalm-verses in which *shav'* occurs, and a rendering of the text
must retain that pathos. Ps. 31:6, then, should read not "wicked vanities"
(Duhm) or "empty idols" (Gunkel), but "vapor-images of mad delusion";
60:11 should read not "vain is the help of man" but "the deliverance of man
is delusion," and accordingly 89:7 should read not "to what nothingness..."
nor even "for nothing..." but rather "to what delusiveness have you created
the children of men." 127:2 means not "it is vain..." or "for nothing..." but
"it is a delusion to you to rise so early." Only in this way can the power of the
fictitious in its manifold misdeeds be juxtaposed vividly enough to reality
across the whole range of the Psalms.

The case is different with words not possessing this emphasis and thick-
ness of association. So, for example, the generally unemphasized *ra'* does
not need to be rendered consistently (our general preference of *arg*
["bad"] comes from the fact that *arg* and its associated words present with
greater intensity than do other roots the required double meaning of "mis-
deed" and "misfortune"). A middle path, on the other hand, had to be
taken when a word did indeed have its own pathos, but its conceptual dis-
tinctiveness was not so marked as to require a uniform rendering. Such a
word is the important but not sharply delimited root *'azaz*. Here, especially
since a single, entirely satisfactory equivalent was not to be found, we were
free to do justice to the manifold character of the concept, which includes
"power," "resistance," "defense," and "victory." In order, however, not to
blur the lines of connection, it was necessary within the groups of associated
poems to establish a linkage, and between the groups to establish transi-
tions wherever possible. (In the process, *ma'oz*, belonging here by popular
etymology if not by scientific, was rendered by compound words to distinguish it from *'oz*.)

The word *ruah* must be rendered uniformly in the crucial passages and in
all the passages related to them; but a uniform rendition of it everywhere
could not *a priori* be regarded as unconditionally necessary, and in the
Psalms the constraints on its rendering had to be eased still further.[8] The

---

8. See also "People Today and the Jewish Bible," "The Hebrew Bible's Direct Influence on
Goethe's Language," "On Word Choice in Translating the Bible," "The Bible in German."

word comprehends in an elemental unity the meanings of "spirit" and "wind." Given the intentions of our translation, it was necessary to retain the concreteness that makes this unity possible, the concreteness not of a thing but of a process. Since, however, the German word *Geist* had long since lost the dynamic concreteness it once had, we had to introduce a word like *Braus* ("surging," "rushing"), which could then be split into *Geistbraus* ("spiritsurge") and *Windbraus* ("windsurge"). But *Geistbraus* was only appropriate where the Bible spoke of *Geist* as the creative, inspiriting *Geiststurm* ("spiritstorm") proceeding from God; it was not appropriate where the Bible spoke of the human *ruah* as something detached and self-contained, which had to be rendered in full embodiment as *Geist.* Similarly, *Windbraus* was only admissible (with the exception of passages where the meanings *Geist* and *Wind* occurred in close proximity and it was important not to blur their affinity) where the natural process was to be felt as coming from above, as a process in which the surge of the creation was still eddying; it was not admissible where only the occurence of a natural phenomenon was meant, and *Wind* by itself was required. In the *Praisings*, despite the creation hymns contained there, that original meaning occurs considerably less often than it does in the Pentateuch, the historical books, or the prophets.

There are cases, moreover, where the style and manner of this book, or of the poetic books of the Bible generally, necessitated more radical alterations in word choice. The root *tamam* here needs to be treated differently than in previous books. In the Pentateuch, *tamim* and *tam* are distinct in meaning; the later can be rendered by "simple," whereas the former, when it deals with a quality of mind, has been translated "whole," which rendering alone could do justice to imperatives like those of Gen. 17:1 and Deut. 18:13. But in the historical and prophetic books the words converge, and in the Psalms (and the two books following) they are altogether fused into a single, essential word, which, encompassing both adjectives equally, as well as the nouns associated with them, attains especially in Psalms the character of a directing concept, the powerful ethos of which necessitates a uniform rendering.[9] This rendering can in the atmosphere of the Psalms be sought only on the basis of "simple," not on the basis of "whole." True, the absoluteness of "whole" is not intrinsic to "simple"; but "simple" has a noble vividness absent from the usual translations "pious" or "perfect."

I was compelled by the altered position of the root *pala'* in this book to make a still more decisive change. We had kept away from translating *pele'* as "miracles" or "wonders," because as in so many other cases the etymology

---

9. This necessary uniformity within Psalms required us to sacrifice also the concordance between the corresponding parts of 2 Sam. 22 and Ps. 18; much the same is true of a number of other words.

offered us something more concrete and more direct, and thus more valuable for our task of a renewed *present-ing* of the Bible—a task altogether
unrelated to that of "modernizing" it—namely the meaning of "singled
out," "drawn aside," "withdrawn," "removed," removed in particular from
both our physical and mental grasp, the meaning then of transcendence
not in the abstract but in full physical presence. We accordingly had the
Bible speak not of God's wonders but of his "removed" deeds and works.
And in so doing, we paid heed to the original when it showed precisely this
concrete sense of the word, whether in the direct experience of these deeds
and works in the unfolding history or in the prophetic vision of the power
reigning there. In the Psalms, however—in which the root occurs far more
often than it does in all the preceding books together—a different situation
prevails: a situation of distance. Man who here celebrates God's *nifla'ot* does
indeed mean something that affects him and his own destiny, something
whose effects he entreats or expects; but he celebrates it in contexts of
which he has heard, precisely through these earlier accounts of experience
and proclamations of vision. *Pele'* has become a poetic term, which, with the
exception of passages like 131:1 in which the original meaning shines
through, is rightly rendered "miracle."

Some roots clearly have undergone in Psalms such a dilution of meaning
only in certain passages. *Zabaḥ* (50:14 and 23, 43:4, and 84:4) is a good
example. *Mashal* should be mentioned here also, as indicating a verse statement made to parallel another verse and therefore needing to be rendered
by something like "likeword," but also sometimes, e.g., 44:15, needing to be
understood more abstractly, as something like "parable."

The case is different with *ashrei*. The word occurs twenty-five times in
Psalms, eight times in Proverbs, and ten times in the rest of the Bible
together. Literally one might translate this "O the blessedness of. . . ." In the
few cases of its occurrence before Psalms, it has been rendered "good for-
tune be to. . . ." But in Psalms, where *ashrei* almost always is used to praise
people in alliance with God, that rendering will not do. "Fortunate," however, is itself neither grand nor pure enough; it dulls the emphasis of the
crucial passages, and fails even in the first verse of the book. Still worse is
the neutral "well for him," the weakness of which is fully revealed when one
tries to use it to render the passages in which the corresponding verb
occurs, 41:3 and 72:17. Nor can these two passages be managed with the
otherwise more adequate *Heil* ["hail," "hurrah," "salvation"] which would
moreover overlap confusingly with *heilig* ["holy"] and *heilen* ["to heal"].
There is only *one* German word that corresponds to what is meant by *ashrei*,
denotatively if not grammatically; that word is *selig* ["blessed"]. We have of
course to strip the word of its surely late connotation of otherworldliness;
we have also, precisely by introducing it into the psalmic contexts ("that he

may be made blessed on earth" in Psalm 41 gives the fundamental tone), to leave the word its natural character of a powerful earthly well-being, a character possessed by the noble middle high German word *saelde* and recurringly by *selig* itself, notably in the poetry of Goethe and his contemporaries.

"THE ETERNAL":
MENDELSSOHN AND THE
NAME OF GOD[1]

Franz Rosenzweig
(July 1929)[2]

The historical significance of the Mendelssohn translation of the Pentateuch is well known. Its success, however, has fallen short both of its historical significance and of its real value. It has been published in Hebrew characters in numerous editions, most recently in 1888 in Warsaw; but this has been largely for the sake of its connection with Mendelssohn's important commentary, the so-called *Biur*, which, situated just at the threshold of our century of biblical criticism—already, that is, in the modern spirit and yet still naive, equally distant from biblical criticism and from neo-orthodoxy—takes up once again the torch of the great medieval exegetes and kindles it anew. In German characters, moreover, after a venture promoted by Mendelssohn himself that only got as far as Genesis, it was published only in 1813 and 1815, then not again until 1845, as part of an edition of the collected works, and since then not at all. When German Jews in the great intellectual surge of the 1830s and 1840s demanded a German Bible,

---

1. Given my technical difficulties and the gaps in the local library, I could not have written this essay without the help not only of Martin Buber but also of a whole array of people who were "there-for-me": above all the doctoral student Nahum Glatzer, and also Dr. O. Driesen, Director of Studies, Frankfurt; Dr. J. Klatzkin, Berlin; Dr. E. Mayer, Syndic, Frankfurt; Dr. M. Soloweitshik, Berlin; Dr. Bruno Strauss, *Studienrat*, Berlin; Dr. Torczyner, Docent, Berlin; R. Wallau, Pastor, Frankfurt.

Our thanks to Werner Weinberg, editor of the Mendelssohn Bible translation and commentary for the Mendelssohn *Jubiläumsausgabe* (Friedrich Frommann Verlag), for a careful reading of part of this translation [eds.].

2. Printed in the *Gedenkbuch für Moses Mendelssohn*, published by the *Verband der Vereine für jüdische Geschichte und Literatur* [eds.: Buber indicates that this note is his rather than Rosenzweig's].

numerous translators strove for the prize: Zunz, Salomon, Johlson, then
later Philippson. Mendelssohn's translation, however, was not considered
to be in the running.[3] Yet it is, objectively considered, one of the great
accomplishments of the classic decades of German translation, of the era of
Goethean "world-literature." Conscious of the "oriental . . . language and
manner of speech," Mendelssohn ventures not only much that is false and
specious but also much that is bold and indeed exceedingly bold, as when
his covenants are neither "concluded" nor "established" but, at least in
Genesis, consistently "cut"—this in close attention to the Hebrew
metaphor, which still reflects the cutting up of the covenantal sacrifice. All
this, however, takes place beneath the cloak of invisibility conferred by the
Hebrew characters, and becomes apparent to the German reading public
only when there appears all at once, as if arisen from nothingness, a generation of accomplished Jewish stylists in German literature and journalism.

Aside from its role in the shaping of German style, however,
Mendelssohn's translation has had a lasting effect on German and world
Judaism in only one respect: its rendering of the divine name as "the
Eternal." This was reproduced in most subsequent Jewish Bible translations; it also made its way into the standard liturgical translations, into ser-
mons, and into all German spoken in and around religious services.
Accordingly, Jewish piety of the Emancipation, even in orthodox circles
(despite Hirsch's magnificently argued resistance[4]), was everywhere col-
ored by it.

So far as I know, it was Mendelssohn who introduced this expression into
Judaism. The older Judeo-German translations that Mendelssohn discusses
in his preface have, as does Hirsch later, simply "God." They, like Hirsch,
avoid the apparently obvious rendering "the Lord." But Mendelssohn's
phrase does have a European and Christian pre-history, albeit an "Old
Testament" one. Its biblical origin lies in the Old Testament in the strictest
sense, i.e., in the part retained only in the Christian Bible as the Apocrypha;
in the Letter of Baruch, chapters 4 and 5—i.e., in the portion that was perhaps written originally in Greek—this phrase occurs no less than six times
as a name of God, *ho Aionios*, "the Eternal." Calvin uses this austere, sublime, genuinely "numinous" term to render the Old Testament name of
God in the French edition he prepared in 1564 of his commentary on the
Hexateuch, from which Reuss[5] reconstructed the "Calvin Bible"—but not

---

3. Philipp Ehrenberg to Jost (manuscript in possession of my mother; Wolfenbüttel,
October 26, 1841): ". . . In reading the subscribers' prospectus for the Mendelssohn *Works* I
find it very surprising that the translation of the Pentateuch is being printed again, and that in
fact subscribers are to be *compelled* to purchase this outmoded work, which today is significant
only for literature and for cultural history. . . ."

4. See his commentary on Gen. 2:4.

5. Reuss, *Bible française de Calvin* (1897; also as *Corpus Reformatorum* 56).

yet in the individual commentaries on Old Testament books published in the 1650s, in which *Éternel* has not yet replaced *Seigneur*, nor in the original form of the Geneva Bible, published by Calvin's cousin Olivetanus in 1535, which only occasionally has *L'Éternel*, nor in any of the Geneva Bibles discussed by Reuss that were published during Calvin's lifetime. It is only in 1588 that Calvin's *L'Éternel* takes over the Geneva Bible altogether, and from that date on it has maintained its place both in the Bible and in Calvinist worship—though two editions of the Geneva Bible published at Lyon in 1550 and 1551, and now in the possession of the Berlin Staatsbibliothek, record frequent occurrences of the term. (We shall have occasion later to discuss another edition, that of 1565, now in the possession of the local library.)

From Geneva the name made its way into the European literatures as well. The earliest source that Littré quotes is the French poet Clément Marot (d. 1540), whose *Fifty Psalms* was published by Calvin; the best known are the passages in Racine's two Old Testament dramas.[6] English too provides some instances, beginning in the 1580s. The Grimm brothers, however, let it slip through the net of their dictionary, though it is familiar in German linguistic history; it occurs not only in the Book of Baruch in the Luther Bible but of course in the Gellert hymn "The Heavens Declare," which was made immortal by Beethoven's music—and whose biblical original has, as it happens, not the sacred name but only the generic word "God."[7]

It seems, then, that Mendelssohn the citizen of Berlin—a city whose strong Huguenot community then and for long afterwards, at least in public worship, kept fidelity to the language of its stepfatherland much as had Turkish Jews to the Spanish of the Inquisition, and Polish and Russian Jews to the Rhineland dialect of the Crusades—is not due much credit in this matter. And yet he did as translator take a step beyond his great predecessor Calvin, a step apparently small but in truth decisive, and in so doing added the dot to the "i" by which the "i" attains its identity.

How did Mendelssohn conceive the problem? Negatively, we can presume that "the Lord" seemed to him too freighted with Christian associations; it had after all through the diction of the Greek and so the German New Testament come to refer not to God but to the founder of Christianity—a reference that even today gives a Christian coloring to the Old Testament. When the devout Christian says, "The Lord is my shepherd," he thinks not of God but of "the Good Shepherd."

6. Jean Racine (1639-1699), French dramatist; the passages Littré cites are *Esther* 3:4 and *Athalie* 1:1 [eds.].

7. No. 4 in Six Songs, op. 48 [eds.].

Concerning the positive reasons for Mendelssohn's choice we have something more than suppositions. The commentator Mendelssohn had found for Genesis had deserted him, and he had not yet found the commentators for the following books; so for Exodus, for the book containing the crucial passage in this matter, Mendelssohn wrote the commentary himself. Now we do not have to look for Mendelssohn's account of the matter at the first appearance of the name, i.e., at Gen. 2:4, as we do for Hirsch's. At that point we find only a reference sending us off to the commentary on Exod. 3:14. And it is in this deferral, in the three Hebrew words of the commentary that in these first chapters is again Mendelssohn's own work—"for there is the place to discuss it"—that we have the germ of Mendelssohn's whole accomplishment concerning the problem, his decisive advance over Calvin and the Protestant Bible, and his head start even over the later Jewish translators who accept his version of the divine name.[8] Exod. 3:14 runs approximately as follows:

> Now God said to Moshe:
> I will be-there howsoever I will be-there.
> And said:
> Thus shall you say to the Sons of Israel:
> I AM THERE sends me to you.

Mendelssohn broadly paraphrases this as:

> God spoke to Moses: "I am the being that is eternal."
> He said further: "Say to the children of Israel,
> 'The eternal being, which calls itself, I-am-eternal, has sent me to you.'"

This, finally, is Mendelssohn's commentary:

> It says in a midrash,
>> The Holy one, Blessed be He, said to Moses: "say to them, 'I am the one who was, and now I am the same and will be the same in the future.'" And our teachers, may their memory be a blessing, say further: "I will be with them in this need, who will be with them in their bondage in the kingdoms to come." (Cf. Berakhot 9b)
> Their meaning is the following: "Because past and future time are all present in the creator, since in Him there is no change and dependence[9] and

---

8. Zadoc Kahn alone excepted, who follows Mendelssohn in every detail.

9. Dr. Torczyner understands Mendelssohn's Job citation here in connection with modern Hebrew usage, as meaning "no variation accompanying the constancy." The word that makes the difference is not, as Dr. Klatzkin assures me on the basis of the materials assembled for his wonderful philosophical dictionary, a term of medieval Hebrew.

of His days there is no passing—because of this all times are in Him called by a single name, which embraces past, present, and future alike. Through this name He indicates the necessity of existence and at the same time the continuous and abiding character of providence. He says, then, by this name, 'I am with the children of men, to be well disposed and to have mercy on whom I will have mercy. Say then to them, to Israel, that I am He who was, is, and shall be, and who practices lordship and providence over all; I, I am the one and I shall be with them in this need, shall be with them in this need and shall be with them whenever they call to me.'" Now in German there is no word that better unites the meanings of omnitemporality, necessity of existence, and providence than does this holy name: "the eternal, necessary, providential being."[10] So we have translated "the Eternal," or "the Eternal Being."[11]

Onkelos translates,[12] "I shall be with whom I shall be" (according to the reading Nachmanides offers), in the sense of, "I am well disposed to whom I am well disposed, and have mercy on whom I will have mercy" (see below on chapter 33). He intends by this to translate with reference only to the aspect of providence, like the second midrash. Saadia Gaon writes that the explanation is, "who is not past and will not pass away, because he is the first and the last." His words are thus similar to those of the first midrash, the one that speaks of eternity. Maimonides in *The Guide to the Perplexed* explains as follows: "the one who exists, who has existence within Him." His reading thus refers to the meaning of existential necessity. In truth the word encompasses all three meanings. But Onkelos writing in Aramaic, and Saadia writing in Arabic, and Maimonides writing in the Arabic of his *Guide,* could find in their languages no word encompassing all three meanings as does the holy name; accordingly, each interpreted with respect to one of the three meanings. And the present German translator decided to render the name with respect to the sense of eternity because for him the other meanings branch out from this central one. Similarly, I have found in Jonathan ben Uzziel a rendering similarly oriented to this meaning: "I-who-am-and-shall-be has sent me to you."

From Mendelssohn's commentary, then, there emerges the surprising fact that even for Mendelssohn this decision in favor of the abstract, "philosophical" divine name, with all the important consequences of that name for modern Judaism, was extremely shaky. The "eternally necessary," the "providential" being—the former found in the name by the classic religious philosophers, the latter by the genuine popular tradition (Onkelos, Talmud,[13] Rashi!)—seem to Mendelssohn meanings equally valid *in se,* and

---

10. In German in Mendelssohn's original.

11. See note 9.

12. From here on Mendelssohn is probably following the material accumulated by his Genesis commentator.

13. The Talmud knows only the "second" midrash (Berakhot 9b).

equally intended by the text. In his decision is an element of an attenuated belief. It is a belief no longer credible to us after the work of Kant the Crusher, to use Mendelssohn's phrase for him; but among the classic eighteenth-century beliefs was a belief in the possibility of a rational theology, and in such a theology, though the connection is in flagrant contradiction to the findings of the history of philosophy, the notion of a being necessarily existent might inevitably imply the notion of a providential one. We today would be able to agree, if at all, rather on the opposite "deduction"— from the providential God to the necessarily existing God. But for pre-Kantian Mendelssohn, "the Eternal"—or, as he prefers in particularly important passages like the one under discussion here, "the Eternal Being"—implies also the God of prayerful petition.

What of the problem considered textually? The conclusive study as of the present moment, I think, and one exemplary in its sober caution, is that produced by Benno Jacob in his essay, "Moses at the Burning Bush."[14] The narrative context of the chapter speaks altogether against the first meaning, the existential necessity, and for the second, the providentiality, of the word in question—which connotes, even on purely linguistic grounds, not the static sense of *being* but the dynamic sense of *becoming*, of *appearing*, of *happening*.

Moses recoils from the role of leader that God commissions him with. So God assures him, "Indeed, I will be-there with you" (3:12). And Moses answers,

> It will be, that when I come to the Sons of Israel,
> and I say to them: The God of your fathers sends me to you,
> they will say to me: What is behind His name?
> What am I to say to them?

And it is in response to this, to the question concerning the meaning of the name—and not, as Jacob demonstrates (and Mendelssohn also in his commentary,[15] though not in his translation) concerning the name itself—that the passage quoted above is intended to respond. But what meaning for the despairing and wretched Israelites would be offered by a lecture on God's existential necessity? They, like this timid leader himself, need rather an assurance of God's being-among-them; and unlike their leader, who hears it directly from God's mouth, they need this in the form of a clarification of the old, obscure name, sufficient to establish that the assurance is of divine origin.

---

14. *Monatsschrift für Geschichte und Wissenschaft des Judentums*, 1922.
15. Calvin also, in his full Latin commentary on Exod. 6:13ff. and 6:2 (*Corpus Reformatorum* 52).

In the narrative context, then, the only justifiable translation is one that makes prominent not God's being eternal but his being present, his being present for and with you now and in time to come. I have shown elsewhere[16] how in the rendering of the thus clarified name this fact can be condensed into the three dimensions of the personal pronoun: the speaker, the one spoken to, the one spoken of. Only in the pronoun is the meaning of the One who is present in one of three ways, the One who is present in one of three sorts of presence, concentrated into a single word. In the pronoun, that is, that is not engulfed in the objectivity of narrative or indirect discourse, but that leaps forth with the explosive force of orality from the always past speech of the book into the present. It is no accident that the two most theologically motivated of all the German translators, Luther and Hirsch, were both unable to solve this problem without rupturing the easy flow of the letters: Luther's capital letters equal Hirsch's *Sperrdruck*.[17] The one who is present to them, is there-with them: *HE*. The one who is present to an "I," is there-with me: *YOU*. The one who is present to a "you," is there-with you: *I*. Precisely the necessary change of persons is the test of this solution to the problem of bringing the rendering of the name into strict relation with the revelation of the name and thus, as will be shown later, of rendering translationally the unity of the Bible as written, and not only as read, which is constituted by just this relation. What Rashi's grandson Rashbam in his commentary presents as hidden beneath the transposed alphabet is in fact nothing but the strict sense of the revelation: "He calls himself, '*I-AM-THERE*,' and we call him, '*HE-IS-THERE*.'"

So Mendelssohn made the wrong choice, influenced as he was by Calvin's example and made susceptible to that influence by the rationalizing, classicizing spirit of his century. (In Mendelssohn's case the spirit of the age made alliance with the Aristotelian spirit of Maimonides, whom Mendelssohn had honored all his life, against the sure instinct of Jewish tradition.) Yet Mendelssohn's error, however fateful for the Judaism of the Emancipation, counts for little against his enormous service: that he was the first translator, and for a long time the only translator, to pose the specifically translational question rightly by linking the rendering of the name to the revelation of the name. The circumlocution "the Lord," prevalent in the countries of Christian Europe after its origin in the Septuagint and its transmission through the Vulgate, did some justice to the uniqueness of the divine name insofar as it was, precisely, a circumlo-

---

16. Appendix I, "Letter to Martin Goldner" [eds.: Buber's note].

17. The word refers to the German (and Hebrew) practice of indicating emphasis not by italicization or underlining but by a slight though typographically distinct separation of the letters of the word emphasized [eds.].

cution and thereby rendered the *transparency* of the name, its saturation with meaning. And no doubt "the Lord" was in one sense a better rendering of the name than "the Eternal," insofar as it had in itself not a limited meaning but one pointing beyond itself; "*the* Lord" is always the Lord of the being set in his presence, the being encountering him—is always, that is, a word of relation.[18] But beginning at least with the Latin *dominus*, this rendering is also in stark contrast to its Hebrew model, the periphrasis of the divine name, which emerged after the return from Babylon;[19] it is the word of a false relation, a ruling and not a helping, an overseeing and not an assisting. The Hebrew *Adonai*, which became in the words of the prophets, of Amos and Isaiah, the aptest word for their consciousness of having been sent—"my Lord"—possessed (and still possesses in Jewish mouths) precisely this inward resonance, charged with a fundamental tone of vocativeness, of direct address and petition, and accordingly was used in post-biblical prayer literature predominantly in the vocative. It glances for a moment up from the middle of the sentence toward heaven, just as the Torah scribe is enjoined before every writing of the name to pause and say that he writes the name in order to sanctify it—and the most pious in this manual labor of piety enact the statement through a ritual immersion. So also the Torah reader is compelled by the traditional cantillation to declaim the name, wherever it occurs, as if it preceded a pause either ending or interrupting the sentence. And beneath *Adonai*, in contrast with "Lord," there lay always and visibly the actual name with its connection to the moment of revelation; and this task, of connecting the name to the moment at which the name was revealed, was discovered by Mendelssohn the translator.

It is precisely here that we find his advance over Calvin. The Genevan Protestants translated the name diversely, but always in connection with the tradition of translation established by the Septuagint and the Vulgate: "I am who I am" (or, with a humanist reference back to the Hebrew original,

---

18. See on this Baudissin's imposingly thorough and thoughtful posthumous work *Kyrios.*

19. Cf. Benno Jacob, *Im Namen Gottes* ["In God's Name"], 1903, "Exkurs." The publisher's notice gives an entirely misleading account of the interesting thesis presented by the first two parts of Baudissin's work. In fact, Baudissin derives both the Septuagint *Kyrios* and the Masoretic *Adonai*, which he considers of later occurrence, from the devotional expostulation, *Adonai!*, "my Lord!" Then, however, he affixes to this integral point of his work the additional point that though the Alexandrians' "my Lord," as he shows conclusively in his two volumes, continues to have the connotation of "my [or our] Lord," the Masoretes' "my Lord," that is, the "my Lord" of post-Christian Jews, takes on the connotation of the coldly sublime "the Lord." This bizarre jumbling of the evident facts is its own refutation—or would necessarily be its own refutation if theology even among the best theologians were not still a militant branch of scientific scholarship. Mephistopheles' point remains valid, even if here the theologian seeks to rob a word of its "jot and tittle."

Mephistopheles' point (*Faust* 1, ll. 1984ff.) is that in theology, as in medicine, there's a lot of hidden poison [eds.].

though understood always according to the Septuagint,[20] "I shall be who I shall be"), or "I am he who is"; and "he who is" (or "I am" or "he who is named 'I am'") has sent me to you. Now once these translators write *Éternel* instead of *Seigneur*, the connection with the revelatory passage is evident; this is very strikingly indicated in the edition of 1565 in the local library, which in general, with the exception of especially central passages, e.g., Gen. 4:1 and 4:26, and Exod. 34:6, has *Seigneur*, but which from the verse revealing the name to the end of the chapter prints *Éternel*, and in its notes explains this name with reference to the verb of verse 14, and then in turn explains this verse as "I shall be it eternally," and "he who is eternal." But in the translation itself, even this edition does not make the connection; the word of revelation, inherited from the platonizing "I am the one who is" of the Septuagint, remains isolated from the actual use of the divine name in the text.

How important it is that this recognition was here expressed in translation is made clear by a contrast with Philo—the first of all those who have availed themselves of the great privilege of humankind, namely to read the book of humankind in the servant's garb of translation as if it stood before them in the royal garment of the holy language. Philo gathered from his Septuagint that only "the one who is" was God himself, and that "the Lord" was a subordinate deity!—and—of course—the deity of divine justice and not of divine mercy.

But Mendelssohn's translational clarification of the relation between the name and the revelation of the name cannot be praised too highly even in its particular Jewish significance. What depends on his discovery of this connection is nothing less than the unity of the Bible. Its unity, that is, as a unified expression and emanation of the revelation of the one God. Or, put more learnedly and thus more comprehensibly: its unity in the principle of monotheism. Biblical "monotheism" does not consist in the perception of a unity of the divine essence; if it did, it would be altogether ordinary. There is no "heathen" belief that does not—and not only in late religious philosophical discourse but in its genuine and original religious perception—gather together its "polytheism," i.e., the fullness of its religious experiences, into the unity of a general "religious" category, in a hierarchy or a pantheon or a catalogue. The singularity of the biblical belief consists

---

20. Unlike Luther, who with a stroke of genius writes, "'I will be that' sent me to you," and so breaks through the Platonism of the Alexandrians to the genuine, unhellenic, Jewish meaning.

Also noteworthy—if the reader will permit me this digression—is the practice of Aquinas. In the *Summa Theologica* (I:13:11), he poses the objection, later of course neatly disposed of, that the name furnished him by the Vulgate, *qui est*, cannot be God's most inward name, since after all God's name must contain a reference to God's creatures, given that we understand God only through those creatures.

in this: that it does indeed presume this "heathen" unity—or, to use the Kuzari's phrase,[21] does indeed presume the God of Aristotle—but perceives this God in his oneness with the personal God of immediate experience— or, again to use the Kuzari's phrase, with the God of Abraham. The "heathen unity" is in this combination not at all subordinate; a God who remained a partial God, say a tribal God, and nonetheless claimed to be "the whole" would be an idol, and thus incapable of entering into union with the God of Abraham (his failure to recognize this is one of Goldberg's[22] central errors). But the heathen unity attains its monotheistic point, so to speak, only through this Jewish uniting of the distant God with the near, the "whole" with "one's own." Only in this fusion do we have the "essence of Judaism"; and it is this fusion, as articulated in the doctrine of the trinity, however broken, however in danger of lapsing into the divided condition that lies before and outside Judaism, that is the essence of Christianity as well. (The gravity and the imminence of this danger are revealed for us now in the work of Barth and Gogarten.) Now this union is the kernel of biblical revelation; it is what makes this book the Jewish Bible. (The difference between the Jewish Bible and the "Old Testament" lies in this: viewed from the standpoint of the New Testament, the God of the "Old" Testament, as compared with the "Father of Jesus Christ," is too easily reduced, in a way, to the God of Aristotle.) And it is precisely this union that, with the fire surging forth from the "*I AM THERE*" called out from the Burning Bush, forges the Bible into a unity in the divine name. Through this union is accomplished at every point an equivalence between the God of creation and the God who is present to me, to you, to everyone—an equivalence whose fire burns hottest in the passages where the name of God [*Adonai*] and the word for God [*Elohim*] beat against each other, e.g., the Eden chapters in Genesis 2-3, or the call to unity of the *Shema*, or more generally in the passages where Mendelssohn is not satisfied with "the Eternal," and attempts in his way, by the rendering "the Eternal Being," to establish solidly the connection of the name to the moment of its revelation in Exodus.

The various historical possibilities may in the light of the findings developed here be sketched more or less as follows.[23] In the Hebrew Bible as we have it the divine name appears in three forms; besides the familiar four-

---

21. The Kuzari (i.e., the king of the Khazars) is the central character in Judah Halevi's philosophical dialogue of the same name [eds.].

22. Oscar Goldberg (1885-1952).

23. For what follows compare the most important of the recent treatments, Driver's essay "The Original Form of the Name Yahveh" (*Zeitschrift für die alttestamentliche Wissenschaft*, 1928). I am in agreement with his crucial thesis, that the tetragrammaton arose as a theological proposition and remained that for some time; I cannot follow him in his account of the trigrammaton.

consonant form, the so-called tetragrammaton, there are also a two-conso-
nant and a three-consonant form—a digrammaton and a trigrammaton,
so to speak. The digrammaton *Yah*, to be prefaced in pronunciation with a
short open o, belongs, as Jastrow has shown[24]—albeit with erring deduc-
tions from the fact—to the group of divine names or epithets that come
from cultic exclamations, or rather acclamations,[25] like Iacchus or Evios.[26]
It would then be one of those interjections, those aboriginal shouts, from
which language itself must have arisen: a primitive word of encounter,
even before the possibility of objectification, a pure vocative before the
possibility of other cases—i.e., exactly what a divine name has to distinguish it from all other personal and common names, not only at the beginning but for all time. This name accordingly never occurs in objective
circumstances, e.g., in narratives, but only in eruptive phrases, of which
the most familiar and common example is the cultic cry of "halleluyah"
("praise Yah"). (This fact speaks against another of Jastrow's theories,
according to which the digrammaton as divine name would be a late product of scholarly reflection.)

The second form of the name, the trigrammaton, is preserved biblically
only in personal names, in the two forms—*Yahu* (with two long vowels and
a mute *vav*) and *Yeho* (with an almost mute e, a long o, and a mute *vav*), as
well as two abbreviated forms corresponding to these, *Yah* (with long a) and
Yo (with long o and mute *vav*). Outside the Bible, however, it occurs independently as a name of God, often in the documents found at Elephantine
of the Egyptian Jews of the fifth century B.C., and on potsherds found in
Jerusalem and Jericho in the fifth and fourth centuries B.C. The word *Iao*,[27]
attested in both classical and patristic sources, and also in numerous, albeit
obscure, gnostic sources as a Jewish name of God, may be taken as further

---

24. *Zeitschrift für die alttestamentliche Wissenschaft.* Marcus Mordecai Jastrow (1829-1903)
[eds.].

25. German *Ausruf* and *Anruf.* An *Ausruf* is an exclamation; component by component it is a
calling-out. When Rosenzweig suggests that what is normally called an *Ausruf*, a calling-out,
would be better named an *Anruf*, a calling-to, he is making in microcosm one of his large
points about the conversational relation between human beings and God. The translation
makes the same switch in the Latinate words that Rosenzweig makes in the Germanic ones; but
the results are not quite the same, so it seemed in order to annotate them [eds.].

26. Cult names for the Greek god Dionysus [eds.].

27. The intimidating scrutiny of the sources in Baudissin's great study "Der Ursprung des
Gottesnamens Iao" ["The Origin of the Divine Name *Iao*"] (in *Studien zur semitischen
Religionsgeschichte*), which even today retains value as a collection of the material then available,
would no doubt have been less intimidating had he at the time—before Elephantine and
Sellin's excavations, that is—been able to refer to an independently existing trigrammaton
and not only to the tetragrammaton. The treatment of the question in *Kyrios* signifies a complete and conscious reversal of position.

Compare also Deissmann, *Griechische Transkriptionen des Tetragrammaton* ["Greek Trans-
criptions of the Tetragrammaton"] (*Bibelstudien*).

attestation of the trigrammaton. It is remarkable that this form of the divine name, through recorded outside the Bible, occurs in the Bible only in proper names and never as a name of God; the Bible preserves only the four-consonantal form, and this fact requires some explanation. That the tetragrammaton is not used in proper names or in secular documents or instruments makes sense, just as does the substitution, for the actual name of the Prophet, of the periphrases Mehmed and Mahmud in Moslem naming, and much as do any of the numerous analogous pious practices; it represents a reluctance to profane what is holy. But the opposite situation, the absence of the trigrammaton in the biblical context, remains puzzling. It makes no difference whether it is an older form of the name of God, subsequently illuminated in the tetragrammaton, or a more recent periphrasis of it; in neither case is it clear why it should not have been as well preserved as the digrammaton. It must have been consciously removed, or consciously avoided, or both.[28]

The tetragrammaton, of unknown or at any rate uncertain pronunciation,[29] is both name and epithet in one.[30] It is thus like all divine names, yet different from them in that in it the name and the attribute are coextensive, so that no part of the name remains unilluminated by meaning (in contrast, say, with all late "explanations" of the names of classical deities), and also in that the fire of meaning does not at any point leap above the surface of the name (in contrast with the "special gods" of Rome). The tetragrammaton becomes a name through its grammatical treatment but also through the restrictions on its occurrence and application; we are taught clearly, however, that it is not ever merely original or merely supplementary from the numerous passages in which the understanding of the name is presented as a great and traumatic event, indeed *the* great and traumatic event, the turning point of world history—passages that in the usual, pseudo-scientific rendering are emptied of any meaning whatsoever. "They shall know that I am Yahweh," "Yahweh is a man of war, Yahweh is his name"—these are perfectly meaningless and become meaningful only when we render the name as a semantic unit, regardless of whether we choose "Lord," or "Eternal," or whatever. Protestant scholarship on the Old Testament holds fast to the use of "Yahweh" in German, by which the name

28. Note in this connection the traditional Jewish practice of not using YH to represent the number 15 in letter transcription [eds.].

29. Besides *Yahweh* there is at least the possibility of *Yeheweh* (see Jacob, *Monatsschrift für die Geschichte und Wissenschaft des Judentums*, 1922). There are even advocates for *Yahoh*; though this, it seems to me, comes into consideration only for the Mesha Stone, which then would be presenting the trigrammaton in tetragrammatic orthography.

30. See on this in Usener's *Götternamen* ["God-Names"] the section "Formale Wucherung" ["Formal Proliferation"], especially the conclusion; and for what follows see the section "Sondergötter" ["Special Gods"].

becomes unrelated, bare, and meaningless. It does so despite understanding the epithetic character of the name perfectly well—one has only to see the excellent account of the question in Gesenius' lexicon. So this degradation of the name of God to the name of an idol[31] is incomprehensible on purely scholarly grounds; rather it is the continuation, with modern means, of the old theological battle against the Old Testament—or at any rate against the claim of autonomy, of biblical sufficiency, which Jews acknowledge in it. The Jewish Bible calls, "Eli, Eli! My God, my God!"—and the Old Testamentarians shake their heads and explain, "he is calling Elijah."

What however is the relation of the tetragrammaton to the two other forms of the name? The two possibilities marked out earlier for its relation to the trigrammaton both yield, however opposite to each other, to the fundamental fact that only the tetragrammaton and the digrammaton occur in the biblical text. Or, put negatively: that the trigrammaton does not occur there. This can only be understood as meaning that in comparison with the trigrammaton the tetragrammaton was never a mere name, but always made its appearance with the full voltage of the theological charge with which it had been loaded at the Burning Bush. Historically one can imagine the process in various ways. If the trigrammaton was an older form—the "Yahweh" of the Old Testamentarians, so to speak—then the tetragrammaton is either the product of a radical theological reworking of the biblical texts or, since it occurs once as early as the ninth century, in the Moabite Mesha Stone, of the biblical texts' earlier layers. Or the tetragrammaton is in this case—and that is my own belief—as old as the Bible, or in other words it is genuinely the trace of the occurrence at the Burning Bush recorded in the third chapter of Exodus (or, for those who believe in literature rather than in occurrences, the trace of that narrative and its "author.") But if the trigrammaton is to be a later periphrasis of the tetragrammaton—though a very old one, as the inscriptionally attested proper names indicate—then historically considered its genesis seems much the same; only in this case the postulated previous form would be either unknown[32] or would be the tetragrammaton itself as a "mere" name. The digrammaton would in all these possibilities be the common archaic origin (if we presume that its classification as a ritual exclamation is accurate). That exclamation would then, to spin out one of the noted possibilities,[33] have become an appellation of God in the trigrammaton through the addi-

---

31. To be sure: Jews too, led astray by the translations "the Lord" and "the Eternal," have suggested to me that our German translation should print *Adonai!*

32. Driver's "extended" digrammaton *Yahwah* or *Yahwahi* seems to me very improbable.

33. Not that proposed by Driver, in whose Assyriological explanation there must be an error, though I who am no Assyriologist cannot ascertain where, since the instances Driver himself assembles in Palestinian inscriptions compel us to a conclusion precisely the opposite of that drawn by Driver from the Assyrian and Babylonian data.

tion of the Old Semitic noun-ending *w*, and this in turn, in the tetragrammaton, through the consonantization of the vowel ending, have become a revelation of the divine—or, for those who prefer to begin from the human standpoint, the recognition of the divine. This name, which is altogether word, altogether word of encounter and presence, was then, when through the development of the language it fell in danger of becoming a mere name once again, fenced round with the periphrastic pronunciation "my Lord" [Hebrew *Adonai*], which makes the name into a silent and yet visible secret and which, by securing it from thoughtless utterance, compels the reading eye to recall its meaning. The periphrasis in its turn indicates the meaning of the name insofar as it names God not as the one who abides in his being, in his essence, but as the one who bends down to be essentially present; at the same time it indicates, through its grammatical incompatibility with the logical flow of the text, how the name as a force of transformation and reformation has transformed the language and formed the book—the name which is itself witness of a moment of revelation, which for the reader now is repeated and renewed in a thousand moments of recognition. Mendelssohn's translation of the name missed both its indication of meaning and its indication of the tension between the meaning-charged name and the context; but with a steady gaze it made, and was the first to make, both aspects of the name a question central to the task of a Jewish Bible translation.

And yet—though it does not render the biblical conception, though it presents the temptation Hirsch indicated, to leave God in his heaven and to establish oneself on earth—even so, "the Eternal" is still animate with the genuine powers of the human soul. "Eternal" is after all for mortals the word of longing, the last word of our *Lied von der Erde*.[34] The great thinkers of human history, from Plato and Aristotle on, have devised fulfillment for this wish of the human heart by showing us a divine sphere in which our longing might repose. The God of the Bible also quiets this longing—not, however, by fulfilling it or promising it fulfillment, but precisely by quieting it, by bringing it to silence. The longing for eternity passes away from those who experience and hope God's becoming present in this world and time. Even that biblical word that is usually translated "eternity" [Hebrew *ʿolam*] means in truth precisely this time of ours till its turning point, till "that day." In the face of living time, the human desire for eternity learns to fall silent.

But precisely because the Bible knows differently—knows something different—it is able to include in its concord even this sound so foreign to it, which is after all a genuine human sound. When Hermann Cohen said,

---

34. Rosenzweig, who was a sensitive and precise writer about classical music and had reviewed recordings some months before he wrote this essay, alludes to the fact that Mahler's *Lied von der Erde*, like our own "song upon earth," concludes with the word "ewig" [eds.].

"the Eternal is my shepherd," his "the Eternal" was only a momentary blazing up of this longing, which was at once inundated by the blessed consciousness of God's bending down to us, by the continuation "is my shepherd." Mendelssohn himself felt as much even in his erring choice of "eternal" over "providential," when he stated that the former implied the latter. And Calvin, the great creator of the word—how hard he works in his commentary to raise the eternal "being" above the level of Plato's "Being," to the level of the eternally powerful deliverer! If the Bible did not have this enigmatic power to transform our errors into its truth, then translating it would be still more risky than it already is. But it is precisely on account of this power that the risk becomes a commandment, and a goal worth any pain; for this transformational energy of the Bible is the secret of its world-historical influence.

LEITWORT[1] STYLE IN PENTATEUCH NARRATIVE

Martin Buber
(From a Lecture, January 1927[2])

By *Leitwort* I understand a word or word root that is meaningfully repeated within a text or sequence of texts or complex of texts; those who attend to these repetitions will find a meaning of the text revealed or clarified, or at any rate made more emphatic. As noted, what is repeated need not be a single word but can be a word root; indeed the diversity of forms often strengthens the overall dynamic effect. I say "dynamic" because what takes place between the verbal configurations thus related is in a way a *movement*; readers to whom the whole is present feel the waves beating back and forth. Such measured repetition, corresponding to the inner rhythm of the text— or rather issuing from it—is probably the strongest of all techniques for making a meaning available without articulating it explicitly. This may involve paronomasia in the strict sense, occurring within an individual syntactic context;[3] it may involve paronomasia more generally, including alliteration and assonance;[4] but it may also involve the sort of paronomasia we are discussing here, paronomasia *at a distance*, working not in immediate juxtaposition but over an extended stretch of text. In all of these cases, such repetition can achieve not only aesthetic value, as manifested notably in the verse-forms of the Elder Edda, but also a special and irreplaceable value of *statement*. This value consists in the fact that the meaning to be stated is por-

---

1. The German term *Leitwort* is retained as a term of Buber and Rosenzweig's art, without any exact English equivalent. See above, "Buber and Rosenzweig's Challenge to Translation Theory," and below, note 9 [eds.].

2. The lecture was called "The Bible as Storyteller," but in its introduction considered the early history of narrative style generally. I print here only some passages from the main section.

3. See, e.g., H. Reckendorf, *Die Paronomasie in den semitischen Sprachen* ["Paronomasia in the Semitic Languages"] (Giessen, 1909).

4. So, for example, J. M. Casanowicz, *Paronomasia in the Old Testament* (Boston, 1894).

trayed without any tacked-on moral, i.e., without any disruption or distortion of the pure form of the narrative. We postulate in saying this that such a form, such a self-contained artistic configuration, is present, but also that a meaning, a message is to be communicated by it—a meaning and a message that transcend the artistic configuration, and which therefore cannot be incorporated into that configuration as a meaning is incorporated into a poem, without any special method, but rather must according to their nature construct their own particular means of expression. Nowhere is this postulate so fully satisfied as when the strictly self-contained epic form meets with a "religious" message infused with the descending spirit.

But nowhere, probably, does this happen with such singular power as in the narratives of the Pentateuch. The strictness of form here arises from the profound intention to report, and *only* to report; and precisely for this reason the message may not impose itself on the form. An edifying account of the religious content transcending the pure report has no place here; the narrative has of its nature no hinges or seams. Message cannot enter here except by acknowledging the narrative law and putting itself under its protection. And that is what it does; without encroaching on the configuration of the narrative, it nonetheless significantly *rhythmicizes* it—by *Leitworte*.[5] Those who listen will hear the higher meaning in the similarity of sound. A connection is established between one passage and another, and thus between one stage of the story and another—a connection that articulates the deep motive of the narrated event more immediately than could a pinned-on moral. Epic diction never overflows, never becomes rhetoric or

---

5. Ed. König, in *Stilistik, Rhetorik, Poetik* ["Stylistics, Rhetoric, Poetics"] (Leipzig 1900), speaks of *Leittöne* ["thematic tones"] in relation to biblical literature; but for him these are a matter merely of rhythmic and auditory aesthetics. A much weightier concept, though one that mixes the notion under discussion here with much that is quite different from it, and much that is intrinsically quite problematic, is presented by Alfred Jeremias' account, in *Das Alte Testament im Lichte des Alten Orients* ["The Old Testament in Light of the Ancient Near East"] (4th ed., Leipzig, 1930, p. 745) of the *Motivwort* ["motivic word"]. Franz Böhl, "Wortspiele im Alten Testament" ["Wordplay in the Old Testament"] (*Journal of the Palestine Oriental Society* VI [1926], 196ff.), gives valuable criticism; he also recognizes that these "plays" on words are matters of "deepest earnest," but has in mind only tendencies of the ancient folk narratives he is trying to reconstruct, tendencies which "the great, prophetic genius of the redactors" sought to erase the traces of. In actuality, however, it is precisely the redactors he thus characterizes who develop and perfect the *Leitwort* style. There are also useful remarks in the collections of biblical paronomasia made by Max Steif, "Wortspiele im Pentateuch" ["Wordplays in the Pentateuch"] (*Monatsschrift für Geschichte und Wissenschaft des Judentums* 69 [1925] 446ff., and 74 [1930] 194ff.) Subsequently Umberto Cassuto, *La questione della Genesi* ["The Question of Genesis"] (Florence, 1934), citing Rosenzweig's "The Secret of Biblical Narrative Form" (below), has developed the notion in my sense of it in a way very fruitful for exegesis, but without discussing it in a manner adequate to its depth of meaning and breadth of occurrence.

An understanding of biblical *Leitwort* style has also found manifold though largely fragmentary expression in Jewish tradition, both halakhic and aggadic, and also in classical commentary.

lyric; the *Leitwort* rhythm is a genuinely epic rhythm, the appropriate artistic *signum* of a mystery stretching around and into the world of aesthetic form.

The *Leitwort* style naturally emerges most strongly not, as in the Joseph story or in Exodus generally, where an individual event has been worked into a continuous narrative sequence and is not separable from it, but rather where the individual event is, as in the first thirty-eight chapters of Genesis or the narrative portions of Numbers, complete and comprehensible within itself. It is from these parts of the Pentateuch that I shall draw my examples.

One prefatory remark seems necessary. When I try to show the meaning presented by *Leitwort* style in a given passage, I am not trying to communicate that meaning in didactic sentences as the "true" meaning of the story— not, that is, trying to produce retrospectively what the Bible forbids itself to produce at all. Neither in this case nor in any case where one seeks the interpretation of the word itself is it acceptable to say, "this equals that." Interpretation by *Leitwort* style can only be interpretation *toward*, demonstration can only be demonstration *toward*—toward something that is to be perceived in its actuality, but not paraphrased in language or thought.

What is to be told is how after the Flood the human race was divided, how the "islands of the nations" were separated, "each one after its own tongue" (Gen. 10:5, 25, 32). Of this moment Deuteronomy sings (32:8) that God on high then divided Adam's children from one another. How did this happen?

The simple story is constructed in two parts (1-4 and 5-9): the human action, then the divine reaction. Seven *Leitworte* make the bridge from the former to the latter: "all the earth," "lip" (i.e., language), the cry "come-now!" "building," "a city and a tower" (of which finally only the "city" remains), "name," and "scatter."

"All the earth" at the beginning, then three times rhymingly repeated, then again at the conclusion of the story. But the meaning of the phrase changes. At the beginning it means the still united human race; at the conclusion, the surface of the earth over which the human race has been scattered in nations. But this second meaning occurs as early as the conclusion of the first half of the story, which then not only begins with "all the earth" but also ends with it—a correspondence that will reveal its significance later.

The united human race has a "lip," a dialect or language. In the first half of the story the word occurs only once. But in the second, where the disruptive, shattering power of God in judgment has its immediate effects precisely on language, the word occurs three times in God's speech, and once again in the summary at the end. The earth, the people of the earth, the destiny of the earth's peoples—these are what the story is about. But language is where it happens.

Its happening is occasioned by the presumptuousness of the people. Their presumptuous action below is answered by superior action from above. "Come-now," they cry, and bake bricks, "come-now" and build city and tower, "its top in the heavens." But then God comes down "to look over the city and the tower that the humans were building," and does so with the same cry. God's answer is an echo. He answers humans in human fashion, but a superior human fashion. We can easily call the divine "come-now" ironic; but it occurs amidst this series of linguistic correspondences between the human deed and the divine response, and all of them are ironic, and none.

The two last *Leitworte* express the impetus behind the human deed. "Name" in the concentratedness of biblical language means the mark and witness of power, outlasting mortal men. Accordingly, a name arises for this work; the name of the world-city opposed to God, the name deriving from the accumulation and confusion of languages: "jumble," "babble," "Babel." And they, for whom the unity of humankind was intended and to whom it was offered, build at the center that touches heaven, so as not to be scattered and dispersed; but precisely in consequence, and only in consequence, they are "scattered over the face of all the earth." Human perversion is itself reversed.

The seven *Leitwort* bridges, then, present for us the connection of rebellion and subjugation at the beginning of the history of the peoples.

An altogether different function is exercised by the *Leitworte* in a story of another rebellion and its subjugation (Num. 16:1-17:5), when Israel was becoming a people in the wilderness: the story of Korah and his "company," as Luther translated the crucial word and as we find it still in the most recent edition of Kautzsch-Bertholet. But this translation destroys one of the two *Leitworte* characteristic of the story; for the word by which the rebels are five times indicated, ʿedah, denotes ten times in the same story the whole community of the people.

A single root, yaʿad, producing two nouns, ʿedah and moʿed, and a verb, is the controlling *Leitwort* of this story; hence moʿed occurs here in a twofold meaning, once indicating the representative assembly of the community— Korah and his followers are at the beginning of the account called "princes of the community [ʿedah]," and "those called by the congregation [moʿed]"—and twice occurring in the phrase ohel moʿed that designates the Tent of "meeting"—the "meeting" namely between God and the people, the Tent of the divine presence, at the entrance to which the ʿedah of Korah is gathered in opposition to the whole ʿedah of Israel. ʿEdah is the congre-

gation or community, living and working as one in the continually recurring encounters of its members. What strengthens and exalts these recurring encounters into a state of community, however, is that the people
engaged in them experience the encounter with God in the *ohel moʿed* as
qahal, as a gathering together, as a totality; they receive his kingly teachings
and so become HIS *qahal* (v. 3). Notably enough, this term in its sense of
God's gathering occurs in the Pentateuch only twice (apart from the
Deuteronomic law), and both times it is spoken by rebels. It is spoken for
the first time here, by Korah and his followers. They, the princes of the
ʿedah and those called by the *moʿed*, "assemble" (v. 3)—the root *qahal* is used
in the story to supplement the *Leitwort yaʿad*, and is subject to the same
inner contradiction—"assemble above" Moses and Aaron, i.e., against
them, so as to defend against their special rights the general rights of the
ʿedah as a whole: "Too much is yours!/ for all the congregation, all of them
are holy,/ and HE is in their midst;/ why do you lift yourselves above his
totality?"[6] This attribution of general holiness to the *ʿedah* is at odds with its
order and structure; it is itself the most dangerous differentiation, founded
as it is in the false identification between those who are "without limit" and
the community as a whole. That is Korah's *ʿedah*: the false *ʿedah* within the
genuine, the usurped *ʿedah* within the properly founded, the *ʿedah speaking*
of God and holiness within the *ʿedah* called anew by God to *become* holy for
him just before this story begins (15:40). That is what Moses means with his
indictment: "so then,/ you and all your congregation/ you are those who
present yourselves together [*noʿadim*] against HIM" (v. 11).

The second *Leitwort* lacks the fruitful inner contradiction of the first; but
it leads us still deeper into the issue presented by the story of Korah's rebellion. It is the root *qarab* in the transitive *hifʿil*-form, meaning "to come near
to," "to let come near," "to bring near to." The almost panarchic claim of
equality made by Korah's people incorporates what is first explicitly
expressed in Moses' answer to it, namely the special claim on behalf of
Korah the Levite to be equal in office to the priests, i.e., when making offering, to "come near to" the sanctuary in the priests' manner. Now "to come
near to" is the most explicit of the biblical notions of offering, almost all of
which point by genuine or popular etymology to the fundamental fact that
the action of offering works by a "lifting up," a "leading toward," a "nearing"
to affect the relation between the one making offering and God, and in particular so as to overcome the distance between them. The most general
term for making offering is *haqreb*, "nearbringing"—hence, precisely, the
general term for the offering itself, *qorban*, "nearbrought." We "bring" the
sacrificial animal "near" to God; but, as the atoning-offering is by the laying

---

6. This is B-R's reading of *qhl* in its nominative form [eds.].

on of hands of the man in need of expiation functionally identified with him, and is presented in his place, so the "nearbringing" contains also our own "nearcoming." The smoke of the offering, "moving near to" heaven, is the visible sign that the distance intervening has been overcome. The same concept is also used, however, to designate the consecration of both priests and Levites for the temple service. Aaron and his sons are "brought near" to "priestize" for God, i.e., to serve God *without intermediary* (Exod. 29:4 and 8, 40:12 and 14, Lev. 7:35 and 8:6, 13, and 24).[7] The Levites also, as having been "given over" to God by the people in the place of their birth, and "taken up" (Num. 8:16 and 18:6) by him, are "brought near" (8:9f., 18:2), but in an unusual way: they are brought only "before" the sanctuary (as once before, in Lev. 9:5, the whole ʿ*edah* was brought), and only "with" Aaron. They are, that is, entrusted only with indirect attendance;[8] they are brought near, but "coming near" the apparatus of the sanctuary itself is forbidden them (18:3), and so is the *activity* of "nearing," i.e., of making offering. Korah's rebellion seems then the crisis in which this limitation on the Levites' domain is maintained as God's will against the claims of men, is validated in the language of catastrophe so as finally to be proclaimed in the language of law (18:1-7).

This problematic of "nearing" in its double meaning determines the atmosphere of the Korah story. The story is fitted between two passages (chapters 15 and 17:1-18:7) that deal with "drawing near" and "bringing near." At the beginning of the first passage, almost exclusively occupied with regulations concerning offerings, we find the conspicuously paronomastic phrase, "let him come near who brings near his nearing." The other, incorporating both the story of the people's grumblings and their punishment and also that of Aaron's sprouting staff, closes with the paronomastic and apprehensive question of the people, "every nearcomer who comes near HIS dwelling dies; shall we die altogether?" Seven times in the fifteenth chapter we find the *hifʿil*-form in the sense of "offering"; once we find it in the rare sense of a secular "bringing near" of a person, in an episode (vv. 32-36) clearly introduced precisely for the sake of this phrase. In chapters 16 and 17 and in their continuation in the ordinances of chapter 18, it occurs nine times; three times in *qal*-form, three times in the adjective derived from the participle of the *qal*-form. This verbal atmosphere, and with it the multiple recurrences of the root "to die" in all these passages, communicates to the reader receptive to *Leitwort* style what is at issue here, and how seriously it is at issue, more compellingly than could any

---

7. See my *Kingship of God*, pp. 125f.

8. This indirect relation, referred to as mere *lavah*, "support," is linked in folk-etymological paronomasia to the name *Levi* (18:24; cf. also Gen. 29:34).

didactic text. Moses' answer must be read on the basis of all this; every occurrence of "nearing" in his answer is marked by it. "Come morning, HE will make known/ who is his and who is holy,/ to let him come near;/ whom he chooses, him he will let come near him." And: "is it too little for you/ that Israel's God distinguished you among Israel's community, to let you come near him,/ . . . near he let you come, and all your brothers, the sons of Levi, with you,/ and now you seek also the priesthood as well!" And then, with the same word, comes Moses' challenge to them to put the "nearing" forbidden them to the *test*, the test that will produce the catastrophe: "take you all your pans,/ put incense on them, and bring you all your pans near before him." (Then, rhymingly, there follows, "two hundred and fifty pans,/ and you and Aaron also with your pans, they all took their pans." In the seventeenth chapter, after the catastrophe, the pans come back— Aaron's too, with which he now stands, burning incense, in mediation "between the dead and the living.") One nearing was authorized; presumptuousness coveted a further nearing; so let the presumptuous come near— and burn.

Moses' answer paronomastically repeats the crucial words of the challenge: "it is too much for you," cried the followers of Korah, and Moses answers, "too much for you, sons of Levi." Korah's followers would speak for "all the congregation"; it is as "you and all your congregation" that they are rejected—they have in fact spoken only for the false *'edah*. "All are holy" is the motto of the rebels; Moses counters this with, "the man whom HE chooses is holy."

With this doubled "whom HE chooses" we encounter a crucial word. As a *Leitwort* it guides us[9] on to the next passage, where death in abundance is followed by the confirmation of life (17:20): "it shall happen,/ that the man whom I choose,/ his staff will sprout."

Leitworte have still another function when what is needed is to hint at the expiation of a guilt without discussing it as such. Verbal correspondences mark the later events in their compensatory meaning; the passages fall together, as it were, and the expiation covers the guilt.

Investigating such a narrative can make us feel that we have discovered a hidden, primordial midrash in the biblical text itself; and we may then be dubious. But the correspondences are so exact, and fit so perfectly into the situation as a whole, that we have to accept the idea: that the roots of the "secret meaning" reach deep into the earlier layers of the tradition.

It is abundantly clear, for example, from a passage like Jer. 9:3 that biblical vision saw clearly enough the problem posed by Jacob's treatment of his

---

9. A *Leitwort* etymologically is a "leadword," a word that leads or guides the reader through the thickets of the text [eds.].

brother Esau, and perceived Jacob's wrongdoing as real wrongdoing; Hos. 12:4 can be understood in much the same way. The task of the Genesis narrative was to comprehend the genealogical development of Israel on the basis of an original divine election and the subsequent selections determined by that election. It had also to present the rejection of the first-born as done under the authority of God, and accordingly could not *discuss* the injustice involved—nor would it as a genuine narrative have space for such an excursus in the first place. But also it had to remain faithful to the leading thesis of the Bible's latent historical theology, namely that God's governance leaves human action free and demands human responsibility for it, that history therefore is not an interrupted monologue but a genuine dialogue. The biblical *Leitwort* style provided as of its own accord the solution to this dilemma—except that here, clearly, that style also affected the choice among various traditions, affected perhaps even the shaping of the tradition itself; here the style worked through *Leitmotive* even before condensing them into *Leitworte.*

To Esau's "exceedingly great and bitter cry" Isaac answers (Gen. 27:35), "your brother came with deceit and took away your blessing." And then Esau: "is that why his name was called Yaakov, Heel-Sneak? For he has now sneaked against me twice;/ my firstborn-right [*bekhorati*] he took, and now he has taken my blessing [*birkhati*]!"[10]

Four motivic words: "deceit," "birthright," "blessing," "name."

In his exile, protected by God but not preserved from affliction, Jacob learns what it is like to encounter deceit in one's own clan. The first *Leitwort* recurs in his complaint; with the same verbal root[11] he asks Laban, "why have you deceived me?" And Laban answers—with the second *Leitwort.* For what was Laban's "deceit"? Just as Jacob, the younger son, presented himself in disguise as the first-born, so Laban gave to Jacob as a wife not the younger daughter but the first-born in disguise. "Such is not done in our place," says Laban, "giving away the younger before the firstborn." *Bekhorah:* first-birth; *bekhirah:* firstborn. "Such is not done in our place," says Laban.

Laban "cheats" Jacob one more time (31:7), but this time God is with Jacob and helps him prevail. After twenty years, divided into "two camps," Jacob returns to his homeland. He wants to meet Esau and be reconciled with him. But first he must undergo the final test, the struggle at night with the "man." Here two things are at issue, the blessing and the name. (The sequence of *Leitworte* here is as follows: "blessing," "name," "name," "name," "name," "blessing," "name.") The blessing he wins is to cover over the bless-

---

10. Here as often, the assonance suggests that the verse is of central importance, and is therefore to be kept in mind in what is to follow.

11. It occurs only one other time in the Pentateuch: Gen. 34:13, of Jacob's sons.

ing he stole: "I will not let you go/ unless you bless me." But then the man
asks his name. "Jacob," he says; and the biblical hearer of the story heard, as
the passage in Jeremiah shows, "Heel-Sneak." It was precisely this, i.e., the
name's confession of wrongdoing, that the man wanted to hear stated. And
now he takes this name of wrongdoing away: "not as Yaakov, Heel-Sneak,
shall your name be henceforth uttered"—indeed, one could almost translate,[12] "no longer will your name be understood as Heel-Sneak"—"but
rather as Yisrael, God's fighter." The bad fight is expiated by the good; the
name of ill repute is redeemed by a name of holiness. The *Leitwort* "name"
follows three times more, and drives the meaning of what has happened
home. In between, there is the blessing, without any speech; probably what
is meant is only the gesture of blessing, but that is enough; the blessing
Jacob has fought for covers over the blessing he sneaked away. Soon (35:10)
God himself will proclaim the renewal of the man Jacob-Israel, and thereby
finally accomplish it. But first the brothers must be reconciled, and this too
happens through the use of the *Leitwort* "blessing": "pray take my token-of-
blessing [*birkhati*] that is brought to you" (33:11)—in this way Jacob asks
Esau not to disdain his gift. When Esau accepts the gift, "blessing" has been
compensated for by "blessing," between one man and another.

The largest pattern of paronomastic style in the Pentateuch—which is also
a pattern of paronomastic *composition*—is the Abraham story.[13] Passages
unmistakably marked by *Leitworte* are joined to passages of a different sort,
altogether free of *Leitworte*, but they are joined in *Leitwort* manner, so that
we have as it were to do with two layers of paronomastic storytelling, which
however cannot be precisely differentiated. It looks rather as if the
paronomastic shaping of the story had taken place at the same time as the
paronomastic linking of it to other stories, adjacent to it or thematically
related to it.

I shall take only a few examples from the abundant material here (there
are considerably more than forty distinct discernible verbal linkages in the
story as a whole), choosing them to characterize the diversity of functions
and forms of *Leitwort* style, a diversity notable in this story in particular.

The Abraham story is constructed of seven scenes of revelation (12:1-4,
12:5-9, 13:14-18, 15, 17, 18, 22:1-19). Between the scenes we find at first only
individual passages bearing on other matters; then, between the next-to-last
and the last, a whole collection of such passages; finally, after the seventh,
after what is the incomparable culmination of the religious narrative, we

---

12. Cf. Ps. 139:20 (Masoretic variant reading) and mss.
13. See also on this my "*Genesisprobleme*" ["Problems in Genesis"] (*Monatsschrift für Geschichte
und Wissenschaft des Judentums*, 1936).

find whatever now remains to be said of a biographical and genealogical character.

   The first revelation is rather a communication than a revelation in the strict sense; in it God lets Abraham experience, not God himself (first Abraham is to "see the land," and only then will God himself [v. 7] "let himself be seen"), but only God's will. Now this first revelation—the drawing of a man out of his natural setting, the call to leave homeland, relations, paternal house—and the last revelation—the drawing of a man out of the earthly contentment of his soul, the call to utmost devotion and sacrifice, even to the sacrifice of his son, his only and beloved son, the son promised and vouchsafed—are by the work of narrative composition brought into close relation to each other; they are made to correspond to each other as beginning corresponds to completion. The compositional means of this effect are *Leitworte.* "Go-you-forth," says the voice of the yet unknown being in Haran, and sends the chosen man into the land assigned to him; "go-you-forth," says at the end of the wanderings the now familiar God to his servant, "testing" him, so as to bring the otherwise unrealizable readiness of his servant's heart into the world. "Go-you-forth"—nowhere in the Pentateuch but in these two places do we find this peculiar idiom, which might be rendered word-for-word by "go, you." Directly after each occurrence we learn what the idiom actually means: after the former, "to the land that I will let you see"; after the latter, "upon one of the mountains that I will tell you of." "Go-you-forth" means, Start off in the given or indicated direction till something happens to indicate a stop. What follows the divine utterance in both cases is the realization of it, without question or scruple; immediately afterwards in the former, after a few preparations in the latter, we find the word *va-yelekh*: "And Abram went," "and he went." A third *Leitwort* creates a further arch from the first text to the last. The summoning in Haran culminates in a fivefold repetition of the root "to bless": the promise of blessing, linked with the commandment to the national father and through him to the nation to become a "blessing" (a commandment to which proclamations like Isa. 19:24 and Zech. 8:13 are linked both in exhortation and in comfort). The summoning at Beersheba contains no mention of blessing, only the simple petition "pray take" (Gen. 22:18), clearly intended as a request rather than an order; but the "messenger"'s final speech to Abraham, after the unbinding of the sacrifice, blesses him in a triple recurrence of the verbal root, and as there the text reads, "with your seed shall all the nations of the earth bless one another," so here it reads, "all the nations of the earth shall enjoy blessing through your seed." Remarkably enough, this divine statement about Abraham is made once more, in between the two actions (18:18): "all the nations of the earth will find blessing through him." This phrase links the predicate of the first statement with the subject of the second—but not in dialogue, rather in God's soliloquy. The statement will be repeated for Isaac with the one verbal form (26:4) and for Jacob with the other (28:4).

Such linking correspondences prevail not only between passages of the Abraham story but also between that story and others—most clearly between the covenant with Abraham and the covenant with Noah, i.e., between the two divine covenants preceding the covenant made at Sinai. First, *Leitworte* parallel the two persons; the *tamim* ("whole") and *hit'hallekh* ("walk") of 6:9 correspond to the *hit'hallekh* and *tamim* of 17:1. We do of course strikingly encounter indicatives in the former place but imperatives in the latter, as if Noah's qualities and attitudes were being assigned to Abraham as tasks; but "to walk in the presence" of someone (17:1) is something more than simply "to walk about with" someone, since the former means not only faithful companionship but precisely the active service of the herald or harbinger, performed by Abraham as he goes through Canaan and calls out God's name (12:8, 13:4, 21:37, the last of which with its proclamation of the *El 'olam* ["God of the man in his generations" (6:9)])is evidently directed to the Philistines)—here I would in all earnest agree with Rabbi Yohanan (Sanhedrin 108a), that this striking expression critically articulates a sense of Noah's limitation—but evidently with an idiom preserved only here, the exact meaning of which we can therefore not ascertain.[14]

As to the covenants themselves, however: one covenant is made with the new humanity after the Flood, one, after the new failure, with the chosen father of a single nation. We should note how difference is embedded in similarity: similarity in the phrase "I will establish my covenant"; similarity in the resounding recurrence of the word *berit* (seven times in God's speech at 9:9-17, ten times in God's speech at 17:1-14 with a triple mention later in vv. 19 and 21), the word in both places (once in the former, twice in the latter) being strengthened to "age-old covenant" (occurring in both places in the penultimate position); similarity in the evocation of the "seed," in the former place once, in the latter, naturally, five times in succession, "your seed after you." And finally, similarity in "the sign of the covenant"—in the former place of course the general human covenant, public, cosmic, and transient; in the latter the covenant particular to a nation, hidden, physical, and lasting; in the former enacted by God, in the latter by man.

I cite only as an example a correspondence establishing a *prospective* connection: the "*I* am he who brought you out of Ur of the Chaldeans" of

---

14. If Benno Jacob is right in his ingenious assumption in *Genesis* (Berlin, 1934; p. 267) that what is referred to in "his generations" is the two ages of the world Noah lived through, then we could understand the phrase as meaning that "for a man of so questionable a transitional period he might be called *tamim*."

15:17—of, that is, the passage in which the Egyptian exile is foretold—and the "*I* am your God, who brought you out from the land of Egypt" of the Decalogue. This correspondence belongs to the series of relations between the lives of the national patriarchs and the history of their nation, which it would be good to have discussed at length.[15]

Several times we encounter a paronomastic mediation between two adjacent narratives. The folk-etymological pun on *miggen* (14:20) and *magen* (15:1) strikes every perceptive reader; before, we have the victory "delivering" over the enemy; afterwards, *after* the victory, we have a clearly deeper fear and the promise of a "shield" against it. Less attention has been given another passage. In the fourth revelation, the one in the middle of the series and the only one the account of which is delivered in the language of the prophetic books—probably because it is the only one indicating the historical future of the people in the precise sense of the word—we find (15:13) the first occurrence in the book of the root '*anah*, to press down, to make bend or bow, used of the behavior of the Egyptians toward Israel: "they will serve them, and will be oppressed by them." In the next story, the story of the Egyptian Hagar's flight, the same word occurs three times (16:6, 9, and 11), and does not occur again until chapter 29. Is it coincidence that an "Egyptian maid" (16:1, and again in 16:3) is the subject here, a maid who is herself "oppressed," and that her story will also close with the word "Egypt" (21:21)? Or do we not here rather have a remarkable connection between the history of the patriarchs and the history of the people? The story of Hagar is to be ranked with the story of Jacob's deceit toward his brother. Given the teleological character of Genesis, Ishmael must be excluded from the consequences of the promise, and Sarah therefore acts rightly and is confirmed in her action by God himself (21:12); but measured by the truth of biblical belief, which resists any shielding of one's fellows by God, and which will not veil human wrongdoing in divine righteousness, Sarah does wrong. As with Jacob, this cannot be said explicitly, for reasons based both on biblical theology and on the nature of epic narrative. But much is said by narrative implication. This Egyptian maid is the first person to whom God's "messenger"—i.e., God's intervention personally manifested—appears and speaks. What importance we are to attach to that is made clear in the thrice-repeated statement, verse after verse, "HIS messenger spoke to her." But not from heaven, as in the first Hagar story, the story of the boy Ishmael abandoned to die, and as also in the story to come in the next chapter of the boy Isaac bound down to die; rather this messenger approaches her in the manner of this world, as equal to equal,

---

15. This has subsequently been done admirably for chapter 14 by Cassuto, *La questione della Genesi*, pp. 365ff.

and speaks to her. His assurance sounds miraculous. That Sarah, the mistress, "had oppressed" her maid when she was "under her hand" (three times the word "mistress" is driven home, six times the word "maid") has already been told; but now the messenger cries to Hagar, "return to your mistress and oppress yourself under her hand." Yet the messenger may say this; he has cast himself down from heaven to the oppressed creature, and what he is recommending is not the mentality of a slave. The last occurrence of the root ʿ*anah* brings the credible reason: "for HE has hearkened to your oppression." Can one hear and hearken to "oppression," the silent state of the oppressed? God can. And at once the messenger ("angel" is what we ordinarily call him, but that obscures the purity of his "messenger-ness"—even a man can be God's messenger[16]) tells her for whose sake she must let herself be oppressed under the hands of her mistress; she will give birth to a son such as her heart dreams of, a wild nomad bowman, who leaping from one edge of the desert to the other will adroitly steal the hard-won crops of the cultivators, and so will "make his dwelling before the face of all his brothers," one after another. At the conclusion of Ishmael's genealogy—and thus at the conclusion of the entire Abraham story—we find noted the fulfillment of the promise, in a phrase paronomastically intensified (25:18): "upon the face of all his brothers did he fall." The *Leitwort* "hearing" mediates between the two Hagar stories (cf. 21:17); but the *Leitwort* "seeing" mediates between the story of Hagar's flight and the revelation made to Abraham immediately afterwards, the revelation of the covenant (17:1). The maid to whom the nameless messenger has spoken now calls upon God himself as the being having spoken to her, and calls him by the name of her experience: "You God of Seeing!" She justifies this in the astonished question, "have I actually gone on seeing here after his seeing me?" Like Moses in the cleft of the rock (Exod. 33:22f.), she "sees" God's "back" (the *aharei* of Gen. 16:13 evokes the *ahorai* of Exod. 33:23), i.e., God's participation in the human world, the mercy that restrains God's judgment (Exod. 34:6f.); she sees that God sees her. More than that no one can see. "Therefore the well was called" (the *Leitwort* "well" also mediates between the two Hagar stories) "Well of the Living-One Who-Sees-Me." God as choosing Israel concurs with Sarah; God as the Living-One Who-Sees-Me looks after Hagar.

This account of naming belongs like all things of this sort to the class of paronomasia in the strict sense, of paronomasia explicitly presenting itself as such. Related to this is the style of paronomastic dialogue: as when Abraham, in the passage evidently meant to substantiate Jerusalem's primordial claim to the rank of worldwide cultic center (14:18ff.), parono-

16. Cf. Hag. 1:13, Mal. 2:7 and 3:1.

mastically takes up Melchizedek's salutatory blessing in his reply to the other king present, namely the King of Sodom. Melchizedek had blessed Abraham in the name of "God Most-High, founder of heaven and earth"; Abraham then performs an identificatory act of considerable significance for the phenomenology of religion, by adding in apposition to the tetragrammaton the divine epithets used by Melchizedek—as if both to express the unchanging self-constancy of the divinity worshipped on Moriah and to acknowledge the name revealed to him as true.

Of a related nature is the peculiar recurrence of the *Leitwort mishpaṭ* in chapter 18—though this does not belong in the class of "presented" paronomasia, i.e., paronomasia attributed by the narrator to the conscious action of his characters. The habit of the casual reader is to treat this recurrence as something ordinary; to avoid this, we have first to realize that the word *mishpaṭ* in Genesis is with the exception of a single occurrence in chapter 40 to be found only in these two occurrences, separated by only six verses. The first is in the divine soliloquy in which God speaks to himself of the promise that in Abraham and in his "nation," "all nations of the earth" will be blessed (only here does the Bible in this way name the one nation and the nations of the world in succession). God says, "I have known him," meaning in biblical language that by electing Abraham he has drawn him into an intimacy of reciprocal relation granted to no one before him and no one until Moses after him (whose relation with God is described in a still loftier expression, Exod. 33:12 and 17). The intention underlying this "knowing" and the condition of the blessing are then stated: "in order that he may charge his sons and his household after him. . . ." What follows names God not in the first person but in the third, and thereby objectivizes him: "they shall keep HIS way, to do what is right and just," i.e., *tzedaqah*—concordance between action and essential task, verification and validation, verity and truth—and *mishpaṭ*. It is for this reason—for the sake, that is, of reciprocity—that God will not conceal from Abraham what he is about to do; he tells Abraham that judgment will be made on Sodom, and concludes his speech with the word "know" in a very different and yet related sense: he wants to familiarize himself with the reality of the sinning people, in the form of his messengers who enter Sodom alone. With this announcement—in which he also discloses to Abraham who the guest was who ate of his bread (humanity even today is nourished by this anthropomorphism, which is not "idyllic" but something even stronger than a sacrament)—he evokes Abraham's haggling plea, by which Abraham becomes the first person in the Bible to address God spontaneously. Only after this and in consequence of it is Abraham validated as the first proclaimer (20:7), i.e., the representative speaker between above and below, able to *hitpallel*, to intervene, to involve himself, to mediate—the word derives from legal discourse, and only secondarily has acquired the meaning "to pray." And now develops that remarkable dialogue that Wellhausen considers a late "excrescence." At issue, finally, is whether a group of innocent people (Abraham's plea goes down only to ten, i.e., the traditional number designating the smallest possible collective unit) can make it possible for God to "bear" the guilt of the guilty community amidst which the innocent live; and the man Abraham wins from God an affirmative answer to this question. The innocent are called *tzaddiqim,* "verified" or "validated"; the word occurs seven times there, and the *tzedaqah* previously mentioned is now as it were developed from it.[17] After the magic number seven has been reached, however, the word is avoided in the following five answers and four questions. The first question, however, closes with a remark that in simple, concentrated audacity surpasses even the Book of Job: "the judge of all the earth—will he not do what is just?" "What is just" is *mishpaṭ.* The play on the first *mishpaṭ* is for the attentive reader unmistakable. This is no "excrescence," but an organic narrative connection. Abraham has not heard God's soliloquy and is not alluding to it; but the narrator keeps hold of the *Leitwort,* and reintroduces it in such a way that we, struck by the connection between the two passages, perceive the reversal of meaning. There God commands men to do justice; here a man, "dust and ashes," challenges God to do the same. It seems to me, however, that the narrator knows silently that even this speech, once it has ended and the man returns "to his place" (v. 33), has been in truth God's speech to humankind.

One might claim that I have ascribed to the biblical narrator too "rational" a behavior. But all genuine poetry is in this sense "rational," i.e., it orders and forms elemental matter in accord with a shaping law of reason. The only question is, in whose service reason is functioning—or, in other words, whether what is functioning is the genuine reason, the reason that understands.

---

17. The adjective, previously used only of Noah, is used in Genesis only once more: in the story immediately following the story of Sodom, where the king of the Philistines asks God (20:4) whether he can destroy a guiltless nation, as if in a weaker echo of Abraham's petition.

THE SECRET OF BIBLICAL NARRATIVE FORM[1]

Franz Rosenzweig
(For Martin Buber, February 8, 1928)

I

When Goethe in *Dichtung und Wahrheit* reflects on the effect made on him and on his generation by the Wieland-Eschenburg prose translation of Shakespeare, he recommends that young people be given prose translations as a general rule, for the sake of the more profound and thorough transmission of subject-matter that such translations do after all offer. He refers in particular to Luther's Bible translation:

> Luther took a work written in a highly varied style, took all its diverse lyrical, historical, hortatory, and didactic tones, and presented them to us in our native language as if all had been cast in the same mold. In so doing he furthered the cause of religion far better than if he had striven to reproduce the various peculiarities of the original. In vain have later translators labored to make Job, or the Psalms, or the other biblical poems available for our pleasure in their particular poetic form. For the great mass of people that one is aiming at, a plain translation is always best; critical translations attempting to rival the original serve only the private delectation of the learned.[2]

Thus speaks Herder's great disciple, the former translator of the Song of Songs—that is, of "the most glorious collection of love-songs God ever made."[3] So Goethe's point here is important, like every point that has cost

---

1. Printed in *Kunstwart*, February 1928.
2. Goethe, *Dichtung und Wahrheit*, Book 11 [eds.].
3. Goethe, letter to Johann Heinrich Merck, October 7, 1775. Goethe is Herder's disciple precisely in accepting Herder's sense of the *poetical* character of the Hebrew Bible [eds.].

its maker a price. In fact, moreover, Goethe touches here on a seminal question in the speaking and hearing of the biblical word; and it is striking that for Goethe, as for anyone who takes the question seriously, the answer seems at first to have to be either one side of a dichotomy or the other. It seems, that is, that since there can be no truce between the claims of religious content and the claims of aesthetic form, the translator must choose between the claims of poetry and the claims of prose.

Goethe's iconoclastic mentality, offering as it does to cut the knot of the problem in two, arises from both personal and historical necessity. But it is of little help toward a lasting solution. Poetry is after all not divided from prose by an unscalable wall. No expression is entirely without form; pure prose is merely a liminal concept. In actuality, as recent investigations of prose rhythm have shown, we are all in a position precisely the reverse of Monsieur Jourdain's: we speak verse without knowing it.[4]

So the line of division between the "religious" aspects of the text and the "aesthetic" aspects has to be drawn otherwise than at first it seemed. Or rather: drawing the line of division is itself a mistake in the first place. An aesthetic object striving to be art for art's sake, a poetry altogether free of prose are of course notions that can arise only in opposition to the wildly extreme notion of a "purely religious" object, an absolutely unpoetical prose. (Moreover: if on the aesthetic side there arises the sin of being only for oneself, then on the religious side the ghastly mirror-image of that sin can arise and be embodied in response.) But where the aesthetic object does not become an absolute, neither does the religious object; it does not reduce itself to a special, religious sub-set of culture, but remains in possession of all its connections with reality—aesthetic reality included. Religious discourse does not then sink into the prose of bare "content"; rather it must—for it cannot do otherwise—avail itself of all means of expression, must sound all tones, must possess all its apparently fixed and prefabricated, independently transmittable "content" only by grace of the transient moment of oral expression. So Goethe's question—which was after all posed in response less to the Luther Bible itself than to the use made of it in Protestant houses, schools, and churches—loses its sharp, either-or quality, and splinters into a whole series of particular questions concerning the means by which the Bible can rescue the immediacy of the word for the mediated and mediable Scripture. This rescue is not the private diversion of philologists that Goethe declares it to be. So much is in any case clear from the fact that the thing at issue is not a form *in se* but rather the numerous particular forms without which the content in whole or in part would simply not be accessible. About

---

4. Monsieur Jourdain, in Molière's *Le bourgeois gentilhomme*, discovers to his great delight that he has all his life been speaking *prose* without knowing it [eds.].

forms *in se*, e.g., the threes and sevens now often posited as units of biblical composition,[5] Goethe would be right, even if such groups were made use of without desperate subtractions from and additions to the poor, suffering biblical text. Forms *in se*—even when they really exist for the author and not only in the imagination of the modern scholar—become important only when we understand their necessary connection with the particular content to be expressed. I genuinely believe that the individual structure of every hexameter in the *Odyssey* has a felt and sometimes perceptible relation with the individual words of that line; to translate is in fact to translate this relation, to make it once again felt and sometimes discernible. This is of course seldom possible; but where translation succeeds, what it renders is not only the "poetic form" but also the living word, the winged word, whose flight leaves both the empty form *in se* and the crippled content *in se* far below it.

The following discussion will treat just one of the problems of biblical expressive form: that of biblical narrative. Martin Buber has discovered this secret of biblical style in translating it, and has taught us how to reproduce it in translation.

II

When do we tell stories? First, of course, when something has happened. The most pressing stimulus to telling a story is present when someone knows something that others do not know, and which they must learn. This situation generally comes into being only more or less immediately after the event that is to be narrated, because later the narrator has most likely been anticipated by someone else. The typical case is the messenger speech of classical and neoclassical drama. In this situation, the narrator's action is perfectly natural and necessary. Both participants, narrator and listener, remain in their real time, in their present; the event narrated is not some indeterminate past but the past of their particular present, and is the past of this present alone, and even of this present only for a moment. The hearer can continue his life only by becoming, precisely, a listener: the story is the lock through which the ship of his life must proceed if it is to continue its journey. The narrator enters by means of his narrative into genuine dialogue, and thus into entirely *present* dialogue, with his hearer. He needs no artificial means to induce the hearer to listen.

Such means *are* needed by the narrator who tells stories from the love of telling and for the pleasure of hearing. He must *create* that intense attention

---

5. Rosenzweig refers here to Eduard Sievers' work on biblical meter; see George Buchanan Gray, *Forms of Hebrew Poetry* (London: Hodder & Stoughton, 1915), pp. 207ff. [eds.].

which attends messengers in tragedy from the moment of their appearance, or at any rate from the delivery of their first words. We are accustomed to say that a narrator must actualize,[6] and by that we normally mean that he must actualize the narrated event. In truth, however, his task is not the actualizing, the making present, of the narrated event but rather the setting of the hearer into a past whose immediately precedent past *is* that event. The hearer must listen as if the narrated event were not some indeterminate past thing but rather that past thing which concerns him just at his present moment; he must then let himself be removed from his actual present and be set within an illusionary present. He is to participate in the matter of the story, but less as someone would who was a direct witness of it than as someone would to whom such a witness was reporting. To facilitate the creation of this illusion, all great epic poetry prefers to set its action in the immediate past, or at any rate clothes its action in the guise of that past. (The historical novel, on the other hand, always seems an anomaly in this regard.) Even the great works of history—before, that is, Ranke transformed the writing of history from the leisure occupation of eminent public men made idle through retirement or otherwise into a learned professional activity—even these works had as their subject the world of active life from which the writer who had now become its historian had just departed. We are always most closely attentive to what has just happened; and where this close relation is not present intrinsically, a fiction has to create it for us.

If there were only this one natural form of narrative, then biblical narrative would be in trouble. Biblical narrative does not, after all, seek to remove its hearer from his own present circumstances, nor to make him forgetful of himself; rather it seeks to address him, and to have him respond, in the full presence of his body and soul. So it must not by any fiction eliminate the fact of temporal distance between itself and its hearer. The heard narrative must not transport the hearer from his own moment to a place beneath the shadow of Sinai; what brings Sinai within the hearer's immediate notice must be the hearer's active obedience—the law, that is, and not the story, Exodus 20 and not Exodus 19. The story seeks to matter to the hearer in his actual circumstances; and precisely for that reason it could not matter to him at all, if the only kind of narrative were the previously described "epical" narrative of the immediately preceding event. But there is another sort of narrative as well, to which the time of the event is

---

6. German *vergegenwärtigen*. Component by component, the word means "to make present," and it is for this etymological sense that Rosenzweig wants the word, since it plays nicely into his thinking about past and present (German *Gegenwart*). The idiomatic sense of the word, however, is "visualize" or "imagine." So it is, as Rosenzweig says, almost a cliché that a writer must *vergegenwärtigen*, as when in English we say that a writer must show rather than tell. "Actualize" is an attempt to suggest both the idiomatic and the etymological senses of the German word [eds.].

entirely irrelevant, and which, regardless of whether the occurrence took place recently or long ago, indeed regardless of whether it ever took place at all, nonetheless moves it into the hearer's immediate present, and so makes it the passage through which the conversation must proceed. We call this sort of storytelling anecdote.

III

"Not only children are nurtured by fairytales."[7] Lessing's Nathan the Wise is not telling about anything that has just happened; rather his story takes place "long, long ago." Yet his audience, the Sultan, listens to him with great attentiveness, as if Nathan had brought with him a pressingly awaited report regarding a recent and as yet unfamiliar incident; and the Sultan after the story is a shaken man, a changed man, other than he was before. Nathan's story is the answer to a question.

This is the other natural form of narrative. Here the narrative does not enter the conversation as an account from elsewhere, as the actualization of fate; rather it grows up within the conversation itself, as the answer to a question, as a contradiction to a statement, as an addition to a sentence. Its occasion, its stimulus, lies in the conversation itself; it acquires its necessity, its presence in the conversation from the narrator's being goaded into storytelling by the stimulus offered him by his interlocutor. Before the stimulus was given, the story was not in his consciousness, only in his memory; after he tells the story, it is the interlocutor's turn to speak.

This sort of story always has a point. A spark must leap between the stimulus and the point if the story is to be brought into the movement of the conversation.[8] If there is a point but no stimulus, the story becomes art-narrative. We see in the conversation of friends and acquaintances how when an anecdote emerges as a natural response, the conversation sometimes dissipates into a wild succession of jokes. The first of these usually takes its stimulus from the anecdote just told in the preceding conversation, whereas its successors have only the weak connection of a general theme—dog stories, Jewish jokes, smut—that after a while is itself felt as a constraint,

---

7. Lessing, *Nathan der Weise,* III:6 [eds.].

8. "Stimulus" translates *Stichwort,* "point" *Spitze.*

Ordinarily *Stichwort* would be translated by "cue." Juxtaposed to "point," however, "cue" evokes not narrative situation but the billiard table. "Stimulus," though more general, avoids this problem.

"Point" is a standard translation of *Spitze.* What Rosenzweig means by it is often what we mean by the "moral" of a story, the sort of propositional gist that anecdote and parable possess but that extended narrative, whether epic or novel, does not. For Rosenzweig that propositional gist is the "teaching" offered by biblical narrative [eds.].

as one story chases another in a meaningless hunt. To avoid such degeneration the great storytellers[9] devise one or many frame stories, these being not epic in character but anecdotal, which become artificial pretexts for an individual tale or for a whole series of them. This technical means of bringing about the natural narrative situation corresponds to the predilection of epic narrative for the immediate past. The storyteller may decline this artificial source of natural occasions for his timeless, anecdotal storytelling. But then he must also decline that natural actualizing of the story which comes about when the spark leaps from the conversational stimulus to the anecdotal point, and hope to substitute for it that artificial actualizing which comes about when the spark leaps from the anecdotal point to a stimulus lying dormant in the hearer's heart. This reversal of the natural sequence of stimulus and point, with the attenuation of the stimulus that it necessitates, corresponds to the imagined movement of the epic hearer or reader out of his immediate self and present into the self and present of a hearer situated in the immediate aftermath of the event. The point of the story becomes, in a sense, itself the hearer's stimulus; and whether the hearer can turn the point upon his own heart is now a matter of chance.

But then this form of storytelling also becomes unusable in biblical narrative. For here too, just as in natural conversation, narrative that is not message, i.e., epic, but teaching, i.e., anecdote, must come second in the dialogue: answer and not question, divine antithesis to human thesis, divine qualification to human statement. As message, biblical narrative may accost man; as teaching, it must be summoned by him. Revelation happens to him; commandment he compels by his action.

IV

Biblical narrative seeks to be both revelatory message and commanding instruction. Only in commanding does it offer revelation; only as message does it teach. Gnosticism and moralism are equally alien to it. How according to all analogy would we imagine a creation narrative? And how unimaginably *other* than our expectation is the creation narrative in the first chapter of Genesis! For that story, which must more than any other story claim the character of revelation, is in fact altogether directed to the normative character of divine action for human beings. The world is made and completed, yes—but the story is told in such a way that we learn from it why

9. German *Novellisten*; Rosenzweig means not novelists but writers like Boccaccio and Chaucer, or the author of the *Arabian Nights* [eds.].

we are to work six days, and why on the seventh, when our work is complete, we are to celebrate.

On the other hand: note how carefully the storyteller avoids, in, say, the account of Jacob's deception of Isaac (Genesis 27), any statement of his moral judgment—which judgment he surely has, along with his insight into the dark and fearful abyss of the *necessity* of the deception—except that judgment which is implied in the articulate course of the events themselves! So also for the account of Abraham in Egypt (Gen. 12:10-20). The biblical storyteller, then, must find a form at once epic and anecdotal, a form to give epic the timeless presence of anecdote, to give anecdote the stimulating, suspenseful character of the novel.[10]

Both the poet's devices, however, both the frame-story and the trappings of the recent past, are denied the biblical narrator; he may not snatch the hearer away from his actual physical and spiritual present, nor magically transport him to the circle of the frame-story, where people provide stimuli for telling anecdotes. The biblical narrator must rather transfer the stimulus into the narrative itself, so that the epic report can, without losing its epic self-sufficiency, nonetheless take on the pointed impetus of the anecdote.

So biblical narrative contains stimulus and point in itself; and each point can become the stimulus for the point to follow. In certain circumstances, moreover, a story is framed around a whole series of similar or formally linked words or formulaic sentences, which hold together, each with that which follows it, like the exchanges of repartee. These are distinguished, precisely by the importance of the *sequence* in which they appear, from the regular epithets and formulaically recurring sentences of Homeric epic, which they might at first superficially seem to resemble. The epithets and the formulae of epic give the poem a unified coloration, which like all visual things should be perceived in a single, comprehensive view; the recurring components of biblical narrative cannot be so viewed, but must rather be perceived in sequence; and where a story or a group of stories is ordered around a recurring formula, the formula must sound more portentous, more richly orchestrated, at each recurrence.

Ties and clamps[11] in biblical narrative can join together passages lying quite near one another, but also passages divided by long stretches; indeed,

---

10. Rosenzweig's shift from epic to novel may seem odd. But he is probably working in Aristotelian categories here; what we call "epic" is a sub-category of what he (and Aristotle) call "epic," i.e., narrative as opposed to lyric or dramatic. The German adjective *episch* can refer to both Homer and Flaubert [eds.].

11. German *Bindungen* and *Verklammerungen*. We might translate this, more abstractly but less jarringly, as "connections" and "linkages." But Rosenzweig's language is deliberately concrete and physical here, in fact medical; *Verklammerungen* are the clamps that hold the edges of a wound together [eds.].

they can compress wholly separate narratives into higher narrative unities. An example of the spark's leaping from stimulus to point over a small space: in Num. 22:29, when Balaam's ass shies at the divine messenger his master cannot see, Balaam cudgels the ass, then says:

> If only a sword were in my hand!
> For then
> I would kill you!

But now the messenger, with his drawn sword in his hand, suddenly becomes visible and pleads the wretched animal's case:

> She did well to bow down before me!
> For then
> you I would have killed and let her live. (v. 33)

The verbal repetitions, above all the manner in which the messenger takes up Balaam's angry "for then" and with sublime irony turns it against him: these purely formal means serve the narrator for the enrichment of an effect that is in the highest sense a part of the story's content—although the narrator has not, even for the sake of that effect, departed for a moment from his purely objective stance.

A clamp over a rather larger area, not as before merely over a small episode, occurs in Genesis when the aged Isaac explains to the lamenting Esau,

> Your brother came with deceit and took away your blessing. (27:35)

Then, two chapters later, just at the moment when Jacob must first acknowledge how scornfully his father-in-law and employer Laban is exploiting him in this strange land, the crucial word occurs again for the first time in a long while:

> He said to Laban:
> What is this that you have done to me!
> Was it not for Rahel that I served you?
> Why have you deceived me? (29:25)

We become suddenly aware of the narrator's linkage of doing and suffering; and yet not once has the narrator stepped out of his role. The betrayed Isaac has unconsciously given the stimulus that his betrayer, now himself betrayed, unconsciously takes up.

The greater the distance between stimulus and point, the rarer, obviously, if both stimulus and point consist in a single word, this single word must be if the reader is to notice it. In recounting the Israelite victory over the attacker Amalek, the text of Exodus states,

> And Jehoshua weakened Amalek and all its people with the edge of the
> sword. (17:13)

The text here employs a verb that occurs only here in all the five books. In Deuteronomy 25, i.e., two whole books away, Amalek's attack is mentioned again, here with a modified form of that same verb, which form occurs here alone in all the Bible; but here the word refers not, as before, to chastisement but to transgression:

> Remember what Amalek did to you on the way, upon your going- out
> from Egypt:
> he cut off the tail of all those grown weak from behind you, since you
> were weary and feeble. (Deut. 25:17-18)

Joshua crippled those who attacked the crippled; thus the second passage tunnels through to the first.

There are of course less obvious connections than the measure-for-measure schemes of the previous examples; these develop chiefly where the stimulus or the point or both consist not of single words but of word-groups. Jacob's nocturnal wrestling with his unknown, unnamed antagonist (Gen. 32:25ff.) is understood by the ancient Jewish interpreters, reasonably and yet also profoundly, as the decisive encounter between Jacob and the divine advocate of Esau. This reading is indeed the only reading that makes sense of the struggle in the place where it is recounted, i.e., between Jacob's apprehension over the ensuing encounter with the brother he once so maliciously betrayed and the auspicious outcome of that encounter. Moreover, it is only this interpretation that permits us to see into, or up toward, the *reasons* for this course of events, reasons which even then defy our understanding but at least command our respect. We may feel, of course, that the ancient interpretation reads something into the text that is not there, perhaps as a rationalization. But this can be shown not to be the case, precisely from the linking of the nocturnal struggle both to the apprehension that precedes and the solution that follows it. The account of the struggle concludes,

> Yaakov called the name of the place: Peniel/Face of God,
> for: I have seen God,
> face to face,
> and my life has been saved. (32:31)

This is anticipated by the conclusion of the account of Jacob's apprehension:

> For he said to himself:
> I will wipe (the anger from) his face
> with the gift that goes ahead of my face;
> afterward, when I see his face,
> perhaps he will lift up my face! (32:21)

and echoed in the auspicious solution:

> For I have, after all, seen your face, as one sees the face of God
> and you have been gracious to me. (33:10)

In this case our insight into the narrative secret of biblical style merely confirms what we can perceive otherwise. In other cases it is *only* in the light that the narrator diffuses over the surface of his narrative by means of these verbal equivalences that the meaning of the thing narrated becomes clear. Thus the account of the building of the "Dwelling," in Exodus 35-40, is shot through with the "he made" of the creation story. Moreover, the creation story concludes with "so were finished the heavens and the earth, and all their array" (2:1); the Dwelling story concludes with "so was finished the service of constructing the Dwelling, the Tent of Presence" (39:32). The creation story ends, "God blessed" (2:2); the Dwelling story ends, "Moshe blessed" (39:43). Again, the revelation of the divine name at the Burning Bush, "I will be-there howsoever I will be-there" (Exod. 3:14), is anticipated by a "here, I will be-there with you" (3:12) and echoed by an "I will be-there with your mouth" (4:15), and by this anticipation and echo is determined in its absolute immediacy, and in the eternality to which this immediacy, this rootedness in the moment, gives rise. This combination of immediacy and eternality becomes the meaning that then in the course of the history of revelation across the centuries becomes the stimulus to all God's further promises of presence to his people.

Or, to take a story quite enigmatic in itself, for which only this attention to verbal equivalence offers even a hint toward understanding: Balaam has at first, at God's bidding, refused the request of Balak's courtiers that he accompany them. Yet he goes with the king's new emissaries, because God bids him. "But God's anger burned, that he went thus." Why? Has the narrator not just told us that God himself gave Balaam his orders? And cannot Balaam now go ahead with a clear conscience, feeling that he will only be doing what God will be telling him to do? The answers to these questions lie in the verbal linkages of the chapter:

Balak commenced anew to send courtiers, more numerous and hon-
    ored than those. . . .
But now
remain here, also you, tonight,
that I may know, what HE,
commencing anew, will speak with me . . .
The she-ass saw HIS messenger,
she pressed herself against the wall and pressed Bilam's foot against the
    wall,
and he commenced anew to strike her.
But HIS messenger commenced anew to cross over
and stationed himself at a narrow spot
where there was no way to turn to the right or the left. (Num. 22:15, 19,
    25-26)

The story of Balaam's expedition revolves, then, around the problem of
"commencing anew," of doing something twice. Ordinarily the proverb is
right: once is not enough. So Balak may indeed make a second attempt,
and commence to send his courtiers again. Balaam thinks so too, when he
commences a second time to beat his ass. He does not of course suspect
that his action takes place in the presence of a divine command that "commences anew" on its own account. In God's sight, once is once and for all;
and the man who, like Balaam, after hearing God's first word makes a further attempt to see whether in the end the proverb is valid for him as well is
punished precisely by its becoming the case that now, for him, once is not
enough in earnest—and now, in fact, "once" for the second time. If we are
not to be satisfied with God's first clear word, but must try what God, commencing anew, will say to us a second time, then God will this time unerringly speak the words of our own heart's demon. So the expedition amidst
God's anger positions itself within the great theme of the story: of the man
who sought to curse and had to bless, because he could, as is said not less
than six times with slight variations in the three chapters, only speak the
words that God spoke to him. He did really seek to curse; his wish for a
"newly commencing" divine word shows his innermost heart clearly
enough.

In the course of this argument we encountered an example of a formulaic sentence. For other examples we need only think of the "there was
evening, and there was morning" of the creation story (Gen. 1:5, 8, 13, 19,
23, 31), or the hardening of Pharaoh's heart after each of the Ten Plagues,
or how after the death of every judge the people continue "to do what is evil
in God's eyes" (Judg. 3:7 and 12, 4:1, 6:1, 10:6, 13:1). What distinguishes the
vital, driving character of these formulas from the pictorial character of
their Homeric equivalents is that they are never fixed in a single verbal

form; they are not the colors of things but the joints of the story. In Homer, all who eat, whether early or late in the narrative, "put their hands to the good things that lie ready before them";[12] and this is a large factor in the great Homeric perception of the unity of man in all times and in all places, a unity which emerges from the Homeric poems from beyond the individual words, from the persuasive power of immediate apprehension. Schiller has expressed this unity in the remark that Homer's sun shines for us also, which despite its simplicity is the profoundest remark about Homer ever made. In Homer too, then, there is a form that reveals the innermost nature of the poem's content, with a power and clarity not to be had by any other means. Form—real form, not "poetic form," and substance—true substance, not apparent, indicable "content"—are indivisible.

V

Probably the form revealed and illuminated thus far is not restricted to the Bible; I would indeed consider the likelihood that such is the case very small even on principle. I believe that almost every element of the Bible can be shown to exist elsewhere as well, if one has sufficiently wide knowledge—knowledge that is of course harder to acquire than is the abstract thesis of universal comparability. The Bible's uniqueness is to be demonstrated irrefutably with respect not to the book as written but to the book as read. The Bible is not the most beautiful book in the world, not the deepest, the truest, the wisest, the most absorbing, not any of the ordinary superlatives— or at least we cannot impose any of these superlatives upon anyone not already predisposed in their favor. But the Bible is the most important book. That can be proven; and even the most fanatical Bible-hater must acknowledge as much, at least for the past—indeed his fanatical hate acknowledges as much for the present as well. What is at issue is not a question of personal taste or spiritual disposition or intellectual orientation, but a question of transpired history.

Thus all the peculiarities deriving from the oral character of this book realize their full uniqueness only through its historical destiny. It is the special destiny of the Bible that this last surviving and yet continually abiding oral book has been preserved for our world and our time, which are a world and time of *writing*. In other books, perhaps, both new books and old, occur forms similarly derived from oral composition; but in other books these forms remain, precisely despite their origin, dumb, because the books in

---

12. Rosenzweig quotes from the celebrated German translation of Johann Voss (e.g., *Odyssey* 1:149); we have substituted the corresponding phrase from the celebrated English translation of Richmond Lattimore [eds.].

which they might speak have themselves been stricken dumb by the law of the time and speak only occasionally and only to individuals and isolated groups. Let us imagine that this formal law of pointed epic[13] prevailed in an even approximately comparable degree of richness and variety of layered linkages in some other book. Today such a law would become only a literary form, and would, precisely because of its oral origin, be a form far less vital than the forms—say, for the sake of a perfectly evident example, the paragraph—which, developed from a written tradition and for a written tradition, lie open before the hastening eye of the reader, rather than addressing the attentive ear of the hearer.

Still more important is another thing. The incorporation of a dialogic element, framing the narrative about an alternation of question and answer, speech and counterspeech, proposition and qualification, has been discussed here as a principle of biblical narrative form. It is in fact present in the Bible not only in narrative but also in the Bible's other genres: in the poetry of the Psalms, in the rhetoric of the prophets, even in the casuistry of the law. But its significance there is of course less. Punishment and promise, praise and supplication and thanksgiving, law and proverb are much less likely than is narrative to be transformed as works of art to the objects of "pure pleasure," and to lose in that transformation their high seriousness and their connection to the real world. Writing drapes them only lightly; when the Psalms are spoken in prayer, when the laws are followed, when the prophecies are believed, they lose immediately their monologic dumbness and gain a voice to call the eternal interlocutor to dialogue: dialogue between man who listens and God who hears. So here it is not so crucially significant that even the one voice alone display a secret duet, a dialogic back and forth. The subterranean didacticism of that secret dialogue becomes important only when the public dialogue moving out from the book into the open air can no longer arise of itself—i.e., in narrative. All history must first show explicitly "to what end" we are to study it, and even then is vulnerable to the critical assessment of its "advantage and disadvantage for life"; even the greatest novel chiefly serves an empty need for entertainment. On the other hand: no love poem, even the worst, no police prohibition, even the most stupid, no manifesto, even the most pigheaded, has to justify its existence; those who first receive it, obey it, subscribe to it are sufficient proof of its right to life. It is of course a right only for a limited time—precisely this present time of being received, obeyed, or belonged to. When this time is past, any interest in the document

---

13. "Pointed epic" is of course for Rosenzweig an oxymoron; "epic," i.e., narrative, is of its nature not "pointed," i.e., instructive. The oxymoronic formulation sums up his sense of the uniqueness of biblical narrative [eds.].

becomes aesthetic or historical—ceases, that is, to be *present*, becomes in the one case timeless interest, in the other interest in time past. But what precedes this stage, if the words of the document have once been spoken from out of the context of a human nexus, is a stretch, however short, of the present, the full and working present; whereas the storyteller, except of course in the two cases of eyewitness-reporting and responsive anecdote, must *a priori* content himself with his hearers' idle hours.

One aspect of the history of the Bible *qua* book is that the parts of it that have arisen from dialogue call back the human partner in that dialogue again and again. Again and again the Psalms awaken us to pray, the laws awaken us to obey, the prophecies awaken us to believe. But this regeneration of audience is not something that biblical narrative can count on, because it has always been, and remains, the narrative of things long past. Biblical narrative must content itself with the hearers whom the law, the prophecies, the Psalms bring it, from among those they have newly awakened to action, to hope, to love. Nor can it make these hearers an audience quick to snatch the word from its lips; if it did, it would have to remain far from them, in the epic past and the picturesque distance. But then it catches these hearers who are distant from it in the net of the secret dialogue that is extended through it; it transforms distant hearers into collaborators, in a conversation that beneath the shell of its epic past extends itself to them in full anecdotal presence. In word and answer, in speech and counterspeech, in proposition and qualification that conversation offers those who are awakened to action, to hope, to love the one thing they still lack, and offers it to them so unassumingly that action, hope, and love are not dogmatically crippled but spiritually winged: it offers them knowledge, it offers them teaching, it offers them revelation.

LEITWORT AND DISCOURSE TYPE: AN EXAMPLE

Martin Buber
(1935)

God's celebrated conversation with Moses after the people's great sin (Exod. 32:7-14, 33:1-5 and 12-23, 34:1-10) is, when considered in context, remarkable both for its structure and for its architectonic complexity. I know no other work of a rhetorical character in which rhetorical eloquence—the nature of which would seem to be at odds with mystery—is in fact so faithful to mystery. But also I know no other in which, as here, again and again bridges of words, and in particular bridges of *Leitwörter*, are erected to support the trembling step above the abyss. Looking even at something so evidently peripheral as the fivefold fugal "now" or "so now" (32:10, 32, 34; 33:5 and 13), or something so evidently incidental as the threefold emphatic "you" in 33:12, in its altogether varied and yet coordinated force—even in these cases we see in control the true signifying force of language.

The central *Leitwörter* are ʿam and ʿalah. They occur five times joined in a sentence (32:7, 33:1, 3, 5, 12), and numerous times separately. Three others—yadaʿ, panim, and ḥen-ḥanan—are arranged with them.

Unlike *goy* (32:10, 33:13), which indicates a physical, bodily unity (cf. *geviyyah*: body, corpse), ʿam indicates the totality constituted by association, by being-together and being-with (cf. ʿim: associated, with, together). Hence the former can be rendered by "tribe" (*shebeṭ* is before Jeremiah never an *independent* unit but rather a branch), the latter by "people." A people can be the people *of* someone who belongs to it, but the possessive suffixes ʿammi, ʿammekha, ʿammo can also refer to the God to whom the people belongs. Hence the possibility for the ʿam-dialectic of our text. "Your people . . . has wrought ruin," says God to Moses (32:7). "Your people" is to be understood here not only as "the people to whom you belong" but also

143

as "the people whom you lead"; so much is clear from the words that follow it: "whom you have made to come up from the land of Egypt."[1] Now comes the recurring characterization the text offers, "I see this people [cf. 2:25, where what is at issue is not, as here, the people's nature but the people's need]—and here, it is a hard-necked people!" (In "this people" we hear, as often afterwards, "this people below"—a connotation indicating variously both contempt and sympathy.) And now God enjoins Moses to separate himself from this people ripe for destruction, lest it be any longer "his" people; then God will single Moses out, as once he singled out Abraham (Gen. 12:2), whose posterity has now gone astray, and "make a great nation" of him (Gen. 12:10; the word here is *goy*, as almost always in Genesis where what is meant is the lineage unit). Moses answers, "*your* people, whom you brought up [not *'alah* here, which Moses does not use in this text, but *yatza'*] out of the land of Egypt"—meaning, You cannot assign this people to me, nor seek to replace it by me; this concerns not me but you, this is *your* people, you are the one who brought it here! And again, in a mnemonic verse distinguished in the Hebrew by suffix rhyme, "turn away from your raging anger [*'appekha*], be sorry for the evil (intended) against your people [*'ammekha*]" (32:12). Now Moses recalls to God, who has just been speaking of abandoning the patriarchs, the oath God swore to them: "that they may inherit (it) for the ages!" *Ve-nahalu*—just as the first of Moses' speeches of reconciliation closes with this word, so the same verb, in the same form (but with a different meaning: *u-nehaltanu*, "make-us-your-inheritance"), closes the last of them. The divine oath proclaims that the people shall inherit, and shall itself be God's inheritance, and the oath holds good in both respects forever. The *ve-nahalu le-'olam* is followed by a sentence of the narrator's that begins *va-yinnahem*, and is thus linked by assonance to the sentence preceding it—the assonance here being an image of the agreement between the two sentences. The sentence begins, "and HE let himself be sorry concerning the evil/ that he had spoken of doing to *his people*" (32:14). Through "letting himself be sorry," God acknowledges, Yes, this is my people, and it will remain my people.

But this is only the first stage of the dialogue: the fending off of destruction. Now, after the tribunal, comes the second (32:31-33:6), in which the issue is leading the people to Canaan. (32:35 is a parenthetical remark of the narrator; it refers to later events and is explanatorily linked to the conclusion of v. 34.) Moses begins by repeating God's "this people"; but in place of the meaning, "this wicked people, which I must accordingly destroy," we have come, by way of v. 21, where in "this people" we hear "this

---

1. I render the *hif'il* form in this way to make clear its *Leitwort*-unity with the *qal*. The renderings given in the versions of our translation so far published are all unsatisfactory.

poor, restless, unsure, fickle people," to the meaning "this indeed sinful people, this easily sinning people, whom you must accordingly forgive"! And then comes one of those magnificent linkages that seem at odds with the context but in fact contribute to the context's deeper meaning: "So now,/ [since they are indeed, like true sinners, dependent on your forgiveness] if you would only bear their sin—!" For the third time in the Bible, after Cain's despairing cry and Abraham's petition, we encounter this ungraspable but gravely meant "bear," which contains already in embryo the uncanny divine proclamation of Isa. 46:3f. Here, however, we encounter it with a direct object: God bears human sin. It is from this passage that we are to understand God's validation, God's "yes, I am that—yes, I will do that" at the conclusion of the dialogue: "God . . . bearing iniquity, rebellion, and sin" (34:7). But what follows the "if," giving for the first time Moses' *personal* answer to God's "you I will make into a great nation," is the "if not": "but if not,/ pray blot me out of the book that you have written" (32:32). Moses does not wish to be singled out and preserved; he remains one with the people, he stands surety for them. And God, at first apparently refusing, but then, with the same "so now" of mercy—earlier a plea for mercy, now a granting of it: "Go, lead the people to the place of which I have spoken to you." And now Moses, who declined grace for himself and stood surety for the people, is for the first time associated by God with the people: "Go, up from here,/ you and the people/ that you made to come up from the land of Egypt" (33:1). This looks like a partial repetition of the beginning sentence in 32:7; but here, set within God's announcement of the "messenger" to be sent, it is in fact its reconciliatory antidote. No longer "Go, down," but Go, lead the people onward, as before, all the way to the land! Not God himself, however, but only a messenger will God "bring up" with them; were God himself to "come up" amidst the "hard-necked" people, he would inevitably destroy it en route (33:3, linked to 32:9ff. by the epithet for the people and by the verb "destroy").

So far the second stage. Now follows the mourning of the people and the indispensable excursus on the Tent in 33:7-11—indispensable because it is fundamentally important at this spot to learn on the basis of *Botschaft*, i.e., theologically, to distinguish rightly between the "face to face" of v. 11, with which the "[Moses] knew God face to face" of Deut. 34:10 is to be compared, and the "seeing of the face" in 33:20 and 23. After these comes the third stage, to which we must in spite of the temporal interruption of 34:4 join 33:12-34:10. What is at issue is whether God himself, and not merely God through a messenger, will bring Israel to Canaan. There will be more to say on this passage; but for the moment let us consider it as regards *'am*. Moses first evokes again, and now for the last time, God's "this people": you have said to me that I am to bring "this people" up (v. 12); but how can I do

this, when you, although "this nation" (*goy*) is of all nations your own people (v. 13), will yourself not manifest this by going with us? And directly
after this "your people" comes twice Moses' "I and your people," fusing
God's "you and your people" and his own "your people." As the unity "I and
your people" he speaks to God: only by going with us will you proclaim that
"we are distinct [*niflinu*, as Israel was distinct within Egypt, cf. 8:18, 9:4,
11:7; the relation to the verb that registers the "removed" character of the
miracles is crucial],/ I and your people,/ from every people that is on the
face of the soil." Here for the first time in the Bible *ʿam* denotes humanity
generally; one thinks of Deut. 4:34, where the liberation from Egypt is
referred to as "the taking of a nation from among nations." Then comes the
entreaty for revelation and the revelation itself; and then, in the middle of
all this, introducing God with an absolutely unprecedented audacity into
his discussion of the limits of mercy, in order to win him for good on the
ground of his own confession of mercy—and, as it were, to catch him
before he says anything more about punishment—Moses "quickly" throws
himself upon the ground and speaks. Now he repeats on his own part, in
validation, "indeed, a hard-necked people is it" (34:9); but then he adds, in
a bold excess of logic, in an inference of the heart, an appeal to the Creator
that the change begin with him: "so forgive/ our iniquity and our sin,/
[alluding to God's speech in v. 7] and make-us-your-inheritance." And God,
as always acknowledging the audacity of fidelity as fidelity itself, answers:
"Here . . . before all your people I will do wonders,/ such as have not been
created/ in all the earth, among all the nations [cf. 33:16]." The phrase
"your people" as spoken by God to Moses is freed of any negative suggestion
by the effect of Moses' having spoken the same phrase to God. Moses' plea
in verse 9, "pray let my Lord go among us!" is answered in verse 10: "then
shall all the people among whom you are, see/ MY work, how awesome it
is,/ which I do with you." God among the people, Moses among the people:
God "being-with" Moses. The sequence begun by "I will be-there with you"
(3:12) is here completed.

Interwoven into this *ʿam*-dialectic is an *ʿalah*-dialectic, which we have
touched on briefly already. *ʿAm* occurs in our text about thirty times, *ʿalah*
less than half as often. *ʿAlah* is not manifested or developed so variously as
is *ʿam*; but it is important. Even in the narrative prologue of the dialogue
(32:1-6), we hear twice the voice of the people saying, "this Moshe, the man
who had us come up from the land of Egypt," and then "these are your
gods, O Israel,/ who had you come up from the land of Egypt." In what follows the relative clause common to the two citations is repeated four times.
This would not be at all striking, however, if the clause did not appear in
this book only in this passage. The *hifʿil* synonym *yatzaʾ* occurs in this book
twenty-four times outside the passage (two times inside it); the *hifʿil* of *ʿalah*

in this sense occurs outside the passage only three times. Clearly, our narrative of sin and expiation is concerned precisely with something special, with "coming up." It is of course clear from many passages of the Bible that referring to the passage out of Egypt toward Palestine as "a coming up" is not only a matter of geography. Here the reference appears at first oddly ironic. To see this we can most easily adduce the significant parallels in 1 Kings 12:28, where Jeroboam addresses the people in ironic wordplay: "Enough for you, to come up to Jerusalem!/ These are your gods, Israel,/ who had you come up out of the land of Egypt." Samaria is high enough, he says; it is to this place that you have been led, and Gerizim is the true mountain of the covenant of holiness;[2] higher than that you need not go. The initial mood of our text is other and yet related. The man Moses has brought us up here, say the people (32:1); yet he himself has gone further up, up to his God up there, and so we do not know what has become of all this—we need God here where we are. And so they get their wish. But then God says to Moses (v. 7), Down with you then to this people that you have brought up so high! And Moses, after the punishment, in the brief passage from 32:30 to 32:34, which is concerned in a special sense with the expiation of sin and in which the root *ḥaṭaʾ*, otherwise foreign to our text except for two concluding occurrences in 34:7 and 9, recurs eight times—in this passage Moses says to the people "so now, I will go up to HIM,/ perhaps I may be able to cover over your sin." And now the people must accept his special going-up as their deliverance. But God, who has granted the possibility of that expiation, now and henceforth in speaking to Moses (33:1) associates him with the people—the irony still plays lightly in the half-acceptance: "Go, up from here,/ you and the people that you had come up." Yet afterwards, addressing the people through Moses, God says, "I will not go up in your midst,/ for a hard-necked people are you,/ lest I destroy you on the way" (v. 3). The true God will remain "up there," the "going up" must happen without him; and that would not then be a "going up." Here then Moses' protest begins (33:15): in that case, he says, do not ever let us "go up" from here. The solution is brought by Moses' last ascent to the mountain, where there appears not only the revelation of mercy but also mercy itself (hence the fact that the sin is again named here, in v. 7 and also in v. 9). The people's talk of "going up" is here truly realized in the actual "going up" of the person standing surety for the people to the height of mercy; this we learn in the triply emphatic *qal*-form of the verb (34:2-4): "Go up in the morning to Mount Sinai . . . no man is to go up with you . . . and [Moses] went up to Mount Sinai." We have here to think back to the triple *va-yaʿal*

---

2. On the claims for Gerizim, see the systematically arranged material in Micha Josef bin Gorion's *Sinai und Garisim* (Berlin, 1926).

of 24:13, 15, 18, to the sole going up *before* the people's sin, in an as yet uncomplicated act of advocacy. Between the two passages lie both the error and the recognition.

Yadaʿ is the next thread in the fabric. In the first parts of the passage we find the verb only once, unemphasized, referring to the "not-knowing" of the people (32:1 and 23). Only in the principal speech does this verb develop its dialectic. In five verses we hear it six times. Here in the third and last stage of the dialogue, after God has consented to lead the people further on, Moses asks that God lead the people on himself and not by a "messenger," that God himself "go with." In a singular way, however, this petition involves also the other petition, for "knowing." One has to look closely at this involvement, and must in the process remember that in the Semitic languages (nor only in them) "knowing" does not take place without contact, without "feeling." Moses says to God, you tell me now to lead the people on, and wish to give me only a messenger in your place, a messenger who however is (and here we have to recall such earlier passages as 14:19f. and 23:20ff.) personally unknown to me—or, as we might say, who is only a power. "You have not let me know the one whom [not just "whom"!] you will send with me!" You yourself have however proclaimed to me that I am intimate with you; "you said:/ I have known you by name" (33:12). (A name is the substance of the person, and to know by name is to touch that substance.) If this is then the case, then lest by being without your presence I be finally bereft of presence altogether, give yourself to me by revealing to me the reciprocal equality of our "knowing"; so that I may be certain of the way, let me grasp your "ways." "Pray let me know/ your ways,/ that I may (truly) know you" (33:13). God is inclined at this moment to grant not this petition but the original one; and soon after he indeed grants it, because his question in v. 14 is answered by Moses' passionate response in v. 16, namely that only in this way can the world "know" Israel's link with God. The last word in God's granting of the petition is then precisely the validation of the words that Moses has represented God as saying: "and I have known you by name" (33:17). This word closes the circle; the verb cannot afterwards be repeated. Now Moses, though jeopardizing God's granting of the community's request, renews his own personal request, which he cannot let drop; but now he speaks not of "knowing" but of "seeing" (v. 18).

What follows (vv. 20 and 23) links this "seeing" with the fourth *Leitwort*: *panim*. The word, previously used unemphatically in vv. 32:11ff., now evokes a passage already discussed, namely the episode of the Tent, which is linked by its *Leitwörter* with our narrative: "And HE would speak to Moshe/ face to face,/ as a man speaks to his fellow" (33:11). (*Rēʿa* is a being with whom one has an *immediate* relation.) In the following speech, however, *panim* appears first in an entirely different sense: in 33:14ff. Moses and God are talking about whether God's *panim* will "go," i.e., go with the people. 33:17 can as noted be understood only as an affirmative answer to that question. What then is the meaning of the "quick" renewal of Moses' petition on behalf of the community in 34:9? Has the petition not after all been granted? It has; but only the partial petition, with which 33:14ff. are still concerned. That God's "face" will "go with" means, since those who see His face will die (33:20 and 23), that God will precede the people, to cast down the enemies in their way—hence Moses' talk in this connection (v. 16) of the impression to be made upon the world, upon humanity, and hence also the "with his face" of Deut. 4:37. Moses' last petition in 34:9, however, "pray let my Lord go among us," has greater scope; it asks that God restore to the people not only his protection, but also the intimate inward presence offered them in 29:42ff. Yet it is precisely this inward presence that is portrayed in Moses' "face to face" speech (the *dabber* of 29:42 and that of 33:11 should be seen together). We cannot "see" God's face—or, in our conceptual language, God's face cannot become our motif. But we can let ourselves be spoken to by it, spoken to in our innermost being, and can stand before it to say our part—or, in our conceptual language, God's face can become our motivator.[3] To our plea (33:18) to be permitted to see God's *kabod*, his *majestas*, we indeed receive a refusal; but the twofold "no" is preceded (v. 19) by a twofold "yes," which speaks of the human face as the "no" has spoken of the divine: "I myself will cause/ all my goodliness/ to pass in front of your face,/ I will call out/ the NAME/ before your face." And this promise is fulfilled: God passes "before his face" (34:6). The man cannot see, because "the hand" shields him; but he hears speaking to his face the voice that expresses the *kabod* of the name.

Here then the last of the *Leitwörter* emerges. Five times in this last stage of the dialogue we have heard of the "favor" that Moses has "found in the eyes" of God, and the repetition might recall the love of repetition in Middle Eastern discourse. But here the love of repetition serves the needs of *Botschaft*. The recurring verbal sequence directs our attention to the heart of the matter; now the heart of the matter is revealed to us (33:19): "that I show-favor to whom I show-favor, that I show-mercy to whom I show-mercy." Or, unconditionally: "God, showing-mercy,/ showing-favor." That is the expressed *kabod* of the name. In it Moses perceives what he had prayed to be permitted to perceive: God's "ways." And when he now moves

---

3. "Motif" and "motivator" translate German *Motif* and *Movens* ("mover"). Clearly Buber understands these two German words not so much referentially as morphologically; they are for him both derived from the Latin *movere* ("to move"), *Motif* indirectly from its past *passive* participle, *Movens* from its present *active* participle. We cannot, that is, take God as standing in a passive relation to us, only in an active one [eds.].

"quickly," to say once again "if I have found favor in your eyes," then he is simply saying, in a last, extreme audacity, So then, do what you are! And God does it.

I have had to lay bare the circulatory system of a great text in order to show in it, vessel by vessel, its circulatory perfection. But into our new reading of that text we must draw not the individual parts of our analysis but only their totality. The network of blood-vessels must now present itself to our reverent gaze as a glowing, transparent whole.

THE BIBLE IN GERMAN: IN REPLY[1]

Martin Buber and Franz Rosenzweig

> I have always found that it is good to know something.
> —Goethe to Eckermann

We do not propose here to enter into the metaphysical or sociological ideas expressed in the review of our translation of Genesis; we do, however, want to discuss for the readers of this newspaper the points at which the reviewer attempts to justify his general thesis through reference to the *language* of the translation. To be sure, a proof that the attempted justification was mistaken at every point would determine nothing regarding the correctness of the reviewer's general thesis, namely that the Bible "in our time" has nothing to say; but the connection the reviewer attempts to make between that thesis and our translation would collapse. We ourselves consider his thesis misleading and pernicious; but we do not wish to develop this view in connection with his attack.

We shall strictly limit ourselves to the examples chosen by the reviewer himself. He seems to have chosen them in a fit of chivalric courtesy; in some cases, at least, we need only adduce the Hebrew original to make clear, even to those unacquainted with Hebrew, that the reviewer's argument is untenable.

---

1. In reply, that is, to a review of the first volume of *Die Schrift* by Siegfried Kracauer, printed in the *Frankfurter Zeitung* for April 27 and 28, 1926, under the title "The Bible in German." The review set out to show the unseasonableness of our undertaking, and reproached the translation for, among other things, "Wagnerizing." Our reply was printed in the *Zeitung* in a somewhat abridged form; it is here printed in full.

On the lively and important controversy centered around Kracauer's review see Martin Jay, "Politics of Translation: Siegfried Kracauer and Walter Benjamin on the Buber-Rosenzweig Bible," *Leo Baeck Institute Year Book* 21 (1976), pp. 3-24, and also Lawrence Rosenwald, "On the Reception of the Buber-Rosenzweig Bible," *Prooftexts* (forthcoming) [eds.].

Luther's "bring clouds" is in Hebrew ʿ*annen* ʿ*anan*, and so in our translation "becloud with clouds." The Hebrew of Luther's "slaughtering" is in the
passage in question *ṭaboaḥ ṭebaḥ*, and so in our translation "slaughtering
slaughterbeasts." Luther's "shall you be our king and rule over us?" is in
Hebrew

> *ha-malokh timlokh* ʿ*aleinu*
> *im mashol timshol banu*

and so in our translation reads

> Want to be king, you a king among us,
> or be ruler, you a ruler over us?[2]

"Lord" would be wrong, because the word used here is also significantly
used by his brothers to characterize Joseph after their rediscovery of him,
when they bring their father Joseph's message; "lord" would be too much
here, as Luther's "master" is too little. We hit on "ruler" because we had
used the associated verb in the account of the creation of man; Luther's "be
lords" in that passage distorts the meaning, which we had rendered strictly
by "they are to rule."

Luther says "to offer burnt-offerings" where the Hebrew—*ha-ʿalot* ʿ*olot*—
says nothing of "burning" or of "offering," but only, as literally as possible,
"to lift up upliftings." We ventured to put "high-gifts" as a clarification of
"upliftings." "Lift-offering" was inadmissible, since the word "offering,"
unlike its Latin root *offerre* (which renders quite well the meaning of the
Hebrew term), in today's language has taken on an unmistakable connotation of surrendering and renouncing—a connotation quite distant from
the Hebrew *qorban* ("nearbringing," "forebringing"). Luther's "burnt-offering" is drawn not from Hebrew but from Greek and Latin. The Septuagint
creates this explanatory term for the noun, while translating the verb
rightly; the Vulgate adopted the term as a Greek loan-word, and Luther naturalized it in German. All three held, as an eminent Protestant commentator says, "to the concept, not to the meaning."

The Latin is also the source of Luther's practice, which the reviewer
praises, of translating the Hebrew functional plural *toladot* by the ontological singular "generation." Our own "begettings," therefore, is not at all the
unintentional functionalizing the reviewer takes it to be, but is altogether

---

2. This is somewhat changed in word order from the rendering printed in the translation.
Why Buber should defend a text that Kracauer has not attacked is not clear, though the
defense would apply to the text Kracauer did attack also. The version in the first edition of
Genesis and the one Buber prints differ in the verb and in word order; an English rendering
of the original version might read, "Being-king, you would be-king over us,/ or governing, you
would govern us?" [eds.]

intentional, arising in fact simply from what is in the Hebrew. The Latin rendering we found interesting, as we did every earlier version; but only the Hebrew could lay down the law.

Also from the Vulgate is Luther's "gates of his enemies." The Hebrew says "gate of those who hate him." We give "high gate" to facilitate the reader's understanding of the singular, which means not just any gate but the gate at which counseling, marketing, and judging take place—a notion that in the Turkish *kapu*, "portal," generally rendered in Europe as "Sublime Porte," extends even into the present day.

The "scent" that so distresses the reviewer[3] comes from Luther himself, who with an alliteration evidently drawn from the runes "as Richard Wagner understood them" writes, "so that this offering of praise may be as the smoke and scent of the offering before." But why do we say "the scent of assenting"? Because the ordinary phrase, "the delightful scent," is Homeric (*Iliad* 8:549f.) but not biblical; the Hebrew word translated "delightful" is no adjective but the genetive of a noun that means "reassurance" or "calming." And why "scented the scent"? In Hebrew: *va-yaraḥ et reaḥ.*

The chief exhibit in the reviewer's argument, however, must be dealt with at greater length. Luther's "and the spirit of God hovered over the water" seems to the reviewer definitive. Luther himself was not so sure; hence the variant, "the wind of God etc." The Hebrew *ruaḥ* that Luther renders so diversely occurs, as Gunkel rightly remarks, only this one time in the entire Bible in the sense that it has here—in, that is, the elemental fullness of its meaning, which everywhere else is divided into "wind" (Gen. 3:8), "breath" or "air" (Gen. 6:17), and "spirit." This one time, however, what is meant is the arch-word that contains all these meanings within it. The Greek *pneuma* and the Latin *spiritus* possess a lesser but similar multiplicity of meaning. In Luther's time, however, the German word *Geist* had it too. That is why he can have God make the host of heaven "by the *Geist* of his mouth." But who today directly perceives the concreteness of that expression? Luther and his contemporary readers still could; hence Luther's thought that he might at the beginning of the creation narrative replace his all-too-unequivocal "wind" with the multivalent *Geist*—still multivalent then, but not for long. He did this, however, without any actual feeling of finality, and indeed without consistently holding to his own solution. In Jesus' talk with Nicodemus (John 3:5ff.), Luther in 1526 joins with his predecessors, including Meister Eckhart, in the suspiciously Wagnerian rendering, "the *Geist geistet* [the spirit spiritizes] where it pleases." But in later editions he writes, "the wind blows where it pleases," so that henceforth in

---

3. German *Ruch*, "scent" or "savor," distresses Kracauer because it is an archaic relative of the modern term *Geruch* [eds.].

his version of the passage as a whole the same word *pneuma* is rendered once as "wind," but immediately before and after as "spirit" ("that a man be born of water and the spirit"), although in the text it is in every case the same word, the arch-word we are dealing with here, meant in the same fashion. "You may well hear its sighing"[4] is not said of the "wind" but precisely of the *ruaḥ*, which here as there does its work above the water—of, that is, the power that encompasses both spirit *and* nature. No thing belonging to the created world can help a translator today to render *ruaḥ*—rather, only by making a noun of the word's connotations of sighing and rushing ("God's surging drawing of breath") can this unity of wind and breath and spirit be rescued for a language no longer familiar with it. "A rushing from heaven" is after all what Luther called the apparition of the spirit at Pentecost.

And our "brooding"? The Hebrew word occurs only one other time in the Bible, in Deut. 32:11; it is used there of an eagle that is either spreading his gently beating wings over his young, or brooding over them. The similar Syriac word means "brooding," and the Syriac Peshitta translates accordingly. This verb is incomparably closer to what the sentence in Genesis speaks of, the hovering over the unformed. The image of the bird over the nest is still present when the Talmud discusses the passage; "brooding" as the appropriate image of the first act of creation is still present in Augustine (*quodam fotu sancti Spiritus sui*, "by a certain brooding of his holy spirit"). In poetry, moreover, in the exalted passages of which the great metaphors preserve their life, the image reaches in captivatingly alliterative verses down to our own time: "When before, above what was about to grow,/ the father-mind hovered, brooding with delight."[5] But "surging," one might say, is after all motion, and "brooding" is stasis; where can they coincide? Precisely here! Here and only here are both in one; for the surging is *everywhere* above the waters. The Hebrew idiom in its brevity means, not at a single place above the surface of the water, but above the surface of the water in its entirety.

It was a gift fallen into our lap that the two German words *Braus* and *Brüten* retained the alliteration of the Hebrew *ruaḥ* and *raḥef.* We would have given the alliteration up if that had been the cost of getting this difficult line, each word of which probably cost us more labor than has this

---

4. I have come subsequently to the view that *phonê*, meaning always "voice" and never "noise" in general, refers to the voice that accomplishes over the primordial waters its work of creating the world, and over the waters of Jordan its work of recreating humankind (cf. the citation from Ps. 2:7 in the original text of Luke 3:22); the same voice appears as the voice of the holy spirit in a tradition preserved only in a fragment of the so-called Nazarene Gospel, but clearly of considerable antiquity (cf. the Targum of Song of Songs 2:23, where the "voice of the turtledove" is similarly interpreted).

5. *Natürliche Tochter* 3:4 [eds.].

whole present dispute, to be pointedly significant in other respects. In other cases, we had trouble avoiding chance alliterations in the German that the Hebrew text did not warrant. Luther's intrinsically splendid "even when the sea raged and roared"—an alliteration that turns out from a comparison with older prints and with manuscripts to be the product of conscious linguistic artistry—we could not accept without reservations.

These then would be the points from which the reviewer's lively imagination took flight for Bayreuth. If the readers of these lines are not prepared to draw the conclusion—a conclusion not maintained, so far as we know, even by the boldest Bible critics—that the Hebrew text of the Bible came into being only after 1876, i.e., the year of the opening of the Bayreuth *Festspielhaus*, then they will have no choice but to see that alliteration and reduplication, i.e., repetition generally, auditorily meaningful and verbally significant repetition, belongs to the essential nature of human speaking. This is confirmed by every child as it begins to speak, by the children's words that precede their actual learning of adult language, and by the learning of this language itself. Repetition is a deep need of human nature; the desire for variation comes only afterwards and in consequence. In linguistic history this truth is manifested in the fact that at a certain stage it becomes a law of good style to vary an expression where possible. But then, of course, the real and concrete specificity of meaning disappears, a specificity rooted so deeply in the vision of this and only this action that it cannot describe it otherwise than with the Hebrew or Greek writer, "becloud with clouds"; in its place arises the elegance of *stylistic* differentiation, which in the mouth of the elegant Latinist Jerome, who even when a church father does not deny that Latin literary style has been shaped by the belletrist Cicero, says rather "bring clouds." In Hebrew itself, when after the biblical period it became a literary language, the peculiar deepening and strengthening of a verb brought about by juxtaposing it to its own infinitive—a deepening and strengthening that our translation seeks to imitate or at least to indicate—was for the most part lost. Luther here as in many details of his translation followed the Latin text; his student Mathesius describes him at the head of his Bible revision committee—at the time, that is, when his knowledge of Hebrew was at its height—"with his old Latin Bible and his new German one, in addition to which he always had the Hebrew text as well." This "in addition to" of the genesis of Luther's translation, in both its negative and positive aspects, is mirrored in the now classic wording of every verse of his translation.

"Cultmaiden" [*Weihbuhle*] is, says the reviewer, a "restoration." We are not sure what exactly is supposed to be restored by it; we do know that the terms available to us, "whore" and "bedfellow," were in no away adequate to the

Hebrew, and the reviewer surely must know this also. The word *qedeshah* is derived from *qadosh*, which of course means "holy," "consecrated"; accordingly it designates a "consecrated" woman, i.e., one prostituting herself in one of the heathen cults, notably that of Astarte—a *hierodoulê* (as the word is translated by most modern theologians, who unlike us permit themselves the use of foreign words). In the Genesis passage it is used euphemistically for "whore." When Judah saw Tamar sitting "by the entrance to Two-Wells," "he took her for a whore," *zonah*; but when he sent his friend to look for her, he avoided the common term and asked, "where is that cultmaiden, the one in Two-Wells by the wayside?"—*qedeshah*. Luther translates both with "whore."

The savagery of "slaughterplace" had to replace the tamer "altar" because *zaboah* means "to slaughter" and *mizbeah* "slaughterplace." "Altar" today leads our thoughts altogether astray; in "altar" we conceive of something at which we kneel and pray. In Genesis people indeed often fall and often pray, but never at a *mizbeah*; that is a place for slaughtering. (To comfort those distressed by the savagery of our rendering, however, we should say that in the subsequent books, where the word is more a technical term than a visual image, so that its root is demonstrably attenuated, we often use the tamer rendering "place.")

For *matzebah*, which Luther renders by *Mal* ["mark"], we give *Standmal* ["standmark"], because the root means "to place," and the term *Mal* is much too indeterminate; one time in ten we had to replace *Standmal* by *Malstatt* ["markplace"] in order to retain the feminine *Zeugin* ["witness"] referring to it.[6] Neither of these words is in the least "restorative"; both are only uncommon, as is the object they denote, and the reviewer's attempts to find them in the vocabulary of music drama will be in vain.

The reviewer does not cultivate his acquaintance with the Luther Bible to the extent that one might expect from such a champion of it; otherwise he would not, in discussing words he finds strewn in abundance through Luther's text, like "verily" (e.g., the exquisite passages in Isa. 45:15 and 53:4), refer them to the "Lowlanders" Dahn and Freytag.[7]

To attest the word *ohne Mass* or *ohnemass* by even a single example from the "dilettantishly antiquarian romanticism of the dying nineteenth century" is a task we fear the reviewer would find impossible; the word even in the second spelling is an altogether sober and contemporary word. No doubt he confuses it with the archaism *unmassen*, which in fact is used by

---

6. *Standmal* is neuter, *Malstatt* feminine [eds.].

7. Kracauer writes of a path "descending from Wagner's heroic high ranges to the nearby lowlanders Felix Dahn [i.e., the German novelist Julius Sophus Felix Dahn (1834-1912)] and Gustav Freytag [German poet, 1816-1895]" [eds.].

Wagner, but would never have occurred to us. Luther, by the way, ordinarily writes *über die Mass.*[8]

Freytag does in truth write "by your leave" [*mit Verlaub*], as we have ascertained by rummaging through the dictionaries; but so does Goethe, with whom we are happy to be classed among the archaizers. In our text the phrase occurs at a particular place, when Joseph's brothers approach the steward in an agitated excess of curiosity, and accordingly with an "agitated punctuation."

"Earthfolk" (actually only "earth") had in Genesis to be put in place of Luther's "all lands" and "all the world" because "all lands" is simply not in the text, and also because a word for world in the sense of the epitome of space is something that biblical Hebrew very revealingly lacks, whereas a word for the epitome of time, for eternity, is something it possesses. To express the idea of world, biblical Hebrew needs two words together; the "cloddish" "earth" and the airy "heaven." How the reviewer in encountering "earthfolk" could lapse into *national* anxieties is to us, objectively at least, incomprehensible. If the League of Nations in Geneva were looking for a concrete word to express its goal, it could hardly do better than "earthfolk."

Several motives determined our rendering of the personal names. Clearly, however, these included neither of the two motives the reviewer attributes to us—in a singular ignorance of our public activity, literary and otherwise, woefully in contrast to the familiarity with it he professes at the beginning of his piece. He attributes to us, that is, a "national" motive (once again!) and an "aesthetic" motive—"a verb that we cannot decline/ we call aesthetically divine." Luther's versions of the biblical names are not, as the reviewer seems to believe, the only ones known in Germany. Luther gives "Hiob," "Jesaias," "Hesekiel," "Isai"; but Catholic German says "Job," "Isaias," "Ezechiel," "Jesse." Even Luther's "Eva" becomes the Catholic "Heva." This split in German usage was itself a reason to return to the original names, the names not shaped by the tongues of Greece and Rome. A further reason was the general tendency of the last century or so to introduce correct names everywhere. Schiller still wrote Jupiter and Juno, but today we would all say Zeus and Hera; since Nietzsche, no one says Zoroaster for Zarathustra. It is perhaps unknown to the reader, and certainly unknown to the reviewer, that this same tendency has made its way into the Luther Bibles available today. Luther's "King Roboam" has since

---

8. The three terms might be translated, respectively, "without measure," "measureless," and "above [all] measure."

The characteristic dispute concerns the status of *ohnemass*, whether spelled as one word or two. Kracauer claims that is a product of archaizing romantic prose, Buber and Rosenzweig that it is "sober and contemporary." Grimm does not list the word at all, nor do any of the big modern dictionaries, so probably Buber and Rosenzweig are wrong here, but maybe so is Kracauer [eds.].

the end of the bourgeois epoch, i.e., since the beginning of the century, been called "Rehabeam." But even this consideration of a demonstrable tendency—a consideration that the reviewer would have to find attractive *in se*—did not for us settle the matter. What did settle it was what the reviewer calls our hyper-Lutherish tendency to Germanize, because the *meaning* of the names, which precisely in Genesis plays so great a role, could only be made apparent by printing the Hebrew names themselves. Eve in our translation is "Chawa" [Ḥavvah]; but this is offputting only at first sight. Only in this way can the connection with the root meaning be reproduced; and reproducing it Germanizes the more alien name with a profundity that made sacrificing the superficial intimacy of the Wagnerian "Evchen [little Eva]" an easy task—devoted Wagnerians as we are. Or consider how on p. 70[9] of "In the Beginning" Yitzḥak's name is created.

"Prophets" could no longer be called by that name, because that Greek word, unlike the Hebrew, means today only a foreteller of the future. The prophets are that sometimes, but not essentially. So, for example, in the one place in Genesis where the word is used (p. 68),[10] the rendering "prophet" is meaningless. "Proclaimer" was in order there, not only because according to the most likely etymology the Hebrew word has that meaning, but also because that rendering directs our thought to the proper point. To "proclaim," unlike "to speak" and "to orate," cannot be used absolutely, without an object. The proclaimer is, as the orator and the speaker are not (both the latter words can take on the meaning of a vocation or office) always the proclaimer of something, is always bound to his proclamation. This word, then, precisely excludes the idea that today is customarily linked with the "prophetic," namely the idea of aptitude or talent—the idea, put briefly and appallingly, of "religious genius."

The word *künden* ("to proclaim," "to herald") did not, as the reviewer suspects, re-enter the language only with Stefan George's *Stern des Bundes* ["Star of the Covenant"]; but it did re-enter it as a verb only with Voss, and as a noun only with Rückert,[11] having disappeared from it for several centuries. This, however, could not hinder our use of it. Of course, language may not archaize; archaizing is against all sense and authority. Language must be wholly present, wholly of today, wholly spoken.[12] But no one confronted with a great linguistic task—and Luther least of all—has ever

---

9. 21: 6. Buber refers to the page number of the translation in order to deny the authority of the late and unauthoritative verse and chapter divisions [eds.].

10. 20:7 [eds.].

11. Johann Heinrich Voss (1751-1826), celebrated German translator of the *Odyssey*, and Friedrich Rückert (1788-1866) best known in anglophone territory for Mahler's setting of his *Kindertotenlieder* [eds.].

12. Language (*Sprache*) must be wholly spoken (*gesprochen*) because in German the two words are etymologically linked [eds].

declined altogether the use of obsolete or regional-sounding linguistic material, and only severe misunderstanding could call such use archaism or provincialism. This is the case, however, on the condition that this internal colonization of the linguistic realm be done with caution and knowledge— in such a way that the new material is viable, and that no already existing viable material is thereby bought off. In a letter to the court preacher Spalatin that the reviewer cites twice but understands not at all, Luther asks for accounts of homely words, *non castrensia nec aulica* ["not of the palace and not of the court"]; but what he means by "words of palace and court"— he is talking in particular of the names of jewels—is the then modern, technical terms, i.e., precisely what the review praises and celebrates as "secular language," in the belief that such language has come into being only in our time, and not rather existed in varying forms in all cultural periods. Luther, on the other hand, seeks and requests *simplicia* ["simplicities"], genuine and long-traditional verbal material.

Having shown that the reviewer's objections to our translation are all in fact objections to the Hebrew text, we are now regrettably compelled to reject also his one commendation of us. Abraham's dying in his good old age is not, as the reviewer maintains, a thing of our imprint, but is there in the text. *Be* is "in," *ṭobah* is "good," *seibah* is "old age."

We would now ask the reader to forget for a moment that the refutation of the reviewer's attempted demonstration is no refutation of his general thesis, and to attend to us—to an unproved thesis against a refuted one. We believe that every moment, our own as much as any in the past, is distant and hostile in relation to the word that in the Bible has become Scripture. We also believe that this word preserves in every moment the power to take hold of those that hear it. The moment is passive, the word active. If we only preserve the word, only conserve it, only let it be borne along by the moment, we blaspheme it. The word wants to speak—to every moment, into every moment, against every moment. We do not know whether that word will take our work of translation into its service, or indeed into what sort of service. We have to attend to one thing only: to be *faithful* to it. Whether the particular words we have brought back to German in the service of that fidelity will be naturalized is for us a minor matter, in comparison with that highest law and its demands.

We are at this time close to completing our work on the second book of the Bible. That book tells the story of how the word at first meets with deaf ears in the people to whom it is offered, "from shortness of spirit and from hard servitude."[13] An unfavorable "metaphysical and sociological situation,"

---

13. Exod. 6:9 [eds.].

as no doubt it would be called, can hardly be described more precisely than
it is described in that line. Of course, the scribes and wise men comforted
their Pharaoh with the thought that, given the situation "in our time," that
word was surely condemned to failure. And then what happened, happened.

CONCERNING A TRANSLATION AND A REVIEW[1]

Martin Buber and Franz Rosenzweig
(March 1926)

When a reviewer doubts the value of a book, the author is obliged to remain silent—however much this obligation may be at odds with his heart and mind. The book is there, it is accessible, anyone can find out what it is like; and this for the author must be enough. If the review diminishes, say, the number of readers; if it beclouds the eyes of such readers as it can prejudice, still the author has available all the unprejudiced readers, whose views, he may hope, his book will clarify and illuminate. He may even believe that "the news will get out."If an eloquent account of a cedar in a stand of evergreens were to assert that the tree was in fact a dwarf pine, the tree's owners would not need to send in a correction.

Things are different when a reviewer distorts a book's governing intention, its ground and motive. This would be like asserting that the root of the tree was rotting, and that the tree itself would soon topple. Who then would dig further to check? Even unprejudiced readers will adopt the hired expert's judgment as their own prejudice. In this case, the author has the obligation to speak: to follow up the reviewer's claim with a correction, and when appropriate to follow up the reviewer's unproven assertion with a

---

1. The review to which our present essay is a reply was written by Richard Koch and published in *Der Morgen* in 1926; the same journal printed the reply as well. The charges made by the reviewer are revealed well enough in the reply itself. I cannot, however, let the reply be reprinted here without adding to it a passage from a letter Koch sent me in 1931, after reading the Jeremiah volume of our Bible translation. The passage reads, "I still think that you were wrong to deny I had the right to judge your translation, simply because I had no access to the original. [We had not in fact done this; cf. section IV of the reply. M.B.] But I was wrong in fearing that this translation would take on all the weaknesses of an artificial period style—a style that is going out of date with surprising rapidity, even in its strongest and most exemplary manifestations."

counterproof. For "proof" is the right word here; even in the realm of letters, fortunately enough, we are not vulnerable to the subjectivism of mere
opinions, however much this may seem to be the case.

The obligation is the greater if the author is not the maker but the translator of a book, and the reviewer's distortion concerns the sources and
motives of his translational activity. For here the author is subject to an
especially strict responsibility—a responsibility, that is, to another being, to
the translated work and to the genius of that work. And if it is precisely the
author's fundamental consciousness of that responsibility that the reviewer
impugns . . . ! It could of course be maintained that the original too is there,
and that the reader need only make the comparison. But in fact the translation is chiefly directed to those not possessing the original language. The
translation may if things go well draw such readers to that language; but
most of them receive the newly published translation with the decisive question—decisive, that is, for the position they will finally take, their choice to
read the book or not to—"how do you handle your responsibility to the
original text?" This question the mass of readers is not in a position to
answer; rather it must let the answer be presented to it precisely by reviewers (and cannot here distinguish between reviewers who know something
and reviewers who do not). Who, moreover, even of knowledgeable readers
will approach the task of examination in full earnest? Who, that is, will juxtapose word to word, sound to sound, image to image? Who will begin (and
without this the task is impossible) himself to translate one or another passage to see what sea was to be fared there, where its cliffs and maelstroms
were, and how the navigation has been conducted? Who will refuse to
accept the decay of the root as a fact, and who will insist on digging further
when the hired expert has assured him of that fact?

This obligation to speak becomes a command when the text being translated is the Bible.

II

In the previous issue of *Der Morgen*, Richard Koch reviews our translation of
Genesis and finds it full of "stylized myths." We use this word "stylized"
when, say, we wish to say of a image in nature that it has been artistically
shaped not in the faithful attempt to create an image of its individual law of
being and growth, but rather in the enterprise of imposing upon that law
the "stylistic" conception pertaining to a notion of form and a striving for
form that are themselves alien to nature. That is: rather than expressing the
elemental meaning of its lines, which have become what they are by descent
and destiny, by nature and nurture, by sun and earth, by affinities and

antipathies, by named and nameless forces—rather than expressing all this in a perceptible form of human contriving, a "stylized" work interpolates an imagined and merely apparent meaning, a construct of aesthetic caprice; in it art is incestuously inbred with itself rather than being married to the created world.

All this is precisely what Richard Koch means; and he says as much quite clearly at the conclusion of his review, where he classifies the "danger" threatening our translation as belonging with the contemporary disease of "willing form"; he warns us against the "error" of thinking "that it is given to humankind to be able to impose forms upon things," and asks us, in continuing our undertaking—with a gesture expressing some doubt of our ability to do what is asked—to "eschew art and artistic effect."

The claim that a translation is stylized, that a translator wills a form, and thinks to imprint a form—this claim means, and cannot be understood to mean anything else, that the translator has proceeded not, or not only, from the text, not or not only in exact fidelity to the text's commands and instructions, but rather, or also, from a will to form that is alien to the text and thus compelled to impose itself upon it.

In the case of the present reviewer, it seems that the milder of these two possibilities—distinguished in the previous sentence by "or"—is the one actually put forth: the "not only" and the "also." This may not be the case; his choice between the two charges may indeed not be clear even to the reviewer himself. "It would be going too far," he writes, "if we were to say that this liveliness had been produced by the deliberate use of artistic trickery. It may be largely the consequence of simple and exact translation." It may. But even then only "largely." So the reviewer has not "gone too far."

And yet—may or may not, largely or not, too far or not too far—no! The reviewer is wrong. It is not a matter of more or less. What we have served casts his weights off the scale. It does not speak in this manner, and cannot be spoken with in this manner. The question formulates itself with ineluctable clarity: have we proceeded from the word that is there, and only from that word, or at moments have we proceeded from our own verbal conceptions?—conceptions that in the presence of the word that is there can only be regarded as verbal delusions! Have we opened our ears and obedient souls to the sound of the speech that became Scripture, or have we mixed in the music of our dreams? Have we served truth alone, or sometimes truth and sometimes demons?

This and no less weighty a question is the true question here. And in truth that question concerns not only us and our present readers.

Richard Koch has himself probably felt the simplicity of that question, its Yes or No—despite his "would be"'s and "if we were"'s. He holds Luther up to us. "Luther," he writes, "surely thought of nothing else but to write in

German what was there in the Hebrew source." We, however—cannot, it seems, be thinking of nothing else. There is nothing in between here. Whatever is not the whole truth is perjury.

III

Such being the case, one thing is asked of us, and that one thing we here do.

We submit the purity of our work to the test of proof. For *what is at issue is in fact provable.*

We know that our translation must contain mistakes; that despite all our pains we have not been able to consider every possibility in every passage; that though we have attempted to take into consideration all the work of our predecessors we have no doubt overlooked some still useful sources of aid. We are grateful for any criticism that makes us aware of such gaps. But for every aspect of our translation to which our attention may be called—an individual word, a letter, a mark of punctuation, a line-break—we pledge ourselves to show that it has arisen, and how it has arisen, from our under-standing, whether great or small, of the words of the text, and from nothing else. We offer to prove that, say, the lively variety of style that distinguishes our translation of Genesis from the noble uniformity of Luther's is the product, piece by piece, of our striving for the exactest rendering possible of what is there—is the product, that is, of Scripture itself, of its discourse, of the sound and history and meaning of its words, of the cadence and structure and content of its verbal sequences. We could then supplement such a proof with accounts of how we ourselves were taken aback by these altogether unexpected results—how, that is, the form of our translation was for us time after time not our intention but our fate. We offer for any pas-sage called to our attention to show, say, that "the strong pictorial charm of the text" arises not from our sensitivity to aesthetic charm but from the text itself, and that even if the reviewer's statement that "the original text in no way sought to exercise pictorial effects" is undisputedly right, it does not at all follow that *we* sought to exercise them, but only that they inhered uncon-sciously in the original text, and precisely therefore inhered also in our translation, concerned with fidelity as none of its predecessors had been.

IV

As he himself notes, Richard Koch does not know the language of the orig-inal text; he can, therefore, be only imperfectly involved in the procedure we have just proposed. This fact does in truth make things more difficult. It is not, however, as if we proposed to deny to those possessing German but not Hebrew the right to judge our book on the basis of the former language alone. Our book is a German work, and can be considered as such *in se*; the reader who comes to it from Luther and Jacob Grimm may indeed see much in it that the narrow Hebraist will not. What is presumed in such a case is only as much of a sense of situation as permits one to presume in simple loyalty that the translation is accurate. No doubt Koch would marvel if someone knowing no English were to reproach Friedrich Gundolf with not having based his German Shakespeare exclusively on a faithful sense of the English original; he would no doubt think that such a reproach could be made *only* on the basis of a comparison between the original and the translation. But since the circumstance in question has not hindered him so far, there is no reason why it should hinder him now in standing up on behalf of his original judgment. He is evidently aware of how serious a matter is ultimately in question here—a matter that, as he acutely writes, "our destiny and our future" depend on. For he knows that "Holy Scripture is more a book of the present and the future than a book of the past." It is now his task to engage in genuine clarification of his views—a clarification that the uncompelled, unsystematic nature of journalistic writing is by its nature simply not capable of.

Our time can recover from its real disease (of which the "will to form" is only a symptom) only if we manage to make devalued human discourse once again compelled and compelling.

A TRANSLATION OF THE BIBLE[1]

Martin Buber
(1927)

The article "Buber's Bible," printed in the *Tage-Buch* for June 18, gives me occasion to make clear, for any readers whom the article may mislead, just what this Bible translation of ours is meant to do. To ascertain this from the publisher's old prospectus—which the reviewer draws on in preference to our own four essays and other writings—is simply impossible.

I

The "Old Testament" has never before been translated by writers seeking to return to the concrete, fundamental meaning of each individual word; previous translators have been contented to put down something "appropriate," something "corresponding." When Luther has Sarah say to Abraham, "Beloved, I pray thee go in unto my maide: it may be that I shall be builded by her," he simply fails to understand the text. Kautzsch-Bertholet says, "perhaps I can attain children through her"; this and similar turns of phrase in other modern versions are not translations but periphrases of the word *ebbane*, which occurs in one other place only, and never in connection with natural childbearing. The verb is derived from the noun meaning "son" (in the plural "children"); it denotes that primitive legal act familiar to folklorists as adoption by feigned birthing, the central Semitic form of which is described in the passage where Rachel speaks to Jacob as Sarah speaks to Abraham: "so that she may give birth upon my knees." The barren woman takes the woman in labor upon her belly, and the act of identification is thereby completed; it is now her belly from which the child emerges, and she

---

1. In response to a review by Emanuel bin Gorion.

is thereby bechilded—to use a term drawn from old German legal discourse. That is what Sarah is saying, and what Rachel says: "here is my slave-girl Bilha;/ come in to her,/ so that she may give birth upon my knees, so that I too may be built-up-with-sons through her." But also her husband who has no children, also Abraham, complains that he will die '*ariri*; and what does that mean? All previous translations say, "without children." The etymology of the word, however, says something else, something more concrete and vivid, namely, "stripped naked"—for to these oriental people children are a living garment and a second body. That is why in Leviticus the "man who takes the wife of his brother" is assigned a punishment corresponding to the sin: "he has revealed the nakedness of his brother, and they will remain naked of children." That is why Abraham calls himself not "childless" but "childbare," "childstripped." To undertake a genuine translation of the Bible entails now and then venturing such words; whether posterity will receive them or reject them is not for the living to know.

II

We have attempted also a second thing not accomplished in previous translations: to distinguish synonyms wherever German permits, i.e., not to render two distinct Hebrew words by one German one, nor—at least within a single sequence—to render a single Hebrew word by two German ones. We have further attempted, in cases where a common root linked various words, to retain that link in German. How much buried treasure these methods can recover can be made clear by a single example, again from the story of Hagar's flight. The same root word occurs three times—in the original text, that is, and in a faithful translation. First, "Sarai afflicted [Hagar], so that she had to flee from her." But then God's messenger finds Hagar in the desert, questions her, and commands her, "return to your mistress and let yourself be afflicted under her hand!" But he also comforts and promises: "for HE has hearkened to your being afflicted." Let us envision the three levels of the scene. First, the afflicted; above her the afflicter, and above her the "Living-One Who-Sees-Me," as the afflicted calls him; and the one above, the Living-One, casts himself down and takes up the one thrown down; he may direct her to let herself be afflicted beneath the afflicter's hands, because that is the way on which he wants to lead her to freedom. But what remains of all this when in place of a single recurring word Sarah wishes to "humble" Hagar but God hears her "misery" (Luther), or even (Kautzsch-Bertholet) when Sarah wishes to "treat Hagar harshly" but the messenger bids Hagar to "bow down" and says that God has heard "how she has suffered"?

Our effort to find strict verbal equivalents of course has its limits—at the limits of the language itself. Hebrew *qol*, for example, means both "voice" and "sound." In the passage the reviewer cites, where Adam and Eve, having eaten of the tree of knowledge, hear God coming toward them, *qol* means not "voice," as the reviewer thinks, but "sound," as we have translated it—for God has at this moment not yet spoken, and what Adam and Eve hear can only be the sound of his steps, as he "walks about in the garden at the breezy-time of the day." (Kautzsch-Bertholet gives "his walking," Gunkel "his steps" etc.—but these are mere periphrases.)

III

The individual word, then, in its original concrete meaning is crucial to us. But that is not to say that the Hebrew verbal sequence is something secondary, something not to be maintained against the conventions of the language into which we are translating. We know of no "content" separable from this form in which it has been transmitted to us, and transferable into a form of a different sort. What matters is to naturalize this form in a qualitatively different language in such a way as the limits of the language allow—the limits, and not merely the conventions. Where Sarah says to Abraham in the Hagar chapter, "the wrong done me is upon you!" this is different both formally and in its entire content and meaning from Luther's "you do me injustice." The substantive difference is clearest in this chapter where the messenger makes promises to Hagar concerning her son. Luther has, "he will be a wild man, and will dwell in the presence of all his brothers." This is a dubious consolation; but the text actually says, and we follow it in saying, "he will be a wild-ass of a man, and will sit in the face of all his brothers." That is the son as the "Egyptian maid" dreams him; that is genuine promise.

This approach to rendering the text does not at all imply the obligation to retain the original word-order; that would often entail doing violence to German syntax. Luther's "let there be light" [*Es werde Licht*] in all its beauty diminishes the force of the elemental word, as Herder saw; but Herder's "be there light" [*Sei Licht*] makes the call that creates *ex nihilo* sound like a conversational imperative. We have to re-order the words to attain the true equivalent in German, with its different sequence of subject and predicate: "Light be!" [*Licht werde!*].

IV

We take seriously not only the text's semantic characteristics but also its acoustic ones. It became clear to us, accordingly, that the text's abundant alliterations and assonances could not be understood in aesthetic terms alone; often if not always it is passages of religious importance in which assonance and alliteration occur, and both assonance and alliteration thus help make this importance emerge more vividly. When, say, God bans Cain from the soil "which made its mouth open" (*patzeta* and *piha*) to receive his brother's blood, something is expressed concerning the violence of that moment that in Luther's "which opened its mouth" remains unspoken. And Luther's "unfixed and vagabond shall you be upon the earth"—magnificent, yes, but it does not represent the words *naʿ* and *nad*, either acoustically or referentially. Neither word is simply an adjective or a noun; both are participles, and the first does not, like Luther's "unfixed," incorporate a negation. Our "wavering and wandering" [*schwank und schweifend*] is not adequate either; but it is the closest approximation I know in any language. ("Wavering" [*schwank*, meaning "wavering" or "trembling"] is not, as the reviewer thinks, a word used only to refer to the swaying of reeds, but can refer also to human movement and steps; and truly there is a wavering sort of wandering or straying appropriate to a man in despair!) Here we succeeded only imperfectly; in another passage, another cited by the reviewer, we succeeded no more than halfway. The passage in question is the remarkable account of how the architects of Babel built of *lebenah*, brick, rather than *eben*, stone, and used as mortar not *homer*, loam or clay, but *hemar*, pitch or asphalt (the reviewer thinks the word means "chalk," but wrongly; neither of the two words has anything to do with chalk). This is no pun; rather the acoustic similarity emphasizes the nature of the situation, in which the builders must discard natural materials for artificial ones, or at any rate for materials that can be brought out of the earth only with considerable effort. The first half of the verse, "so for them brick-stone [*Backstein*] was like building-stone [*Baustein*]," worked well enough; but the second half needs improvement.[2] Especially in the first volumes we shall find a lot to improve, though not as strikingly often as did Luther.

V

It goes almost without saying that our notion of fidelity led us to reject the usual euphonizing and Latinizing of the biblical proper names, and to introduce into our version the biblical names themselves; the time of saying "Zoroaster" in place of "Zarathustra" is past, and the time of saying "Ezechiel" or "Hesekiel" for "Yehezkel" will pass soon enough. Here too,

---

2. An improved version has been introduced in the one-volume revision of the Pentateuch (the so-called Lodge Edition, 1930), not yet available in bookstores: "raw-earth pitch [*Roherdpech*] was for them like red-earth mortar [*Roterdmortel*]."

however, there were limits: widely known geographical names were not to be made unrecognizable, as by writing, say, not Egypt but Mitzrayim—because the earth is after all there, and the people have died. This inconsistency is part of the nature and fate of this unprecedented work, whose goals and limits are established not by some abstract principle but by the reality of a book and the reality of two qualitatively different peoples and languages—by the full reality of these things, that is, and not by anything smaller.

Because this is the case, the greatest reality of the Bible, namely that of the divine name (there being only one, with the others only characterizations or attributes) had inevitably to signify both our clearest goal and our most solidly fixed limit. The goal we believe we have attained in our version of the conversation at the Burning Bush, where the name is revealed. The limit is wherever the name encounters us, the name that is not to be spoken and—precisely because it is revealed in the one passage—not to be translated. We were not free to introduce into the spoken Bible, the Bible "aloud" that we had in mind, any soundless sign; nor were we free to use any of the usual fictions, like "Lord" and "Eternal." (It is not true that "the popular etymology of the name Yahweh contained in the Bible derives it from 'he who is eternal.'" The truth is to be found rather at the passage in question of our translation.) We were free only to indicate the barrier wherever it presented itself, so that, as in the Hebrew, behind the barrier the goal could be seen to shine. For scholarship is only one of the presuppositions of our work, and not its master.

VI

We have, as I said, had in mind the Bible "aloud." We proceed from the notion that the Bible is a product of living recitation, and is intended for living recitation; that speech is its nature, and the written text only a form for preserving it. Hence our method of rendering its rhythm. Our translation is the first *colometric* translation (though Jerome had already seen the necessity for it), i.e., the first that gives the text its natural division into lines of meaning as these are determined by the laws of human breathing and human speech, with each line constituting a rhythmic unit. It is not a question of "blank verse," as the reviewer thinks; and thus also not, as he thinks, a question of diverse meters, indeed not a question of meter at all.

In the case of the New Testament, scholars have desired a colometric configuration of the words for some time, both in editions and in translations; and to some extent this desire has been realized. Thus the eminent philologist Eduard Norden writes in 1913, "if colometry was already desired by the ancients, whose ear could aid their reading, so much more must we desire it, who are accustomed to read with the eye alone"; the theologian Roland Schütz then specifies in 1920 that what matters is "to hear, in a way, with the eye, and thereby to find a way through cold typography to the harmony of the *cola*."[3] The characteristics of a colometric rendering of the Old Testament required, given its special problems, a separate discussion. This was made still more complicated by the diversity of style even within the prose, a diversity manifested in the rhythm; but it was facilitated by a tradition of rhythmic division already possessing both a written and an oral form of expression: the former in the system of the so-called accents accompanying the Hebrew Bible word by word, the latter in the conventions of Sabbath recitation. To what extent we could adhere to this tradition, and to what extent not, are made clear in Franz Rosenzweig's "Scripture and Word"; to read and apply that essay would have done far more for the reviewer's task than has his treating the publisher's prospectus as the translators' last will and testament.

To assess what we have achieved is possible only on the basis of an impartial understanding of what we have attempted: to transmit the reality of the Bible to western men and women in a western language. This cannot be done—regardless of what greater accomplishments may follow our own— by an "entirely different ordering" of the text; we cannot dissolve the unity of this book, whatever its genesis, into its component parts without robbing it of its life. Rather it can be done only along the path we have taken, only by remaining true to the words, the sentences, the rhythms, and the structures of the book.

---

3. Norden, *Agnostos Theos,* p. 361; Schütz, "Die Bedeutung der Kolometrie für das neue Testament," Zeitschrift für Neutestamentliche Wissenschaft, 1922, pp. 161ff. (Buber cites these passages in a manuscript fragment on biblical rhythm now in the Buber Archive at the National and University Library in Jerusalem) [eds.].

A SUGGESTION FOR BIBLE COURSES[1]

Martin Buber

I

A Bible course should lead students to the biblical text, not past it. What matters first, then—and also last—is to teach students to understand what is there. And for that, we ourselves must take what is there seriously—its wording, its meaning, its sequences and connections.

II

No matter how difficult a wording the text presents, we must struggle as hard as we can before deciding, with the melancholy of inevitable renunciation in our hearts, to alter the text in even a single vowel—i.e., to confess to ourselves and others that here we have no access to the text and cannot devise one. Nothing is easier or cheaper than to consider the text erroneous and to presume we can get behind that text and thereby reach a true one! But we should acknowledge that whoever was responsible for the text as we have it knew as much Hebrew as we do. It is our task to grasp what *he* meant by that text, and how he understood it. To seek to get behind him is a pointless self-deception; for even where, say, the ancient versions concur in a reading other than that given by the Masoretic text, we cannot be sure that even then someone was not simply attempting to ease an oppressive

---

[1]. From the third circular of the Central Bureau for Jewish Adult Education, of which I was director; written early in 1936. I have here drawn together the principles arising from my experiences in a whole series of Bible courses, given for teachers and directors of youth groups etc., between the spring and winter of 1934 and then since the late autumn of 1935, in various parts of Germany.

difficulty. The "letter of the text" is, however problematic it may seem, a strict reality, in comparison with which everything else is only appearance.

III

The text, then, is to be accepted, except in those extreme cases where infidelity to it is a painful necessity. But it is to be accepted, and understood, precisely as *the* accessible, verbal form of its meaning. We are not talking here about a content that acquired this form but could support another form also—about a What that could be separated from this How and joined to another—about something that "could be said in other words as well." It cannot be said in other words without becoming another thing! And if it becomes another thing, then it becomes precisely something altogether different, something of a different order, something—unbiblical. The biblical word is never merely the "expression" of an intellectual or spiritual concern, whether "ethical" or "religious," or of a historical or legendary transaction; rather it is a transmitted and traditional *word*, a word once *spoken* and then transmitted in its spokenness—spoken once as message, as law, as prophecy, as prayer, as narrative, as instruction, as confession, as conversation, and entrusted as such to the organic memory of generations, preserved there, and maintained, forever new, in living speech, not noted down or at any rate still existing in company with its own notated form, and ready, even after everything has been noted down, to arise again from the written Bible in its original spokenness. The pattern etched into this word is its very nature, its unique quality; we must not efface it. Its rhythm is the necessary form in which it has been distributed to, and imposed upon, the collective memory. Its repetitions of sound are relations established between passage and passage; and even where it seems to be joking, it is making a point—"play upon words" is here done in earnest, in the deep seriousness of the verbal world itself.

IV

"Spoken" means: spoken in a specific situation. The biblical word cannot be separated from the situations of its spokenness; otherwise it loses its concreteness, its physicality. A command is not a maxim but an address—spoken to the people, heard always by the generations as having been spoken to that original generation, but never to be lifted out of time. If it becomes a maxim, if it is moved from the second person to the third, from the obligatory relation of hearing to the optional relation of interested reading, its flesh and blood are gone. A prophecy is the speech of a man speaking under commission to a human group at a particular moment, in a particular situation; its effects depend on the decision that the group will take in response to it at this moment—or not take. Precisely in the held breath of this vastly decisive moment lies the secret of the eternal validity of the prophetic word. The biblical stories are only to a small extent mere transcribed chronicles; in most of them we hear still the voices of their storytellers, exhorting, compelling, exemplifying, warning. Many psalms exhibit the character of liturgical poetry, some the character of litany; but the fundamental tone is that of the lived immediacy of cries of need and jubilations of thanks—the speech of personal speakers, who precisely when and because they mean the "I" of the genuine person can as choral leaders of the community speak of the fate and salvation of that community in their song. This concreteness, born of the situation and fitted to it, must be retained for the biblical text; the text must be taught not as pieces of a literature, but rather as parts of a vast, multivocal conversation, arising from the first cause of the creating and revealing word, and issuing back into that first cause again in the form of prayer. That is why it is not so important to learn from the historians when, or where, or in what circumstances this or that text arose; historians, even those who constitute and interpret history, are confined to the realm of the mediated, and restricted to the means that realm offers. The important thing rather is to learn from the text itself the things concerning its particular situational rootedness that it and it alone can tell.

V

Biblical texts are to be treated as texts of the *Bible*—that is, of a unity, which though having come into being, having grown from numerous and diverse whole and fragmentary elements, is nonetheless a real organic unity, and can be comprehended only as such. The consciousness that established the Bible, selecting from the abundance of a presumably far greater textual repertory what would fit that unity, and selecting in particular the versions of that material appropriate to that unity, began its work not with the actual assembling of the canon, but long before—in the gradual bonding of what belonged together. The work of composition was itself "biblical," even before the first notion of a biblical structure arose. It sought a synoptic view of the various parts, it established relations between this excerpt and that, between this book and that; it revealed fundamental notions through passage upon passage, took the secret meaning of an action only dimly visible in one story and revealed it fully in another, illuminated image by image and symbol by symbol. Much of what we call "midrash" can be found in the Bible itself, in these traces of a work of selection and coordination aimed at creating biblical unity—a work whose strongest technique was the discretely consistent application of repetitions, motivic words, and assonances. In this area we are only now coming to any methodical understanding. What matters is to sharpen our sense of these correspondences and linkages, and in general our sense of the unified functioning of the Bible. We will then find far other patterns than those of the "source-texts" to which the Old Testament scholarship of the previous centuries has sought to trace the structure of the Bible; we will find greater variety and greater communality, and understand the dynamic growth of the latter from the former. That is not to say that we should not familiarize ourselves with the theses of modern scholarship. We should; but we should also know what is that we gain from them. Theses come and go; texts remain.

FROM THE BEGINNINGS OF
OUR BIBLE TRANSLATION[1]

Martin Buber
(February 1930)

The history of our Bible translation began five years ago this spring. But before that there was also a pre-history. I had been thinking for many years of venturing such a work, on the basis of the current state of the language. My belief at the time was that it could only be undertaken by a partnership, and in particular a partnership of people closely connected with one another, and so able to help one another in the work more profoundly than is ordinarily possible. Such a partnership was already in formation before the war; there had even been an agreement made between it and a major German publishing house, which was to publish the translation gradually, in individual books (but not in the canonical order of the text). Among the participants were Moritz Heimann, Efraim Frisch, and I; and the three of us had already settled on what text each of us would begin with. The war thwarted this plan—among many others. But it was only in the following decade that the plan as I thought about it finally matured, and was theoretically and methodologically elucidated. I understood only then, that is, what sort of book this was—in meaning, in language, and in construction. I understood why in spite of everything this book sought to be integrated anew into the present human world—meaning by "anew" something like "renewed in its originality"—and understood not only why but also how. In 1923, Franz Rosenzweig was working on his translation of the poems of Judah Halevi, and often turned to me for consultation. We soon began to move in our conversation from the particular examples at hand to the nature of translation generally and the problems of the translator's task.

---

1. Originally published in the Rosenzweig memorial issue of *Der Orden Bne Briss*; I have somewhat altered the conclusion.

176

Gradually certain questions presented themselves, first as the sometimes bright but mostly only glimmering background of our conversation, but then more pressingly as its magnetic center: Is the Bible translatable? Has it been in fact translated? What remains to be done? Little? Much? The crucial element? How can it be done? In editing a classic translation? In a daring new beginning? Does the age have room for a new beginning? Does it have the calling, the energy, the support, the ear? And above all: *How* is the Bible to be translated? How is it to be translated at this time?

Rosenzweig's fundamental view at the time (as can be inferred from the Afterword to the Halevi translations) was that Luther's great work had necessarily to be the basis of any attempt at a German translation of the Bible, and, therefore, that what was to be undertaken was not a new translation but only a revision of Luther's—though an incomparably more comprehensive and rigorous revision than any previous one. My view was that our questions could be answered only by the experiment itself, requiring and using the whole person of the experimenter—only by an approach making straight for the goal, recognizing and using all previous translators without committing itself to any of them.

And to that approach events unexpectedly led. I received one day a letter from Dr. Lambert Schneider, a young publisher then unknown to me. He wrote that he wished to begin the work of his newly founded publishing house with a translation of the "Old Testament," but only on the condition that I would undertake the work—whether a new edition, an editorial revision, or my own new translation. This letter written by a Christian of pure German ancestry[2] struck me as a sign. I read it to Rosenzweig; I added that I was inclined to accept the proposal, but only on the condition that he collaborate on it with me. I noticed that this both delighted and disturbed him. Later, I understood why. He was not then, as he had been in the first period of his illness, expecting to die in a matter of weeks or months; but he had given up thinking of the remainder of his life as occupying any great measure of time. Now, however, he was being offered (and thus trusted as being capable of) participation in a work that, as he recognized far more quickly than I did, would require several years of extremely intensive work. What was at issue for him, then, was permitting himself another mode of reckoning his future.[3] For Rosenzweig too in all sobriety believed in signs, indeed still more strongly than I did. He said—or, more precisely, since he had not for some time been able to speak, he indicated with an unsteady finger on an elaborate machine two or three letters of each word, where-

---

2. He remained admirably true to our common enterprise afterwards, even when the work had been transferred to Schocken.

3. But the phrase on the title page, "a translation *undertaken* etc." is Rosenzweig's, and implies a steady concentration on the final goal.

upon his wife guessed the word and spoke it aloud—" Well, let's just try it."
What he meant was clear: we should settle the controversy practically, by
testing both methods on a chapter of the Bible and thus finding out
whether either of them was usable for us, and if so which of the two. "Which
chapter?" I asked. He answered, "The first."

We naturally began by attempting to revise Luther. We took one verse
after another and altered what seemed to our linguistic sense and knowledge to need alteration. After a day's work we found ourselves with a heap
of ruins. Clearly, we would get nowhere on this path. Clearly, Luther's "Old
Testament" would remain in perpetuity a magnificent structure; but for our
time it was no longer a Bible translation.

I now undertook to draft a translation of the first chapter of Genesis in
accord with my own conception. When Rosenzweig had read the manuscript several times, he wrote, "The patina is gone, but now it's bright as
new, and that too is worth something." This sentence was followed by extensive remarks, and had been preceded by a whole series of other remarks,
together composing a masterpiece of constructive criticism. The joint work
had begun.

The form of our collaboration remained the same till the end. I would do
a translation, and then would send the pages of my first version (the so-
called quarto manuscript), for the most part in chapter units, on to
Rosenzweig. He would send back his remarks: objections, suggestions, proposed alterations. Whatever I found immediately plausible I would use at
once to make changes in the text; on the rest we would correspond. What
remained in dispute would be discussed at our Wednesday visits. (I lectured
every Wednesday at Frankfurt University, and spent the rest of the day at
Rosenzweig's home.) When we were done with the first version of a book, I
would go on to produce the second version, a clean copy ready for the
printer (the so-called folio manuscript), and the process would begin again:
again there would be a whole series of comments. The process would be
repeated again in connection with the first proofreading, and with the second; after this we would read the book together, and make a joint comparison; again there would be extended conversations. After the third
proofreading we would send back our *imprimatur.*

To make Rosenzweig's task easier, I would indicate on the quarto manuscript wherever necessary the reasons for which I had translated in one way
and not another; and, since he had to be spared any unnecessary thumbing
of books, I listed in connection with every difficult passage the various interpretations, from the ancient commentators to the most recent essays in the
scholarly journals. Even so, our correspondence would often continue for
weeks in connection with a single word.

"My role here," Rosenzweig wrote me at the beginning of the work, "will probably be that of the muse of precision (Diotima and Xanthippe[4] united in a single person), as yours was with Judah Halevi. But that role, as you can see from that example, is no small matter." "His role" became, though he held throughout to the image of the muse of precision, a hundred times greater than the "example" would suggest. The pages that went back and forth in these years yield together a remarkably vital and alive commentary: the Bible is illuminated in the space of our interplay.

What sort of interplay this was I can characterize here only in connection with a few principal questions.

1. We agreed immediately that, in accord with our rightly conceived philological task—"We always do pay heed to scholarship," Rosenzweig once wrote me, "but the scholarship we pay heed to is our own"—we had to stick as much as possible to the Masoretic text, as being the only objectively graspable text. We also agreed that where it was a question, say, of the connections of various portions to one another, we were not to consider the matter with reference only to this or that apparently isolable source, but had rather to reproduce the literary totality lying before us—or, to use the terms of modern Bible scholarship, we were to think not of J (the "Jahwist") or E (the "Elohist") but of R (the "Redactor"), i.e., the unitary consciousness of the book. We reinforced each other in this recognition, continually learning in the course of the work from the work itself; and the recognition rooted itself in us more and more deeply in the course of our interplay. It was something we had in common, then, that Rosenzweig expressed in his significantly witty remark that we took R to stand not for "Redactor" but for "Rabbenu."[5]

2. I had come long before the beginning of our work to the conviction that in translating the Bible one had to go behind the *writtenness* of the word, and had then to return to its *spokenness*—a spokenness at once original and made audible anew in every genuine reading aloud of the text. It followed that the text of the translation was to be divided into natural speech-units, dictated by the laws of breathing and delineated according to meaning: the so-called *cola* (hence the word *colometry* to describe the typographical patterns). Each unit was to be an easily speakable, easily perceptible and thus rhythmically ordered unity—as indeed all early oral tradition works toward what is easily speakable and easily perceptible, and thus works by the formation of rhythms. This view of mine Rosenzweig soon made his own, and in his essay "Scripture and Word"[6] beautifully articulated it and

---

4. Xanthippe was Socrates' nagging wife, Diotima (in the *Symposium*) his prophetic instructor in the art of love [eds.].

5. See above, "The Unity of the Bible" [eds.].

6. Reprinted herein [eds.].

gave it its rationale. *Cola*-structure was however the one matter where he never tried to talk me into anything. "I couldn't produce a single *colon*," he would say.[7]

3. We both noted that many instances of "paronomasia," i.e., of the use of verbal or auditory similarities, were very often used by the Bible not for stylistic ornamentation but as an articulated signal of the special importance or significance of a passage, and that therefore such things as alliterations were to be reproduced wherever possible. Rosenzweig then kept close watch over these matters—with the pedantry of genius, one might say. But soon in the course of the work I came to feel that these principles of repetition and correspondence in the Bible were even more widely significant, both extensively and intensively. When the Bible tells a story, it does not to be sure add to the account of the event any explicit "moral"; but by slight or extreme repetitions, now only varying a single word root, now multiplying whole sentences in a sort of refrain—by, that is, setting two or more passages in relation to one another—the Bible directs our organic attention to the meaning of the story that is to appear to us. If, for example, what is to be said is that the divine messenger confronts Balaam in precisely the way in which Balaam has confronted his donkey, then the Bible says this by using in both cases the same phrases—in part the same very rare phrases. This "formal secret of biblical style," which I had "discovered in translating" (to use Rosenzweig's language), Rosenzweig again presented in an essay of his own, further developing my conception, called "The Secret of Biblical Narrative Form."[8]

4. Our interplay was manifested most strikingly, however, around the issue of rendering linguistic peculiarities. In response to my first sketch, Rosenzweig had written, "It's remarkably German; Luther in comparison is almost Yiddish. But maybe now it's *too* German?" He soon began—at first only indirectly, but then more and more emphatically—to combat the "too German." Thus when I had inexactly rendered the conclusion of Gen. 2:16, he wrote,

> I would try to render all these inner infinitives. So, for example: "you may eat, yes, eat." But this has to do with the fact that if I were to go beyond Luther I would seek to surpass him in Hebraicizing the syntax, whereas you, in a dehebraicized syntax, seek to surpass him in excavating the Hebraic context of the individual word.

It was clear to me that his striving for syntactic imitation—subordinate of course to the unhebraically determined laws of German—was justified, and

---

7. Actually, the *Arbeitspapiere* are full of Rosenzweig's suggestions for making *cola*, so it's not clear what Rosenzweig could have meant by this statement [eds.].

8. Reprinted herein [eds.].

accordingly I made it my own. Some time later, when we were deep into our joint work, I had occasion to discuss in a letter, in connection with a brief essay of mine on Karl Eugen Neumann's renderings of Buddhist texts,[9] the difference between the principles Rosenzweig had worked from in his Judah Halevi translations and those from which I was proceeding in this attempt to translate the Bible. Rosenzweig responded, "You are still forgetting that you have converted me—and in the most fundamental way, namely, through my own work" (August 14, 1925). But in fact we had converted each other.

5. Rosenzweig had correctly seen that one of the essential tasks of the Bible translation was for me "the excavation of the Hebraic content of the individual word." I had in the course of my decade of reflection come to the realization that one had to reach behind the conventional, ostensible meanings that one finds assigned to the biblical words in the dictionaries, and seek their original concrete and sensory meanings, to the extent that these can be inferred from Hebrew etymology—and sometimes also from the etymologies of other Semitic languages, though these have to be used cautiously. In this search one must always remember that the so-called synonyms of a language often differ sharply from one another in their sensory content, and also that corresponding ideas in different languages have in many cases little sensory content in common, indeed that it is precisely in this divergence that the particularities of national character proclaim themsleves with special clarity. One must also of course remember that the original sensory meaning of a word need not emerge in translation everywhere to the same degree, or ever with undue force. Rosenzweig did not simply accede to this inclination of mine to "excavate"—rather it was precisely in this area that he managed his most independent and productive contribution. He sought above all to deliver cultic and theological terms from the faded state into which they had fallen, and to restore to them their characteristic fundamental color. In certain cases of this sort he rightly worked not from scholarly etymology but from the popular etymology reflected in the Bible itself. He strove passionately on behalf of his discoveries, sometimes so fanatically that I—here as in other matters—had to function as the admonitory frontier guard of the German language, or even as the advocate of the putatively understanding reader. But our dueling was only a secondary phenomenon; the most characteristic aspect of our work was a joint struggling for equivalence, yielding precisely at the highest and most decisive points a joint victory—within which it was no longer possible to ascertain what arose from one man's thought and what from the other's.

---

9. See below, Appendix I: "Making Plain."
This alone of all the cross-references in this essay is Buber's [eds.].

When I had sent Rosenzweig the last portion of "In the Beginning" (in the first version), I received this poem from him:

> That all beginnings ends may be:
> this I now know.
> "Into life," I wrote, of writing's task now free;
> in two years, though,
> the action-willing hand grew lame,
> the discourse-willing tongue, the same;
> all that was left was writ.
> But my beginning came then from this end:
> what I wrote there
> has not—for this my thanks, dear friend—
> stayed writing bare.
> We wrote the word of the Beginning,
> prime act that gives the End its meaning.
> And so began the Writ.[10]

The phrase "into life" is drawn from the conclusion of Rosenzweig's "life-book," *The Star of Redemption*. The line following that quotation, however, was in a sense corrected eight days later. I had in the meantime proposed to him to use *Du* between us,[11] and added that I hoped it would not be difficult for him to accustom himself to the practice with a man almost nine years older than himself. On September 29, 1925, Rosenzweig wrote me as follows:

> My dear friend,
>
> It is not at all difficult; moreover I have said *Du* to you in silence all too often already.
>   The distance between us comes not so much from the difference in age, though that difference is augmented by ten years' span of virile experience of the world—for you[12] were already a public figure at twenty, while I at thirty still danced to Rumpelstiltskin's tune—but comes rather from a feeling in me, to which I have hitherto given expression through

---

10. The verse-translation is primarily Everett Fox's work, tinkered with by Lawrence Rosenwald.

In a talk given at the ceremony to celebrate Buber's completion of the Bible translation, Ernst Simon suggested that this poem of Rosenzweig's echoed Goethe's account of Faust trying to translate John 1:1; see above, "Buber and Rosenzweig's Challenge to Translation Theory," Section III-A. The talk, titled "Ssijum—Schlusslernen," is printed in "'Die Schrift'—Zum Abschluss ihrer Verdeutschung" (Tel Aviv: Bitaon, n.d.) [eds.].

11. Such a proposal to use the familiar rather than the formal pronoun was a very weighty matter in the Germany of 1925 [eds.].

12. Here and throughout the letter Rosenzweig addresses Buber as *Du* [eds.].

my usual salutation.[13] I almost regret that that salutation is now out of order; it remains present, however, as an undertone, just as a silent *Du* was present previously.

As I thought over my verses again tonight, I noted that in them I had been in them somewhat too ungrateful to providence. The text should not read "just two years," but "just three." I wrote the last words of the *Star* on February 2, 1919—and then of course rejoiced, mismanaged, and enthused the rest of the year away. It wasn't until I'd found Edith[14] that the position in Frankfurt[15] became available, and my sword found a grip.[16] Hence the inaccurate number—which wasn't, however, simply an error.

Afterwards we would sometimes exchange poems at the completion of a book. These verses came after the completion of the second:

As "Book of Names" this book is known,
Within a naming circle grown.
It opens with a dozen names—
whence spring a people and its claims
on fate—displayed above one heart
on breastpiece stones, engraver's art.[17]
But in the circle may be found
within this book where names abound
an inner circle hov'ring, where
the Unnameable One, in moment rare
lights up into an "I" His "He,"
that Name might like Existence be.
Then when this book comes to an end
the Name appears, appears again,
now doubled, radiant in its might,
Existence in creative light.
Twelve names, beneath which quakes One heart,
One Name, of Thirteen Attributes a part;
the naming-book that tells of revelation
reveals divine and human name-creation.[18]

---

13. Rosenzweig had always before begun his letters to me with the salutation "Honored friend."

14. Rosenzweig's wife.

15. He means the *Freies Jüdisches Lehrhaus* ["Independent Jewish House of Study"], which he founded and directed.

16. Cf. the motto of the *Star* in connection with the 45th Psalm.

Readers may appreciate an elaboration of Buber's laconic note. The motto of the *Star* is drawn from Ps. 45:5, which reads, in an English based on Buber's German, "Prosper, and ride in the service of fidelity." The verse that precedes this is, "Gird your sword, hero, upon your hip, gird your worship and your glory" [eds.].

17. "Engraver's art" is not in the German text of the poem; it is used here for rhyming purposes, building on the description of the High Priest's breastpiece in Exod. 28.11 [eds.].

18. Poem translated by Everett Fox, with suggestions from Lawrence Rosenwald [eds.].

APPENDIX I

APPENDIX

Making Plain:[1]
In Memory of the Orientalist
Karl Eugen Neumann[2]

Martin Buber
(1925)

A Chinese folktale begins by telling how in a pagoda there once stood two clay statues: on the left a statue of Lao-Tse, on the right a statue of Fo, i.e., Buddha. A Buddhist priest came by, saw the statues, and said angrily, "Great is the congregation of Fo; why should his image stand to the right of Lao-Tse's?" (In China the left side is the place of honor.) So the priest shifted the statues about. Afterwards a priest of the Tao came, looked, and said, "My congregation too is a noble one—why is Lao-Kiun placed to the right of Fo?" And at once he moved it to the other side. This went on till with the constant shifting both statues were ruined. Then Lao-Tse said to Buddha, smiling, "It's not that we two couldn't put up with each other perfectly well—it's these fools' fault that we're treated this way!"

Is this or something like it not the case of translators and commentators, especially in regard to sacred texts? They think to put the speakers they are concerned with on a pedestal of special honor, and thereby destroy them— or at any rate destroy their clay images. They venture to bring out their "individuality," and thereby distort their truth. Great speakers, however, are concerned only with truth, and not with a particular accent for declaiming it, which they would consider merely an aspect of their mortal fate—if they ever bothered with it in the first place. They can indeed put up with one another perfectly well—in the authenticity of their word. That authenticity lies

---

1. German *Schlichtung*. The verb *schlichten* can mean "to arbitrate," but also "to level, smooth, plane"; the adjective *schlicht* means "plain" or "simple." A more literary translation of the title would be "Pla(i)ning" [eds.].

2. Written for a memorial volume planned by the R. Piper Verlag; printed in advance of book publication by the *Frankfurter Zeitung* for October 18, 1925.

above any isolable content; it is engendered in the human articulation of the broken word by the speakers' communality in the one unchanging truth, i.e., the truth of the one unspoken word. This authenticity, altogether different from all "originality," is where ordinary translators and commentators fail.

It is in this context that we feel most strongly what we owe Karl Eugen Neumann, who made clear and present to us the authenticity of the Buddha—not by a periphrastic description of it, since all such description is in vain, but by the recreation of Buddha's word in German, "being intimate with the ten thousand instruments belonging to a language of great ancestral wealth."[3] He, like the master he served, was concerned with truth—the saving truth of humanity, the truth of being and word and "way," rather than the truth of intellectual or religious content. Because this was the case, however, because he was committed to nothing but fidelity to truth and authenticity, he was also able to shape from the material of our language the fated imprint and accent of the person. One example of many may show how Neumann's renderings differed from the usual ones, and also how he himself worked in the service of pure form. The stanza in question is translated by an eminent scholar as follows:

> To water fields, we dig the stream a trench;
> the arrow-makers shape the arrows straight;
> the carpenters must bend the boards to fit;
> but sages—hearken!—conquer their own fate.

Neumann at the beginning of his work translates the same text as follows:

> Aqueducts hold the water in;
> bowmen bend arrows hewed to sharpness;
> carpenters carve hard wood;
> their own hearts do wise men tame.

But at the end of his work, the stanza has attained this purer form:

> Farmers make plain paths for water-channels;
> bowmen plane sharp arrows smooth;
> carpenters plane the rough places of narrow beams;
> their own selves, in truth, do wise men make plain.

Here we have both simple, seamless form and perfect fidelity; as in Pali, so now in German, the one word is metamorphosed into its various incarnations. What has happened? A farmer, a bowmaker, a carpenter, a wise man have all been at work together.

---

3. We have been unable to locate the source of this phrase [eds.].

A Letter to Martin Goldner[4]

Franz Rosenzweig

June 23, 1927

Dear Mr. Goldner!

Do not, please, expect to find in this letter any "Jewish or personal" reasons for our rendering of the divine name—at least no more than are implied by the fact that the translators are after all Jews and persons. Your reasoning here is in fact much closer to ours than you think.

At first we used "Lord." That became less and less acceptable, because it is simply wrong. Then we said to ourselves that actually we should do the reverse—should say "God" for the name, and "Lord" for *Elohim*. "God" has for us something of the character of a name, while "Lord" has the generalized, conceptual quality of *Elohim*. So Luther too in chapters 2 and 3 translates *Hashem Elohim* as "God the Lord," evidently for this same reason. But such a reversal, we saw, would only clarify the problem and not solve it. Then, suddenly, just as "Lord" was becoming desperately unacceptable, the present rendering occurred to us. At first we received it hesitantly; but then, on examination, we found it seeming more and more right. Finally there remained only the problem—which will especially interest and divert you— of using the capital letters in such a way that they would not attract the reader's eye prematurely, and yet could not be overlooked when the reader had in fact reached the word. This entailed several experiments to find the rather complicated rules we eventually settled on—where an initial capital was needed and where not, where spaces were needed and where not.

Such was our voyage of discovery. The story of such a voyage is, as you will know from your own experience, always shorter than the subsequent cartographical survey of the territory discovered. But only the latter is important, only the gain for geography. In this case, then, what matters is the objective rightness of the solution, as this developed in our experimentation and reflection, and not the subjective means through which the sudden insight came. An interest in the voyage of discovery is a purely romantic interest— "for young adults."

---

4. The following letter refers to an account Goldner gave of the Bible translation to a study-group of "Die Kameraden."

We have first to be rid of the conviction that the right translation is actually "Yahweh." Perhaps—though *only* perhaps—this would be true for a pre-biblical stage of the tradition, a stage however that from the sources as we have them can never or as good as never be reconstructed with any confidence. (And if such a reconstruction were possible, it still would not be clear whether the tetragrammaton belonged to this original tradition or rather had arisen precisely at the moment of the biblicizing, the book-making, of the pre-biblical material.) In the biblical text as we have it, and even in the hypothetical sources into which scholars seek to dissect it, the tetragrammaton is already no longer a mere name but a name that is also an idea, i.e., a name that cannot be treated as a noun—it cannot, for example, be put into the plural—but which one cannot read without having to conceive a meaning, a meaning altogether filling the name and not one simply retained in part within it—as we sometimes note that *Friede* ("peace") is contained in *Friedrich*, without its being the case that *Friedrich* must therefore be thought of as essentially cohering with *Friede*. Here and only here: *nomen* is entirely *omen*.

It is not the case, as I once thought, that all this begins to be true only at the time when the name is first replaced by the substitute name, regardless of whether this takes place in the Hellenistic era or, as Jacob argues in an interesting excursus in his youthful work *In God's Name*, directly after the exile. Rather even at the time when the name was still spoken, whether as "Yahweh" or—for even this is not certain—as "Yeheweh," it could not be spoken without evoking the name's meaning—even at that time, that is, the name was wholly transparent. We have a very clear proof of this: the phrase *Adonai shemo*, no doubt familiar to you from at least the Song of the Sea. This phrase becomes nonsense if it translated, "his name is Yahweh." A battle-cry in this form—"his name is Mars!", "his name is Zeus!", even "his name is Wilhelm" (though the case is different with "his name is Napoleon," since here, because of the first Napoleon, the name has to some extent become a concept)—would be met by the hostile army with a simple "so?" or "so what?" But meaning enters in when a noun is introduced, as in Luther: "Lord is his name!" Or in the Vulgate: *omnipotens nomen ejus*. And Friedrich Leopold von Stolberg translates the phrase rightly as "His Name is, I-am!"

"Rightly," because the meaning suddenly shining through the opaque surface of the name is of course to be ascertained only in the self-witness concerning the name that the biblical text itself records, in the central passage of Exodus 3. That passage, however, must be rightly understood. Stolberg and all those who find here notions of "being," of "the-one-who-is," of "the eternal," are all Platonizing. It is not that such notions are not connected with the name; but they are, precisely, connected with the name, and latent in it, as philosophical consequences. The immediate meaning is different—much more pointed and more direct. You will find it briefly stated in Rashi's commentary on the passage and in *The Kuzari* IV:3, and stated as fully as could be wished in Jacob's magnificent treatment of the matter in "Moses at the Burning Bush," in the *Monatsschrift* for 1922. God's self-naming evolves directly from the previous passage (p. 14, *colon* 18[5]). God calls himself not "the-one-who-is" but "the one-who-is-there," i.e., there for you, there for you at this place, present to you, with you or rather coming toward you, toward you to help you. For the Hebrew *hayah* is not, unlike the Indo-Germanic "to be," of its nature a copula, not of its nature static, but a word of becoming, of entering, of happening. The merely copulative sense of "to be" is expressed in Hebrew, if at all, by an interpolated *hu'* or *hi'* or whatever. Only because this one-becoming-present-to-you will always be present to you when you need him and call upon him—"I *will* be there"—only for this reason does he become in our reflection, our afterthought, also the ever-being, the absolute, the eternal, separated thus from my need and my particular moment—but only thus separable because any future moment of any person could take the place of this present moment of mine. His eternity is made visible only in relation to a Now, to my Now; his "absolute being" only in relation to my present being; his "pure being" only in relation to the least pure being of all.

How then can we translate this? It would be altogether mistaken to replace the secondary adjective "eternal" by, say, a primary adjective like "present," because even then the crucial matter would be absent, namely the simultaneously sounding "present-to-you." And "he-who-is-present" would no less than "the Eternal" or "Lord" be *only* meaning and not, as is essential to the tetragrammaton, a meaning-bearing name. A name comes alive only in being named; the vocative is its real subjective case, and even the nominative case is for it an objective one. This is made clear by a look at the good origin of the bad translation "Lord" in the Hebrew substitution *Adonai*. The Hebrew word does not mean "Lord"; rather it is a vocative, which retains the vocative quality even when it is used in other cases, much like French *Monsieur*. This vocative quality brings into the recited text, everywhere except in the clearly vocative instances of the name, a tension directing us to the nominal quality of the name; it is precisely this tension that is missed by rendering *Adonai* in western languages by the mere word "Lord."

This quality of relatedness, of reciprocity, inherent in the divine name first simply because it is a name and then in particular because of its special

---

5. That is, line 18 of page 14 of the first edition of the Exodus translation, which in chapter-and-verse notation is Exod. 3:12 [eds.].

meaning, must rather be rendered on the basis of the other side of the relation—the side of the one who speaks and names. The "present-to-you" of
the original must be rendered by a "present-to-me" of the translation. The
vocative solution is forbidden simply as being too grotesque; what is bidden
in its place is the personal pronoun, which in its three persons means precisely the three dimensions of "present-to-me": the capacity to be spoken to,
the capacity to be spoken to by, the capacity to be spoken of. The second
person has priority here, since it is the source of personhood of the other
two—only him whom I am prepared to speak to do I accept as an "I," and
only him whom I have spoken to do I accept even in his absence as a person. Or conversely, only from being spoken to does there come my objective and subjective self-consciousness, my "he-consciousness" and
"I-consciousness"—both in the psychological singular and the sociological
plural. Only because he is my "You" do I perceive the one-present-to-me in
his "I," and can speak of "Him."

But enough for now. It is just now Shabbat, and everything has in any
case been said, albeit briefly.

Yours,
Franz Rosenzweig

From Martin Buber's *Kingship of God*[6]
(1929)

Moses then resists somewhat, and asks the being speaking to him from the
Burning Bush, the being sending him on this extraordinary mission to
Egypt, "Here, I will come to the Children of Israel/ and I will say to them:/
The God of your fathers has sent me to you,/ and they will say to me: What
is his name?—/ and what shall I say to them then?" (Exod. 3:13). Scholars
have rightly posited that the question "What is his name"[7] has to do with
primitive beliefs concerning names; "It was then a common conviction that
through a knowledge of a god's name one could have the god himself in

---

6. *Königtum Gottes*, 3d ed. (Heidelberg: Lambert Schneider, 1956), chapter 5, "JHWH der
Melekh," pp. 68-70; English edition *Kingship of God*, 3d ed. (New York: Harper & Row, 1967),
chapter 5, "JHWH the Melekh," pp. 104-106 [eds.].

7. The closest analogy is Deut. 6:20, where also the question is not, "*which* laws are these?"
but "*what* are these laws [familiar to us]?"

one's power."[8] But we must also add that these beliefs were stronger among the Egyptians than among any other ancient people;[9] among the Egyptians it was thought that through knowledge of a hidden god-name one could oneself *become* a god. Moses is not assuming that his people will, when he says he is sent by the God of their fathers, then ask "so what is his name?"[10] Such nonsense would be incomprehensible in any people, let alone in this people, whose consciousness of its own tradition the author of the Burning Bush episode is surely not calling into question.[11] Perhaps that author was, as scholars now claim, ignorant of, say, Abraham's evocation of the name YHWH in Genesis; but surely the Redactor was not, and such passages, given a subject of such importance, must have influenced the Redactor's selections of texts.[12] The question Moses expects from his people concerns not the letter of the name but its secret, its particular articulation, its magic use. The afflicted will, Moses thinks, want to know (in accord with what they see in Egypt) how they can invoke God with power, so that he will appear at once to them and help them. God's message will not be enough for them; they will want rather to possess *him*. What, Moses asks, shall he answer them? And YHWH answers him with his *ehyeh asher ehyeh*, which reveals in the first person what the name conceals in the third—conceals, that is, only now in this its developed form, since the tetragrammaton grows from the original "Godshout,"[13] *Yah* or *Yahu*, and from the primordial acclamation-

---

8. Gunkel, "Jahve," in *Religion in Geschichte und Gegenwart*, 2d ed., II: 10.

9. See for example Lefébure, "La vertu et la vie du nom I en Egypte," *Mélusine* 8: 223ff. (1896-97); Budge, *Egyptian Magic* 2 (1901), 157ff.; Lexa, *La magie dans l'Egypte antique* (1925), 1: 113ff.; Obbink, *De magische beteeknis van den naam inzonderheit in het oude Egypt* (1925), especially 79ff.; Foucart, "Names (Egyptian)" in the *Encyclopedia of Religion and Ethics* IX: 151ff. (Foucart's entry in the same work, "Body [Egyptian]" [II: 764], calls the theory of names the foundation for more than half the religious ideas of Egypt.)

10. That is the interpretation of Kautzsch-Bertholet.

11. Even if, as the reigning interpretation of 6:3 would have it, only the name Shaddai had been passed on to the people, they would at least have known that name, and so would have had no occasion to ask Moses the question he imagines being asked. But in fact 6:3 refers not to the revealing of the tetragrammaton *name* but to the disclosure of its *meaning* that has just then occurred.

12. The problem is not solved by distinguishing among the sources (cf. Galling, *Die Erwählungstraditionen Israels* [1928], 57ff.).

13. Rosenzweig, "The Eternal"; see also Driver, "The Original Form of the Name Jahweh," *Zeitschrift für die alttestamentliche Wissenschaft*, Neue Folge V, 1928, 24. Both essays adduce in comparison the Dionysus acclamations "Iacchos" and "Euios"; to these might be added Sabos-Sabazios and Eleleus (see Perdrizet, *Cultes et mythes du Pangée* [1910] 59, 77ff., and Theander, "'*Ololugê* und *ia*," *Eranos* XV [1915] 99ff., especially 120ff.). On the general problem see the valuable section "Urlaute und Urtermini des sensus numinis" in Rudolf Otto, *Das Heilige, bzw. Aufsätze das Numinose betreffend*, retitled *Das Gefühl des Uberweltlichen* (1932), 203ff., which makes reference (p. 210) to Driver's explanation of the tetragrammaton [English edition Rudolf Otto, *The Idea of the Holy*, 2d ed. (London: Oxford, 1950), John Harvey, tr., "Original Numinous Sounds," pp. 190-193; Driver is not quoted by name].

name (Exod. 4:26, 12:8, 13:4, 21:33, 26:25),[14] and in the tetragrammaton
name and epithet nearly coincide.[15] The word does not, that is, mean "I am
who I am" or anything similar, since *hayah, havah* in biblical language
means "is" only (and only secondarily) in a copulative sense, and never in
an existential one—biblical language has no concept for that existential
sense of "be"—but principally means "become," "happen," "be-there" or
"be-here." *Ehyeh* in our passage means precisely what it means in the same
story both before (3:12) and after (4:12 and 15): to be present to someone,
to be with someone, to assist someone—except that here the verb is used
absolutely, without any specification of *whom* the one-who-is-there is there
for.[16] God does not by this make any theological proposition that he is eternal or self-sufficient; rather he offers to the creature he has made, to his

---

In contrast, Mowinckel, in a letter to Otto that Otto cites 326f. [not quoted in the English
edition], presumes an original form *Ya-huwa*, i.e., "Oh He" (*huwa* is the Arabic form of the
third person personal pronoun); he accordingly sees the tetragrammaton not as an expansion
but as an abbreviation of the original acclamation. In working out our rendering of the name,
Rosenzweig and I had even in 1925 begun from the postulate that it contained a "He!"-excla-
mation, from which was made a "He will be there!" or a "He is there!" (Compare our translation itself, in particular Exodus 15.) The notion of a divine name *Hu'* contained in the
tetragrammaton seems also to exert some effect even on talmudic tradition, *b. Shabbat* 104a;
see also the passages cited by Marmorstein, *The Old Rabbinic Doctrine of God* (1927) I: 84. Otto,
p. 210 [English ed. p. 193], rightly adduces also the dervish-cry *Ya-hu* and the "I know no other
but *Ya-hu* (Oh He) and *Ya-man-hu* (Oh He who is)" of Jelaleddin Rumi (see Nicholson, *Selected
Poems from the Divani Shamsi Tabriz* [1898], 126f. and 282). One might also cite Friedrich
Delitzsch, *Wo lag das Paradies?* (1881), p. 166.

14. This fact alone forbids us to see in the proper name YHWH *in se* as such any evidence of
an original Jewish polytheism. Gressmann, *Mose* 426, writes, "the naming of a divinity in such
a way as to distinguish it from other beings has meaning only on the presumption of polytheism." But in fact proper names are originally used not, in general, to *distinguish* one person from
another, but rather so as to be able to *address* the divine person, and in particular to address
that person in such a way that it alone feels itself addressed, and that it alone will answer.

15. Rosenzweig, "The Eternal." A similar opinion is voiced earlier by Hehn, *Die biblische und
die babylonische Gottesidee* (1913), pp. 228ff. Max Weber, in *The Sociology of Religion* 3:131n., holds
it impossible "to consider, as Hehn does, the name as a theological principle of Moses', since
Yahweh was not worshipped in Israel." Aside from the complexities of the historical issue Weber
touches on, however, it is clear that what is at issue here is not the name as such, but its transformation into the *tetra*grammaton; and regarding this latter there can be no doubt that we find
it in non-Israelite texts exclusively as the name of Israel's God. Van Hoonacker, *Une commu-
nauté Judéo-araméenne* (1915), pp. 69ff., has also shown that the tetragrammaton is a "secondary
formation," arising from the "development" of the shorter name; Burkitt, "On the Name
Yahweh," *Journal of Biblical Literature* 44 (1925), 353ff., has then sketched the role of Moses in
this development. Yet Konrad Müller, apparently without knowing either Hehn's work or Van
Hoonacker's, had with reference to Otto's work, already argued, in "Jah—ein numinöser
Urlaut?" *Kartell-Zeitung: Organ des Eisenacher Kartells Akademisch-Theologischer Vereine* 31 (1921),
150f., that "Moses' religious action" was "by a small phonetic extrapolation to have given the ir-
rational and contentless primal numinous syllable 'Yah' a rational and significant meaning."

16. See recently, *inter alia*, Skipwith, "The Tetragrammaton," *Jewish Quarterly Review* 10
(1898), 662ff.; Spoer, "The Origin and Interpretation of the Tetragrammaton," *American
Journal of Semitic Languages* 18 (1901-1902), 33f.; Hehn, op. cit., 214f.; Driver, op. cit., 246; and
especially Jacob, "Mose am Dornbusch," *Monatsschrift für Geschichte und Wissenschaft des
Judentums* 66 (1922), 131f.

person and his people, the assurance that they are in need of and that renders all magical feats both void and superfluous. The first *ehyeh* says simply, "I shall be-there" (with my host, with my people, with you)—so you do not need to conjure me up; and the next *asher ehyeh* can according to all parallel passages[17] mean only, "as the one I shall always be-there as," "as who I shall on this or that occasion be-there as," i.e., just as I shall on this or that occasion want to appear. I myself, God says, do not anticipate my own manifestations—and yet you think by some means or other to constrain me to appear here and not elsewhere, now and not elsewhen, so and not otherwise! Or, in summary: you do not *need* to invoke me; but neither are you *able* to invoke me. What is here reported is, in the context of the history of religion, the demagicalizing of belief—in the self-proclamation of the God present to his own, abiding with his own, accompanying his own.

A Reply[18]

Franz Rosenzweig
(End of May 1929)

My Dear Rabbi,

Your reservations belong for the most part in the category of our own self-criticism, so we find it only right to have them expressed. I have recently put the matter to myself as follows: for the translator there is neither good nor better, only bad and less bad.

In particular matters, however, I would offer a few remarks, because I have promised them to you. In the orthography of the proper names our chief motive has been to direct the reader to the least wrong pronunciation possible—rather "Shmuel," that is, than "Shemuel."

Your remarks on the *vav*-connective raise a serious problem. As chance

---

17. See in particular Exod. 16:23 and 33:19; 1 Sam. 23:13; 2 Kings 8:1; Ezek. 12:25. See also Arnold, "The Divine Name in Exodus 3:14," *Journal of Biblical Literature* 24 (1905), 127f., who however grasps only the sense of the pronoun and not the sense of the verb, and therefore declares the whole utterance an incomprehensible "midrashic gloss" on 14b. Jacob, op. cit., understands the passage more comprehensively.

18. To a review by Rabbi Josef Carlebach, which Rosenzweig had seen before its publication in *Der Israelit*, the reply appeared in the same journal.

would have it, I have just now received a letter from Fritz Goitein in Jerusalem, in which he writes,

> As to one point I am finally not yet convinced: the asyndeton. True, when you hear the Fellaheen here tell stories, it's your translation exactly—they speak in just that way. But as regards diction and language, it seems to me that there was a terrific shock in this country's history—I mean by that not the Arab conquest but the Aramaic flood that buried the old classic ways. Talmudic storytellers are magnificently asyndetic; Aramaic-Arabic is one world. But this original noble Hebrew shuns all disconnectedness, and in your translation that is not at all clear.

We were guided by the consideration that the *vav*-connective is normal in Hebrew and not specifically "biblical," i.e., not to be rendered with the "and" that because of Luther took on the character of a specifically biblical diction.

We diverged from the vowels and consonants of the Masoretic text only with the greatest reluctance, and on principle only where we thought a lot was to be gained. (1 Kings 7:36 is by the way meant not as an emendation but as an attempt to do justice to the Masoretic reading.) We were somewhat freer in altering accents and such. In 1 Sam. 4:1, we wanted to remove from Samuel the burden of special responsibility for so unfortunate an undertaking.[19] (What, by the way, is your opinion of 1 Sam. 13:1? Do you not agree that relineating the verse genuinely rescues the Masoretic reading?[20]) Our experiment in Gen. 2:4 is intended to rescue the half-verse that modern criticism has cast doubt on, making it not some insignificant retrospective remark but rather having it begin the series of "these are the begettings" with the significant remark that what the pagan world understands as "begetting" ("cosmogony"[21]) is in truth creation.[22]

---

19. In a Bible translation making use of the traditional scheme of chapter and verse, Sam. 4:1 reads "and Samuel spake unto all Israel" (Geneva Bible), as if Samuel's word were spoken on Samuel's initiative. Buber and Rosenzweig, however, link 4:1 to the preceding verse 3:21. In the Geneva Bible, 3:21 reads, "And the Lord appeared againe in Shiloh: for the Lord revealed him selfe to Samuel in Shiloh by his worde"; Buber and Rosenzweig's rendering of the passage as a whole reads, "HE continued to let himself be seen in Shilo,/ for in Shilo HE revealed himself to Samuel in HIS word,/ but Samuel's word came to pass before all Israel." The linking of God's revelation to Samuel with Samuel's speaking to Israel does in fact "remove from Samuel the burden of special responsibility" [eds.].

20. Buber and Rosenzweig split 13:1 in two; the first half, "Saul was then a year old in his kingship," ends a section of Buber's text; the second half, "when he had been king over Israel for two years," begins the next section [eds.].

21. Rosenzweig puts the word in quotations marks to indicate that "cosmogony" means by etymology "the procreation of the universe" [eds.].

22. Buber and Rosenzweig split Gen. 2:4 in two. The first half, "these are the begettings of the heavens and the earth: their being created," they take as the concluding verse of the creation story; the second half, "on the day that HE, God, made earth and heaven," they take as the beginning verse of the story of Adam and Eve [eds.].

In theory you are also right in warning us of the dangers inherent in our intrinsically legitimate probing of deep verbal content. In this case it's I who am "at fault." Daily by letter, and once a week orally, Buber passionately and ironically presents the poor reader's case against me. But do believe that nothing of what remains is occasioned by connoisseurship; rather it is occasioned by *rabies theologica.* We translate on the basis of the Torah. We attempt to make plain the Torah's conceptual system even in its books of narrative. We are convinced that the Bible seeks always to instruct, even in the "narrative" and "poetical" portions—sometimes explicitly, but more often by the powerful and yet inobtrusive means of linguistic allusion. Hence our battle for a terminology. . . .

A few more particulars. *Mizbeah* does indeed occur in a weakened sense in some passages. We respond to this in, for example, Leviticus, by translating the word merely as "place" except where in accounts of sacrifices "slaughtering" occurs in close proximity to it. But ought we to have left out "slaughter" from Exod. 20:24 and 2 Chron. 33:16, where it is clearly intended? And similarly in many other cases.

The "overwatched night" [Exod. 12:42] (which by the way can be justified linguistically—see Lagarde, Barth, Ibn Ezra) is not meant as mythologizing, but the reverse—it was for God a night of watching over us, and so it has become for us a night of remaining watchful. And that is after all something that you too could accept.

The verb "to king" (German *königen*) is common in Middle High German—it's only within modern German that Grimm gives only one example.

Regarding *ba'al*—the translational problem here, in all its appalling theological significance, is best understood on the basis of Hosea 2.

Tamei'—theologically it is at once clear that this is not a purely private notion: the *ruah ha-ṭum'ah* (Zech. 13:2) is not simply a lack of purity. So the word simply cannot be translated "impure," "impurity," "impurify"—even aside from the fact that we do not allow ourselves to render two different words of such importance by a single equivalent. We worked hard to find an adequate term; and I would maintain that no fitter equivalent in German can be found. . . .

Franz Rosenzweig

From a Letter to *Dozent* Josef Wohlgemuth[23]

Franz Rosenzweig
(End of January 1926)

Our thanks for having sent the proofs. But really we have nothing to say in reply. To be discussed with so thorough a consideration of detail is how we would wish to be discussed always. One sees then what it means when a critic has himself confronted the difficulties. We shall ponder your censures in earnest, even those that are only such censures as we believed we had considered already, when we come to make a new edition.

At the beginning of your essay you explain very thoroughly the prejudices existing against us as Bible-translators; but this too can only be welcome to us, since the subsequent *post*-judice of us, the judgment after the fact, is only thereby made weightier. The question, Whom were we thinking of in the translation? is not easy to answer. In the actual activity of translating, no one—as you know from your own experience, the *pasuq* [verse] stands so gigantically before you with its difficulties that behind it the figures of readers are invisible. When one pauses for breath, one does think of future readers, and imagines them in all sorts of forms—least of all, however, in the form of aesthetic youths. The publisher may be thinking of such things when he estimates the size of the edition and the lowest possible price that this size permits; but to think of them during or even between moments of work could spoil the activity altogether. But beside the expert and the teacher, one thinks also of the many simple souls among Jews and Christians, who have lost access in the one case to the original and in the other to Luther. It is these people—serious, painstaking, striving—whom one wishes as readers: the Jews so that that they can find their way back to the original, the Christians so that they can again feel the living word behind Luther's text that their clergy have spoiled for them. . . .

Do bring your warm and fruitful interest to future volumes as well! . . .

---

23. In reply to the galleys Wohlgemuth had sent of his thorough review of the first volume of *Die Schrift*; the review subsequently appeared in *Jeschurun*.

A Letter to the Editor

Franz Rosenzweig
(not sent)

Frankfurt, February 19, 1926

. . . I have just received the review you brought over of the first volume of our new Bible translation. The scholar to whom you gave the book for review assesses "in various passages from the beginning on" our fidelity to the text. He proves this in the following way: "'Surge of God brooding all above the waters' or 'vault be amidst the waters' hardly corresponds to the Hebrew original." Since we considered precisely these sentences ideal examples of literal translation, we would be grateful to your reviewer for pointing out our mistakes here so that we could correct them in later editions. He might perhaps find this difficult to do quickly, given the enormous literature on the first sentence—ancient, medieval, and modern both Jewish and Christian. I would however be equally grateful for instruction regarding the second sentence, concerning which he might, if he reads vocalized Hebrew, to some extent inform himself from the ordinary lexica, under the words *hayah, raqiʿa, tavekh,* and *mayim.*

Very Sincerely Yours,
Franz Rosenzweig

From a Letter to Hermann Gerson

Martin Buber
(January 1929)

Wilhelm Stapel, in *Antisemitismus und Antigermanismus* (1928), had characterized the language of our Bible translation as "half-jargon," arguing that
in reference to that language one could "most easily" understand "the difference between the German linguistic manner and the Jewish." In support
of this claim, Stapel wrote as follows:

> A few examples, then, of German linguistic form and of the German-
> Jewish "renovation" of our language. Luther: "let them go themselves
> [*selbst*]"; Buber: "be it they themselves [*selber*] that go." Luther: "for they
> go idle"; Buber: "they are only slack [*schlapp*]." Luther: "let someone
> afflict these people with work"; Buber: "let servitude weigh upon the peo-
> ple." Luther: "you are to do no work"; Buber: "make no [*nicht mache*]
> labor." Luther: "and the Cherubim shall stretch up their wings on high";
> Buber: "and the Cherubim are to be made spreading wings upward."
> Luther: "tablets . . . that were inscribed on both sides"; Buber: "tablets,
> inscribed on from both their surfaces." Luther: "grew vexed in anger";
> Buber: "burned then Moses' anger up." (The skittering tempo of this last
> phrase is especially characteristic; it exhibits a particularly Jewish gesture.
> Luther's *German* Moses "grows vexed"—this we understand at once. As to
> Buber's *Jewish* Moses, however—it is not possible to say, "his anger burned
> up," because a fire that "burns up" is a fire that consumes and quenches
> itself.[24] Buber misuses "burn up," because in the nature of his Jewish ner-
> vous agitation he needs this word rhythmically and tonally, and needs it
> in the sense of "flamed up" [*emporflammte*] or "blazed up" [*emporlohte*].
> But he cannot use either of these words, because Jewish anger neither
> flames nor blazes, but burns. Between the two possibilities, then, between
> "flamed up" and "burned up," he chooses the second, partly because it
> begins more quickly, with the accent on the first syllable, partly because it
> fits better with a guttural language than does the labial *empor*.

---

24. Stapel's point is that German *aufbrennen*, like English "to burn up," normally means "to
consume with fire" or "to be consumed with fire." His point is right as far as it goes; but so is
Buber's subsequent response to it, since the German verb can also be used like the English
phrase "to flare up," where no idea of consumption is implied. We have, however, found no
English phrase of which both Stapel's point and Buber's response are true; the English rendering "burn up" supports Stapel's point only, and thus makes it seem truer than it is [eds].

My student and friend, Hermann Gerson, asked me why we had translated as we had the passages adduced by Stapel. What follows is my answer.

1. Exod. 5:7, *hem yelekhu* does not mean "let them go themselves [*selbst*]," but rather "be it *they* themselves [*selber*] that go." Our *selber* is moreover a better word than the unorganic *selbst* (see Grimm's *Dictionary*, 10:1 Sp. 430 and 445[25]); moreover, as Stapel clearly does not know, *selber* is a word Luther is fond of using. Here Luther writes *selbst*, which is still a good and uncorrupted form. So our translation is better German than what Stapel cites, and is moreover the only one to render the original in its full force; "let them . . . " diminishes the gravity of the Hebrew phrase.

2. 5:8, *nirpim hem:*—*rafah* has nothing to do with "idle"; the words denote not a situation of inactivity but a corporeal condition, made clearest in the phrase *va-yirpu yadav* (2 Sam. 4:1 and often), which means not "his hands became idle" but "his hands grew lax" (Luther, less accurately, "grew weary"). What Pharaoh wants to say is that the Israelites are so to speak slackening themselves, that they have a mental disposition corresponding to the physical condition of slackness. That is precisely the meaning of our good German word *schlapp* ["slack," "sloppy"], which is the Low German form of High German *schlaff* ["slack," "lax"]; cf., for example, Lichtenberg's "a slack [*schlapp*] heart," or Schiller's "the slack [*schlapp*] century of the castrati" (from *Die Räuber*); Schiller in his youth was very fond of that energetic word.

3. 5:9; Luther's translation is simply wrong. There is no "someone," and no "afflicting," no relation between person and person. Rather Pharaoh means that servitude (not "work," since ʿ*avodah* has here the specific sense of "slave-labor") must lie as such a burden upon the the people, must so "weigh" upon them, that etc.

4. 20:10: a typical example of Stapel's total ignorance of the text. The text here turns around the great correspondence between *loʾ taʿaseh* and the ʿ*asah* spoken by God in verse 11. As God, who "made" the world, rested on the Sabbath, so you also are on this day not to "make" any labor more— "labor" and not "work," because *melaʾkhah* is, in contrast to ʿ*avodah*, the real labor of human hands, but not the result of that labor, not the "work"— which *melaʾkhah* means only when the subject is precisely the labor by which the work is produced (e.g., 1 Kings 7:40). As for our unusual placement of the *nicht* at the beginning of the sentence—compare, for example, Lessing's *nicht rühr an* ("not to touch") as a rendering of *noli me tangere*.

5. 25:20; Luther pays no attention to the peculiarity of the participial con-

---

25. Grimm points out that the "t" of *selbst* is an "unorganische" addition to the original form *selbes* [eds.].

struction, which is however extremely important. The text means not that the Cherubim are to do this and that, but that they are in their sculpted presentation to be made in such a way that they etc.

6. 32:15; Luther translates *tzad* and *tzela'*, *pe'ah* and *ketef*, and finally also *'eber* with the one word "side," while we have as far as possible reserved "side" for the word that actually means it, namely *tzad*. "Surface" is an appropriate rendering of *'eber*—what is unidiomatic about it I cannot see (cf. Grimm 10:1, p. 385, l. 11f.[26]). Our harsh but not inadmissible retention of the "from" responds to the text's evident intention to allude to a mystery of the divine "finger"; the abundance of haggadic interpretation is centered around a real exegetical problem, which we can best approximate by the formula, "written once and once only, yet written on and from both sides (and therefore legible on and from both sides)."

7. 32:19; a passage subject to discussion, but only to discussion. *Hara* we render by "burn up" only here, and elsewhere by "burn" or "burn away"; in the later volumes we prefer "flame," "flame up," "flame out," since we reserve "burn" for *saraf*. In the second edition we will say "flame up" in this passage also. But as regards "burn up" (*aufbrennen*), Stapel shows an inadequate knowledge of German. The passage speaks not of fire that is burning up but of anger. For *aufbrennen* as an intransitive verb Grimm (I: 627) gives only "*ardescere* [Latin 'burn'], *flammen* ['to flame'], *auflodern* ['to blaze up']." Among Grimm's examples: "at this name the stoic[27] flared up" (Wieland); "and so his senses flared up like wisps of fire" (Jean Paul). The meaning *igne consumere, inurere,* "burn away" "consume with fire," is a meaning only of the *transitive* verb. So it is not at all true, as Stapel maintains, that a fire "burning up" means a fire "consuming and quenching itself," since the intransitive form of the verb does not possess that meaning at all. The whole tirade on the "Jewish Moses" turns out to arise from ignorance of the German language. As regards Luther: what he gives here is simply not a translation of the text, which speaks not about Moses but about his anger, i.e., that it "burned" or "blazed" up; moreover, he is here for once not even speaking good German, since "grew vexed in anger" is a dubious pleonasm—indeed the phrase "in anger" only weakens the word "vexed."

In summation, then: in the passages in question, we have, unlike Luther and all other translators hitherto, preserved the essential qualities of the text—among them a gem like the point of 20:10—precisely by being willing to approach the limits of the German language, though without passing beyond them.

---

26. Grimm in the passage Buber cites notes that *Seite*, "side" is often used of the two *Fläche* ("surfaces") of a *Tafel* ("tablet") [eds.].

27. Grimm gives *Stoiker* ("stoic"), which makes sense; Buber gives *Stöcken*, which does not, and probably results from a mistranscription of Buber's handwriting [eds.]

APPENDIX II

The How and Why of Our Bible Translation[1]

Martin Buber

I

Franz Rosenzweig began writing the *Star of Redemption* in the summer of 1918, in the Macedonian trenches, as the forces there prepared themselves to defend at close quarters against an evidently impending attack. He spoke of the work in a letter to a friend, saying this was not yet "his own book"— that, he said, he would not write until the time he could, and was free to, and had to.[2] (In the year before his death he elaborated on this vague indication in a letter to his physician: he would write the book "at seventy," because he could not before then have "accumulated the necessary knowledge."[3]) The *Star*, he said, was only a preliminary study; and yet by his own account it was also his "system." Yet what sort of book could it be to which the system was intended only as a preliminary study? He explains in the same letter to his physician that this other book was to be a Bible commentary, the first part devoted to the weekly portions, the second to the *haftarot*,

---

1. Buber wrote this thoughtful and beautiful essay around 1938, probably just after he arrived in Palestine. It was a time when the task of finishing the Bible translation must have seemed peripheral, but also, and for that same reason, a good time to look back on what the translation had meant.

The German essay has never been published in a commercially available edition, though a transcription of it appears in Anna Elisabeth Bauer's Freiburg dissertation, (published in 1992 by Peter Lang, Frankfurt am Main, in the series *Europäische Hochschulschriften*), and no English translation of it0 has ever been made. Buber himself made a Hebrew version, published in *Darko shel Miqra'* (Jerusalem: Mosad Bialik, 1964). The German manuscript is in the Martin Buber Archive of the Jewish and National University Library in Jerusalem, Arc. Ms. Var. 350, Bible 46a gimel.

The translator wishes to thank Judith Buber Agassi, director of the Martin Buber Estate, for her amiable willingness to grant the right to publish a translation of the essay (and for a long morning's exhilarating conversation); Anna Bauer, for lending a copy of her dissertation; and above all Margot Cohn, of the Manuscripts Division of the Jewish and National University Library, for showing him the essay in the first place, and for listening, after he had read it, to his enraptured enthusiasm for the project of translating it.

All notes to this essay are the editors'; they are for the most part restricted to identifications of the works Buber quotes, in the cases where Buber gives enough data to make identification possible.

2. Letter to Rudolf Ehrenberg, September 4, 1918.
3. Letter to Richard Koch, September 2, 1928.

the third to the festival readings and the Five Scrolls. Later, however, when he had finished the *Star*, it seemed to him that in that book, in which he now saw "the sum of his intellectual being" and "his most authentically personal work"—so that he saw his future as consisting "only of life, and not any more of writing"—he had in fact written "the commentary without the text." That is of course not meant strictly; it is intended to mean that the *Star* had helped to reveal the world from which and for which Scripture is spoken, i.e., the true and divine world that has since the time of Scripture become obscured. Some actual pieces of commentary, however, excerpts from a theological Bible commentary, found their place in the work also. In the second part, the part on "the path," i.e., the way that leads from creation through revelation to redemption, there is at the conclusion of the first book, "Creation," a "grammatical analysis of Genesis 1"; at the end of the second, "Revelation," an analysis of the Song of Songs; and at the end of the third, "Redemption," an analysis of the 115th Psalm. "Grammatical" here refers to a theological grammar; for Rosenzweig thought of language as the power that shatters the shell of secrecy.

In these passages of commentary he of course proceeds from the original text, and repeatedly notes peculiarities of the text that could hardly make their way into a translation. But he reads the original text through the lens of the customary translation—not Luther's exactly, rather the genre of customary translation of which Luther's translation is merely an especially characteristic example. So, for example, at the beginning of the Scriptures, he understands *tohu va-bohu* as the translations do. He does not understand the words as nouns, indicating the chaos that precedes the creation but abides after it, below the world that is made, and above which the earth is suspended (Job 26:7) (though it can at any moment break through into it at God's command [Isa. 34:11, Jer. 4:23]); rather he understands them as adjectives denoting the qualities of "without form and void," as the first adjectival utterance concerning the inanimate world, concerning a darkness "in which all qualities show only the single gray color of 'without form and void.'"[4] In the same chapter he does not understand the sentence *na'aseh adam* as predicated of a pure We; rather he proceeds on the basis of the translation, which with its "let us make a man" introduces a grammatical second person foreign to the text. Rosenzweig knows of course that God does not, in the version we have, speak to some mythical assembly—a fact emphasized by the fact that the "in our image" of this verse is followed by the "in his image" of the next. Nonetheless he speaks of an I "that, as indeed the German translation indicates, has its Thou unmediatedly within it."[5] But

---

4. *Star of Redemption*, section 139.
5. Ibid.

no—God does not here speak to himself even once, rather he speaks only from himself, from the totality of fundamental energies that is in him—or, as Rosenzweig says, in the plural of absolute majesty. No Thou can be found in the original text here, and however beautiful the customary German translation is, it is also false. The theological grammar here is still the grammar of languages other than Hebrew. In the end, however, the problem is not in the translation but in the tradition of common Bible-reading generally, Hebrew Bible-reading included—in the traditional superficiality of Bible-reading, which does not take earnestly enough the difference between what is written and what is not.

It was only later, in Frankfurt am Main, when Rosenzweig had moved from the proud structure of his system to the humble but altogether real work of building his small Jewish community, that he came to grips in earnest with the Hebrew Bible as it is. The outward impulse toward that encounter was, by Rosenzweig's own account, the Bible class of his new friend Eduard Straus, who was then helping him found the *Freies Jüdisches Lehrhaus*. In this class Rosenzweig was, as he said, "for the first time in his life actually standing before the pure text in its nakedness, without its traditional garments." Until that point he had, as he said, been reluctant to read the Torah and the Prophets except in the context of the millennia— the Jewish millennia, he said; but he would have been more nearly right had he said, as noted, the millennia generally. Only now in Frankfurt did he dare "to take his place before the text and the text alone." Everything that the Bible became to him, everything that took place within the Bible, had its origin in this "naked" encounter.

II

My own way to the Bible was different. I grew up in my grandfather's[6] house, and as a child had known the original text for years before I ever saw a translation. The reading of this translation—the one edited by Zunz— had as its consequence that I began to get angry at the Bible. Stories that I had previously received as self-evident became unbearable; the story of Samuel's killing of Agag I bore for a long time like an open wound,[7] and even today that wound is only scarred over and not healed. Psalms in which the speaker in all innocence complained of his enemies, Psalms that before I had not even noticed—even these now began, in Michael Sachs' beautiful translation (his earlier translation, less beautiful but more true, I got to

---

6. Midrashic scholar Solomon Buber (1827-1906).

7. Cf. "Samuel and Agag," in Paul Arthur Schilpp and Maurice Friedman, eds., *The Philosophy of Martin Buber* (La Salle, Ill.: Open Court, 1967), pp. 31-33.

know only later, through Rosenzweig) to seem to me in my torment like shameless vituperation. It was for me like what happens in a fairy tale, when a wicked spirit drapes a veil over a maiden and transforms her into something dreadful; and I have similar experiences here in the streets of Jerusalem sometimes, when I catch sight of the face of an Arab woman all covered by some multicolored veil and it seems to me the face of a ghost. Later, when I got to know Luther's German Bible, the charm of the language reined in my anger; but soon after—shortly after my Bar Mitzvah—I suddenly noticed that I was reading the Bible with literary pleasure, and that fact so shocked me that I did not pick up a Bible translation for many years. I tried to return to the original text; now, though, it seemed to me hard and alien, the words had lost their easy and familiar movement, they darted before my eyes, and again and again I had to marvel that there was a book like this on earth and that I had been forged at it.

It took thirteen years for anything new to happen. I had come home from Herzl's funeral, and to lighten my heavy heart I opened one book after another—in vain, nothing spoke to me. And then, casually, without hope, I opened the Scriptures—it was the story of how King Jehoiakim cut section after section from Jeremiah's scroll and threw them in the brazier's fire[8]— and it went straight to my heart. I began again to read in the Hebrew Bible, not continually, only a passage from time to time. It was not familiar, as it had been in my childhood; but neither was it alien, as it had become afterwards. Every word had to be won, but every word could be won. From that time the Bible has meant in my heart nothing else but the untranslated book. I read it aloud; and in reading aloud I got free of the whole Scripture, which was now only *miqra'* and nothing more.[9]

One time—again after several years—as I was in the middle of speaking a chapter aloud it seemed to me that the chapter was being spoken for the first time, that it had not yet ever been written down, that it did not at all need to be written down. The book lay before me; but the book was melting in the voice.

In the years before the Great War I had been a member of a Berlin *Stammtisch,*[10] which met once a week over a glass of wine, and to which a number of important people belonged. The relation between the German and Jewish members of the *Stammtisch* was one of openhearted camaraderie. But some of the Jewish members seemed sometimes to themselves like excerpts of a Hebrew book read in Luther's translation; it seemed to

---

8. Jer. 36:21ff.

9. Buber distinguishes between two names for the Hebrew Bible: German *Schrift,* "Scripture," i.e., "what is written," and Hebrew *miqra',* "the calling," i.e., "what is spoken."

10. A small club, called *Stammtisch* ("habitual table") from its meeting regularly at the same place.

them that what counted in the camaraderie was not the *Urtext* of their being but the translation, the translation that was more beautiful than true. Luther had translated the Hebrew Bible into the German of his New Testament, into a language stamped by Christian theology, and no translator, not even a Jewish translator, had been able subsequently to get free of it. Were not we ourselves, however intimate we were with our German friends, accessible to them only in a Christian translation? Something was wrong. We felt more and more the need to correct it. Any direct attempt, though, would have been dilettantish and hopeless. We had only an indirect way to proclaim our truth: a faithful translation of Scripture. We had no choice but to evoke the troubling truth. From that, anything might happen—but it would be to us ourselves in our real being, and not to a semblance of it, that it would happen. Yet our impulse came to us from a historical depth that I then merely intuited, and only later saw in the whole of its connection with our time.

Paul de Lagarde had been the one profound thinker among German anti-Semites, and the seed he had planted was then flowering in Germany in the form of an intellectual movement that aimed at a "Germanization of Christianity" with a "German God" and a "German Christ"—goals that had as their first postulate a radical severance from the "Old Testament." (This movement should not be confused with its grotesque epigone,[11] which has in our days through its entry into political power gained a reputation in inverse relation to its inner significance.) Lagarde's movement derived ultimately from the ideas of Marcion, the great Christian gnostic of the second century, who undertook to separate the two attributes of the Jewish-Christian God, i.e., justice and mercy, and of them to make two distinct gods, and thus also to divide the two "Testaments" from each other absolutely. These ideas had in their turn been derived from the work of a still greater man, Paul of Tarsus, who brought to the gentiles the aspect of Judaism they were ready to receive: messianic redemption without the Torah of the revealed and revealing God. The church preserved both Testaments together as the canonical Bible; but the validity of the law—including of course the law contained in the prophetic books—was annulled, though not the validity of its documentary source. Hence the abiding discomfort in the conscience of gentile peoples, who from generation to generation learned of a law that had been the original law of their God, a law that at its center was a law for the right conduct of a people, a law that we cannot even today read in earnest without hearing it say, "So must a people live to be a people of God." And this original law, which they read of as a law annulled by God, annulled in its turn, through its tendency toward

---

11. The Nazi movement.

the consecration of every aspect of life, the dualistic foundation of the existence of the Christian people: the division of being into a holy sphere of the spirit and a profane sphere of the world. In the epoch of rising nationalism this discomfort reached its height. For a people to attain an independence that could not be disturbed by the prickings of conscience, one had to tear the sting of the "Old Testament" out of the flesh; and this became the first, negative goal of the movement.

But the generations of these peoples had not learned the real form of the Scripture; they had learned the Christian reworking of it. The real form was less European, less cultivated, and wilder; it was also greater, more rigorous, and more challenging. It came upon its readers in formidable encounters, and it was not to be evaded.

The German Jews who wanted to present the reality of Israel had to try to present the real form of Scripture. They had to show that the spirit hovering over the waters was an eagle,[12] not a dove. And that enterprise might well aid these new Marcionites in their work. But then, one day, the eyes of the people would open, and they would be astonished at what they could now see, and amazed at themselves.

All this, as noted, we felt only vaguely then; I myself, who had taken the initiative in the matter, came only afterwards, during the war, to see it clearly, and then only gradually. Our translational plan, moreover, went no further than the ordinary principle of unconditional fidelity. We had, on the other hand, at least divided up the first tasks, and had interested a big German press in publishing the work. Then the war came, and undid everything. Not long afterwards I left Berlin.

In the quiet of my new residence in Heppenheim, I read the Scriptures all over again, in order, not skipping a single verse even when it appeared unimportant. I let no obsolete word by without thinking of its original power; I took no abstract word as merely abstract, but tried to trace the physicality at its root, and then of course its change in meaning; I penetrated into the construction of the sentences, till the whole sentence in the peculiarity of its structure said something to me that could not be discerned in the sequence of its words alone; and with the aid of my assisting voice I presented to my ears and my wondering heart that rhythm in which alone the biblical message could attain complete expression. Many years again passed in this way. I was no longer bold enough to think of a translation; it was all too great for that. I contented myself with reading and glossing Hebrew or German passages from Scripture for my friends, both Jewish and Christian, and also for the young people who came to see me, again both Jewish and Christian (Christians, among them theologians, were coming in increasing numbers).

---

12. Cf. Gen. 1:2; Deut. 32:11.

Yet all this time the central insights were imperceptibly taking form, the insights that Rosenzweig called "the fundamental points" of our translation and which he said he had learned from my "theoretical remarks" and my "practical procedures"—though, to be sure, without the great, critical-creative intellectual passion that Rosenzweig received them with they surely could never have become the constitutive principles of a translation.

III

Franz Rosenzweig came with several other young people to visit me in the spring of 1914, but I did not on that occasion really get to know him; I did not really see him. Now, in the autumn of 1921, when he and his young wife came to visit me in Heppenheim, I saw him at first glance as the man he was. And at the same moment I was astonished at how close we were. In my first and of course insufficiently attentive reading of the *Star*, a good many of his individual thoughts had indeed seemed close to mine, but not the substance from which the thoughts grew. The crucial thing for what was to come later was that I now found in him, in the form of a precocious grace, a relationship to being that I myself had won only after long and diverse but always productive journeys through decisive personal experiences. These experiences, beginning in the first year of the war and ending a year after it, brought me from a timeless and languageless sphere into the sphere of the moment, where between one strike of the clock and the next everything depends on perceiving what is being said to one, now, in one of the innumerable languages of life, and on answering in a language appropriate to the situation.

This belief based on language, in which all verbal language becomes language based on belief, I found again in Rosenzweig. And in that belief was the germ for our later collaboration: the rendering of one of the verbal languages into another, but not, precisely not, of *any* language nor of the language of *any* book, but of *the* book that alone among all books presents to us the history of humankind as a conversation—and that can present it as such because it has drawn from the language in which it is written or rather spoken the innermost power of acclamation, of command, of proclamation, of lamentation, and of thanksgiving. We had in common the realization that one believes not *in* the Bible but *through* it, and throughout it. "*Schrift* [writing, Scripture] is *Gift* [poison]," Rosenzweig wrote in a letter a few months before beginning the Bible translation, "holy *Schrift* included. Only when it is translated back into orality does it suit my stomach."

That expresses precisely what I too meant, and mean now. But it also indicates the line at which the new Bible translators must do battle with

Marcion and the Marcionites. Marcion's God is silent, or speaks from a chartless distance and does not reach us; only God's son, the "Son of Man," speaks and is heard. Our God makes himself a world with his word; and the heaviest of the trials he imposes is the thirst for his word, a thirst he promises to quench. For he is not, like Marcion's God, the alien or distant God; nor is he, as Marcion says of the Jewish God, imprisoned in the activity of the demiurge. He is the God who dwells both "in exaltation and in holiness" and "with the crushed and lowly in spirit": the "Far-and-Near," in the phrase Rosenzweig uses for the title of his translation of Judah Halevi's *Yah anna' emtza'akha* ["Lord, Where Shall I Find You?"]. Where far and near are together is the realm of the spoken word. Faithful Bible translation is an attempt to translate back into the oral, to reawaken the spoken word. For Christians? For them and for Jews, so many of whom have in the familiarity of the biblical word—the biblical word so often misread aloud—forgotten to hear and to understand it as a spoken word.

Rosenzweig's translation of Judah Halevi's poems is among the greatest works of the linguistic conscience that I know in all literature—of the linguistic conscience of the translator, who in relation to the mystery of two languages is responsible for his attempt to bring them together in unison. In 1923 Rosenzweig would often ask my advice in this project, and I could see with what elan and tenacity he was, despite his worsening bodily paralysis, wrestling with the spirits of both languages to win their blessings. There was something extraordinarily exquisite here, something I myself did not possess and is generally uncommon among us: the grace of consistency, of warranted obstinacy. Then, in April[13] of 1925, a young German publisher I did not know wrote to say that he wanted to inaugurate the work of his press with a translation of the Old Testament, but only on the condition that I undertake it, either as an edition or adaptation of an earlier translation or as a new translation of my own; and it was then inevitable, once I had seen that I could not refuse the offer, that I went to Rosenzweig and said I would do it, if necessary, provided he help me.

The publisher's letter thrilled me but also shook me; from this unknown figure had come a confirmation of my vision, but at the same time a challenge. And I could see the gravity of the challenge even then, since it seemed likely from the beginning that what was at issue was a new translation. My proposal clearly had an equally mixed effect on Rosenzweig, both thrilling and shaking him also—but at a deeper level of life, perhaps the deepest of all. He had prepared himself for his gradual dying with a purer and clearer resoluteness than I had seen in any other human being—and now came this paradoxical challenge, which demanded of him, if indeed everything was to be done anew, a very long period of labor. He had con-

---

13. Buber is mistaken here; the letter (now in the Buber Archives) is dated May 6.

sidered the Judah Halevi translations "the last work of high quality that he would do";[14] and now he was to accomplish a labor of the highest possible intensity. I have no doubt that my proposal touched not only his soul but also the very sources of his life. And from those sources his answer came (he had for some time not been able to speak, and could only indicate, with great effort and uncertain fingers, the essential letters on an alphabetical chart, which letters his wife filled out into words): "Well, let's give it a try."

What did he mean?

Rosenzweig at that time considered the Luther Bible the one legitimate translation, legitimate because validated by history; as he indicated in the Afterword to the Judah Halevi translations, he asked nothing of a Bible translation but what Luther had given. When he heard in January of 1925 that the Jewish community of Berlin was planning a translation, he wrote that "precisely as a German Jew" he considered that "a new, official Bible translation was not only impossible but also forbidden, and that only a Jewishly revised Luther Bible was either possible or permissible."[15] He even thought of writing a long essay against the plan. I represented to him my conception, deriving from the aforementioned experiences of my childhood but developed by subsequent study, that a real Bible translation had never been undertaken, aside from the honorable but unsuccessful and long-forgotten attempts of Aquila and the *Vetus Latina*; and, therefore, that the possibility of such a translation could be determined only by an experiment risking one's entire being. The "try" Rosenzweig now spoke of was intended to settle the controversy practically; we would first in all earnest attempt to revise a single chapter of Luther—would, that is, alter Luther wherever according to our notion of a faithful rendering of the text a revision seemed necessary.

Our initial positions here were of course different, at least theoretically. For Rosenzweig as for me what mattered was to "render the foreign tone in its foreignness," as he had written in the Judah Halevi Afterword; but Rosenzweig felt that Luther had for the most part done precisely this to the extent that it was appropriate and possible, and had in any case done it to such an extent that one could by careful examination and revision of his work attain to a faithful reconstruction of the biblical text. This I could not believe; but I entered into the proposal ungrudgingly and in all earnest, ready to do my best for the task of revision and ready to be convinced by my own work even if it bore witness against my own critical stance, acquired intuitively twenty years earlier but only afterwards developed by study. We made the attempt together, with the utmost precision and thoroughness. It was a day of great labor; and that night, before I traveled home, it was clear that nothing could be done with revision, that what was at issue was not

14. Letter to Joseph Prager, September 18, 1923.
15. Letter to Buber, January 25, 1925.

details but a system of life. Rosenzweig formulated the reason a year later in his essay "Scripture and Luther," stating rightly that for Luther as translator the real point of departure had been not the original text but the Vulgate, and that in figuring out the meaning of the Hebrew text Luther thought not Hebraically but Latinately. I have in my subsequent research on the Gospel of John found on the other hand that Luther in his translation of the New Testament thought not Latinately but Hellenically, though as is widely known he learned Hebrew first, in his youth, and Greek only some years afterward. In other words: what the great Germanist Konrad Burdach called "the national appropriation of the Bible" took place for the German people only in the New Testament, not in the Old. And this covenant with the Hebraic spirit was in fact struck as a covenant with the ancient form— since it is true in Scripture if anywhere that spirit and form cannot be severed without harm to being. Burdach knew this. As the volumes of our translation were published he would almost always send letters expressing his enthusiastic support, and in our last conversation his exact words were, "only now has the appropriation become possible." He knew of course by that time something else as well, which we too had learned: that the appropriation would not take place, not now, not in this time. Rosenzweig had intuited this even at the beginning of our work, as I myself did later but less clearly. Even after we had begun to work on Genesis he wrote to me to say, "Is it in fact clear to you that the situation that the new Marcionites have striven for is *de facto* here? By 'Bible' today the Christian means only the New Testament—and maybe the Psalms, though he thinks for the most part that they belong to the New Testament too. So we will be doing missionary work."[16] Five months later, though, he wrote in that aforementioned letter to a friend, "I fear sometimes that Germans simply will not put up with this all too un-Christian Bible, and that it will be the translation by which the Bible undergoes the expulsion from German culture that the new Marcionites have striven for, just as Luther's was the translation by which the Bible conquered Germany. But after such a *galut babel* [Babylonian exile] a new return might follow, seventy years later, and in any case—the end is not our business, but the commencement and the commencing."[17]

The encounter with Luther continued throughout our work on the translation. The basis on which it took place was an encounter between one situation of belief and another. Not, though, between a Jewish situation and a Christian. Rather between the situation of two Jews of today, in the meeting between Franz Rosenzweig and myself, and the situation of the German Christian who had translated the Scriptures four hundred years before us.

----

16. Letter to Buber, July 29, 1925.
17. Letter to Eugen Mayer, December 30, 1925.

Luther was led to the Bible by his "fit" in the Wittemberg tower; and in that fit, Habakkuk's words[18] about the verified man who will live in his own confidence and trust—the words that sum up the idea of how "belief" is realized in "life"—came to Luther as refracted through the Pauline interpretation (Rom. 1:17) of the "justification" that is revealed "from faith to faith," i.e., as refracted through the doctrine of the perfect severance of the world of faith from the world of works. And then, as he himself says, Luther would in translating Scripture consider at every passage "dark" to him whether it dealt with grace or with law, with anger or with the forgiveness of sins, which it "would rhyme best with"; for him as for Paul it was toward this duality, toward the overcoming of the Law by Grace that the Gospel was directed, and when he was presented with the interpretation offered of this or that verse in Jewish tradition, he demanded of that interpretation that it "rhyme with the New Testament." We, however, had no such predetermined perspective. Scripture was for us, as Rosenzweig says, "everywhere human." But we also knew this: that "everywhere these human traits can, in the light of a lived day, become transparent, so that suddenly they are written for this particular human being into the center of his own heart, and the divinity in what has been humanly written is, for the duration of this heartbeat, as clear and certain as a voice calling in this moment into his heart and being heard." We had, then, no choice. "We do not know from what words teaching and comfort might come; we believe that the hidden springs of teaching and comfort might someday break through to us from every word of this book." We had, therefore, to "humble ourselves in a new reverence toward the word," a reverence that "necessarily must renew our reading, our understanding, and our translating."[19]

This, then, was the case: for Luther, the real and spoken word is put under the doctrinal authority of "the Word of God," the *logos*; in Luther's translating all that matters is to make available to perception whatever seems to "practice" that Word, i.e., "practice" Christ. We however felt no obligation but to free the real, spoken, and speakable word that lies caught in Scripture, and to let it sound again in the world. It does not matter what it says; what matters is for the world of this moment to hear it.

IV

"Translators," says Luther in his *Table-Talk*, "should not work alone; good and true words don't always occur to a man by himself." So he consulted

18. 2:4.
19. See above, "Scripture and Luther."

several others, Christians and also Jews. But sometimes several are fewer than one. Our work could only be accomplished by two: one who wrote and one who read. This second translator, moreover, who read and tested and altered, needed the qualities Rosenzweig in fact had in this last phase of his life: the daring of the man who in his translations of poetry had ventured to the limits of his language; the devotion of the man who in his belief sought nothing else than to serve the object of his belief with all his strength, till the day he would enter into the eternity he believed in; and the infinite patience of the active martyr. Through these qualities the impossible became possible. The man who could not hold his head up unassisted read with awe-inspiring strength and diligence all the sketches, fair copies, and corrections I sent him; the man whose tongue had been struck dumb, whose arm lay inert in a sling, whose hands could not reach out, whose fingers could barely move—he with the aid of his wife, who had become in a way his second and functioning body, filled page after page with his remarks: objections, suggestions, proposed alterations. Often the exchange of opinion over a single word went on for a week. But the most miraculous thing was that he wove into these remarks not just considerations on eternal matters and accounts of daily matters but also poems on various occasions, and even anecdotes and jokes; over the pages there always hovered the smile that again and again shone from his inert head into his eyes, and sat poised on his lips. In his soul the power of belief was made kin to the power of humor. If the former let him feel that the hand that struck him also cherished him, the latter let him stand in the air as if on solid ground. It was from him that I ultimately learned my life's teaching: that belief without humor is a fearful thing, that humor without belief has no foundation, but that both together let us bear the pain that there is to bear.

After the attempt at revising Luther had failed, I sent Rosenzweig the first draft of my own translation of the first chapter, and he after several readings of it replied, ironically, "the patina is gone, but it's bright as new, and that's worth something too."[20] The patina of "biblicality" that the centuries had laid over the bronze tablet—which in its origin sought only to preserve the spoken word, lest it be obliterated—had vanished, and not by infidelity but by fidelity; if each "and" beginning a sentence was gone, it was only by this means that some analogue in German to the "Cyclopean" syntax of the Hebrew could be brought into being, the analogue to which Rosenzweig had referred as early as the Afterword to Judah Halevi. And the point was precisely to find an analogue, i.e., something to evoke the intended impression with the means of the other language, not to make a copy. Only one "and" had, as Rosenzweig recognized, to remain at the beginning of a sen-

---

20. Letter to Buber, May 1925.

tence[21]—because what it binds to the first verse is not the second but rather "all that follows, to the last word of the twenty-fourth book." This is one great example of Rosenzweig's creative criticism. So also the radical severance between the first, cosmological creation story and the second, anthropological one, a severance defended by him with arguments one ought to read in the letters. And so on.

He remarked on the fair copy I had sent him of my revised version of the beginning of Genesis, "It's now amazingly German; Luther by contrast is almost Yiddish. Perhaps now too German?" I was led to think back to this remark even during Rosenzweig's lifetime; Wilhelm Stapel, the most perceptive of our antagonists, had seen clearly what danger to his conception of a "Christian statesman"—i.e., a sham Christian offering religious sanction to all the violences of the state—would be entailed among the German people by the dissemination[22] of the actual Scriptures, which demand the shaping of society on the basis of belief. He called the language of our translation "half-jargon"—thereby revealing his remarkable ignorance of the German language itself, and also falling prey to the misfortune that all the locutions he adduced as proofs could in fact be found in the classic authors of German literature. So later, in a presentation he made three years ago at the "Scientific Working Conference" of the "Research Division for the Jewish Question of the Imperial Institute for the History of Modern Germany," he contented himself with baring the dark secret that "Jewish translation is intended for ritual purposes," that its goal is "to have the 'German' text"—composed of course in a "Hebraic German," in "the strangest German that was ever written— chanted ritually just as the Hebrew text would be." "This seems to us," he writes, "the most characteristic product of the period from 1918 to 1933: the artificial attempt to make the German language into the Hebraizing language of a cult. The reasons for which this new-fashioned German was admired by the Germans of the Weimar Republic are evident."

In fact my resolve to reveal the natural rhythm of biblical discourse—by dividing biblical prose into *cola*, i.e., units corresponding to the breathings of the human speaker, as poetic texts are divided into verses—derived from an altogether different intention: to break "at any cost," as Rosenzweig put it, "the chains that hold all written German today in bonds of silence,"[23] namely the chains of punctuation, and thus to loose the bonds of the reader's tongue by means of the reader's eye. What is achieved with this method—which even Jerome knew, but which neither he nor any subse-

---

21. The *vav* with which the second verse of Genesis begins.

22. German *Verbreitung*; Bauer's transcription reads *Verbietung*, "prohibition," but that makes the sentence nonsensical.

23. See above, "Scripture and Word."

quent translator carried out—can only be understood when the method is tested by reading aloud. Even Rosenzweig only saw what had happened when I read him some passages aloud in this fashion. "The reading," he wrote me, "enraptured me; it has really worked."

No unjust reproof vexed Rosenzweig anywhere near as much as did false praise of the translation as "artistic." "Those who expect a work of art," he wrote me, "*cannot* understand us. Though it is one. But it is visible as such only to those who are not seeking for it there—just as the elegance of a mathematical proof is revealed only to those who approach it with a mathematical interest in it, not to those looking for elegance." Equally ignorant were those critics who castigated our alliterations and assonances as aesthetic[24] devices, as if we had learned them at Wagner's feet; they only showed thereby that they did not know, or at any rate had never read aloud, the biblical verse we had shaped our sound-patterns in accord with—and we had shaped them in accord with it only because in such similarities of sound and in the recurrence of the same sound the Bible usually intends some indirect lesson. It does not attach a moral to a tale; rather it avails itself of the "strong and yet unobtrusive means of linguistic allusion," it underscores the lesson of a passage by repetition of sounds, and by repetition in diverse passages of the same rare words or word-roots it allows each passage to comment on and supplement the lessons of the others. We find hints of this great expressive method in other, originally oral Semitic texts; but in the Bible it has been developed to an unparalleled degree, because here each author grew up in the auditory environment of the words that are spoken onward to him; and when his mission touched him, he saw himself called to enter into those words with his own heard and spoken offering—to make reference to what had been said, to link new associations to what was old and long familiar by means of sounds and words, to link himself as speaker with other speakers in a common linguistic service for the sake of the teaching. That is what Rosenzweig called "the unaesthetic-superaesthetic aesthetic of the Bible." And we had now undertaken to act in its service.

In that service we sought also to draw out the elemental meaning of individual words, i.e., their original concrete sense, wherever by the use of the word, indeed sometimes even by its formation and re-formation, there was expressed a fundamental fact of teaching and belief—wherever, that is, there was a clearly prevailing intention to reveal or to preserve for the reader, or rather the hearer, some element of teaching in all its concrete presence. Within the field of notions of sacrifice, for example, it was important to render on the one hand the general Semitic term *zebaḥ*, which expresses the rit-

---

24. Some illegible adjective precedes *Ästhetizismen*, "aesthetic devices."

ual slaughter of the animal, and on the other such specifically Israelite terms as ʿolah, which expresses the ascent of the thing offered in smoke up to heaven, and the late and comprehensive qorban, which expresses the bringing near and presentation of the gift to God; we could not use phrases haphazardly, but had to try to preserve what precisely had been said. In no other area of our work did Rosenzweig reveal so inventive a passion as in this one. His work here culminates in his interpretation of the tetragrammaton, expounded and argued in his essay "The Eternal."

It is clear to me now that in our rendering of the divine name we were right to let ourselves be guided not by the conventional substitution *Adonai* but by the mysterious acclamation *ani va-ho*, which had moved me deeply ever since my early youth; I am convinced now that at the origin of the tetragrammaton stood some exclamatory pronoun, some "taboo word" (as Hans Bauer puts it) for referring in inspired enthusiasm to an ineffable divinity.

V

"The people who wrote the Bible," Rosenzweig says in a letter, "seem to have thought of God in a way much like Kafka's."[25] It is true that Kafka has given us the greatest Job-interpretation of the century; but that interpretation breaks off where God begins to speak. Kafka knows that the place where he has laid himself to sleep is a place of awe, though he has heard no voice and though the ladder he has seen in his dream is broken, and reaches nowhere near heaven.[26] Kafka is indeed the type of the stubbornly unyielding Jew, who though he feels with pain the contradiction of the world cannot be deluded by Marcion; the fact that the voice does not reach us, and that in its place we hear only a confusion of mad imps, he attributes not to some demiurgic antagonist but to a miraculous disorder in the transmitting apparatus of the servant powers.

The people who wrote the Bible, on the other hand, seem to have thought that if the voice does not break through, *im ein ha-dibbur nifratz*,[27] the cause lies in our ears, which have been "pierced" (Ps. 40:6) but all too often remain "uncircumcised" (Jer. 6:10). No decision in this dispute is going to be found at this moment. We the translators of Scripture have a more modest task: to take care that a human ear which the voice reaches from any passage of Scripture be able to receive that voice more easily and more clearly.

---

25. Letter to Gertrud Oppenheim, May 25, 1927.
26. Cf. Gen. 28:11ff.
27. Heb. "if the word [of God] is not widespread," playing on 1 Sam. 3:1, "Now the word [*dabar*] of God was rare in those days; visions were not widespread."

INDEX[1]

---

1. The index focuses on the matters Buber and Rosenzweig held central: particular biblical passages and terms, which are indexed in detail. More abstract topics, e.g., "the nature of translation," are indexed on a broader scale.

The editors' introductions are not indexed. In general, references to Buber and Rosenzweig are not indexed, nor are instances of proper names where the figures referred to are not discussed; in general notes are indexed less closely than text.

2. For an explanation of this term see 27n.

3. For an explanation of this term see xxxix-xlii and 120n.

---

4. In principle, only those passages are indexed that are in fact discussed, not merely cited or quoted. Where this distinction is hard to make, the passage has been indexed.

221

---

5. These include Hebrew terms; German renderings of these Hebrew terms that Buber and Rosenzweig discuss and which the English translation retains; and English terms rendering Buber and Rosenzweig's German terms.

---

6. For relations between the Buber-Rosenzweig translation and other particular translations, see entries under the names of the translators.

Martin Buber (1878-1965) was born in Vienna and raised by his grandfather, the noted Midrash scholar Solomon Buber. He studied in Berlin with William Dilthey and Georg Simmel, taught at the University of Frankfurt from 1925 until 1933, then emigrated to Palestine in 1938, where he taught at the Hebrew University until 1951. Buber remained active as an educator and cultural and political critic until his death. In the course of his long life, he played an important role in almost every area of Jewish life in Europe and later in Israel. In Zionism, he represented what he called "Hebrew Humanism" and advocated peaceful coexistence between Jews and Arabs. In religious thought, he was known as an interpreter of Hasidism; in philosophy, as the exponent of the philosophy of dialogue, which influenced Christian as well as Jewish thinkers. In Jewish learning, he was an innovative interpreter and, in collaboration with Franz Rosenzweig, a seminal translator of the Hebrew Bible.

Franz Rosenzweig (1886-1929) was born in Kassel and raised in a cultured but largely secular home. He studied with Friedrich Meinecke in Freiburg and with Hermann Cohen in Berlin, fought in World War I, and when the war was over, finished his philosophical *magnum opus*, *The Star of Redemption*. In July of 1920, he helped found the highly influential *Freies Jüdisches Lehrhaus* ("Independent Jewish House of Study"), and later became its director. In January 1922, he began to be affected by the progressive paralysis of amyotrophic lateral sclerosis, which confined him to his home from July of that year onward. During the remaining portion of his life, he was active chiefly as a rigorous translator and visionary theorist of translation, first in his versions of poems by Judah Halevi (1924), then in collaboration with Martin Buber, in their epoch-making translation of the Hebrew Bible.

Lawrence Rosenwald is Associate Professor of English at Wellesley College. He has written extensively on American diaries, notably in *Emerson and the Art of the Diary*, and on the theory and practice of musical text-setting, and has published translations from German, Yiddish, French, and Latin.

Everett Fox is Associate Professor of Judaica and Director of the Program in Jewish Studies at Clark University. He is the author of *Genesis and Exodus*, a new English translation (with notes and commentary) informed by the Buber-Rosenzweig principles. He is presently completing his work on the remaining books of the Torah.